AF573940

MacAskill

Seascapes and Sailing Ships

MacAskill
Seascapes and Sailing Ships

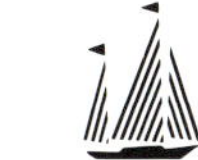

Nimbus Publishing Limited

Published by:

Nimbus Publishing Limited
P.O. Box 9301
Station A
Halifax, N.S.
B3K 5N5

The publisher gratefully acknowledges assistance for this publication from the Nova Scotia Department of Culture, Recreation and Fitness.

General Editor: Dorothy Cooper
Photo Editors: Michael Cartwright
Earl Conrad
Ann Risley
Design: Earl Conrad
Film and Printing: Atlantic Nova Print

Printed and bound in Canada

Acknowledgements

"W.R. MacAskill: The Man and His Time" is copyrighted by Harry Bruce and reprinted by arrangement with Bella Pomer Agency Inc.

"The Schooner Races" is excerpted from the Introduction to *Race to Fame,* by Claude Darrach, published by Lancelot Press, Hantsport, N.S.

Prints of photographs used in this book were supplied by National Artworks Ltd.

Canadian Cataloguing in Publication Data

MacAskill, Wallace R., 1893-1956
W. R. MacAskill : seascapes and sailing ships

ISBN 0-920852-78-5

1. MacAskill, Wallace R., 1893-1956.
2. Photography — Marine. 3. Photography — old sailing ships. I. Cooper, Dorothy, 1939-
II. Title.

TR670.M33 1987 779'.37'0924 C87-090079-X

Contents

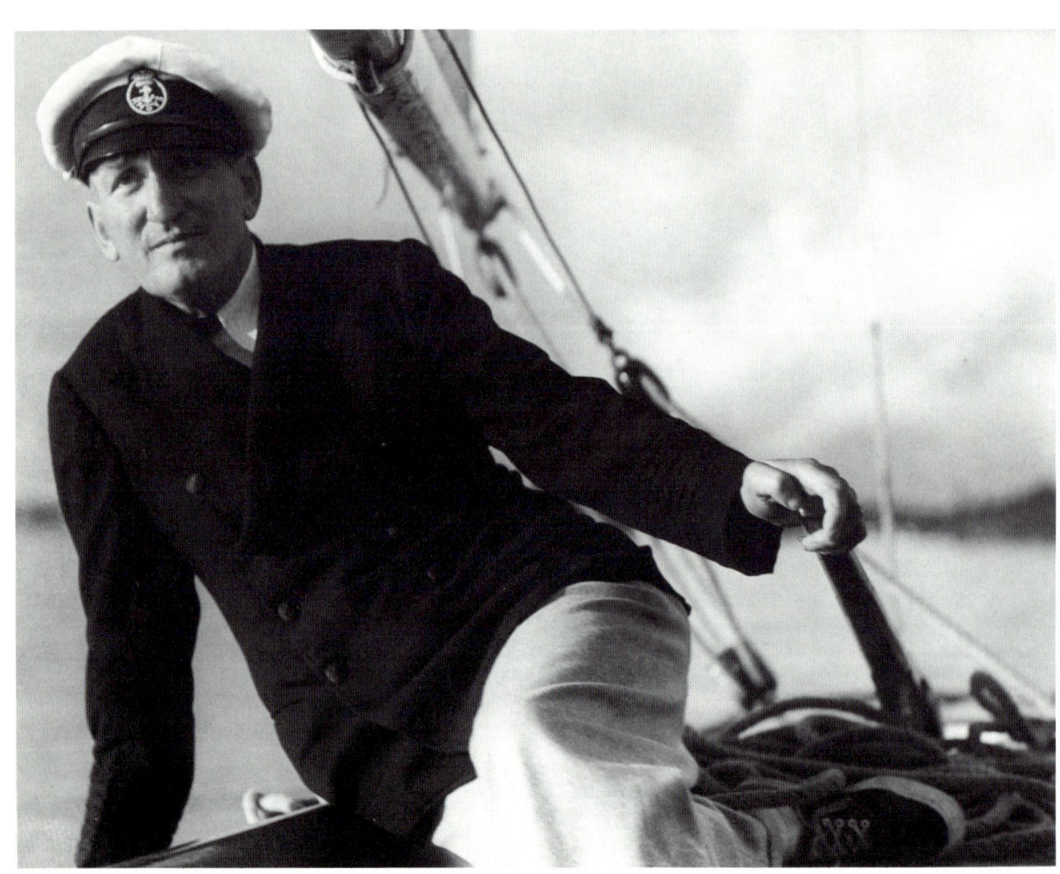

Wallace MacAskill at the tiller

Foreword

The style of any art is usually more significant historically than any particular artist working in that style at any specific time. There are, however, some artists working in the style who redefine its terms and limitations. W. R. MacAskill was just such an artist.

He possessed that drive and curiosity which transforms itself into greatness. Always willing to extend the search for that third dimension of emotion and sensitivity, it was through the adaptation of a soft-focus portrait lens to his style of photography that we have been given some of his most emotional statements of life and the sea. MacAskill images are not just a documentation of his time, culture and subjects; they transcend that. Each image is a clear, precise non-ambiguous statement reflecting his innermost feelings and thoughts. His best images evoke an even greater dimension of thought in the viewer: a sense of being there; being a small part of a greater expanse. The viewer senses that MacAskill was a man who worked free of compromise in his life and did not succumb to the prejudice of existing pictorial photography.

W. R. MacAskill set the benchmark for nautical pictorial photography thus far in this century. His perception and ability to see both composition and light have given him a rightful place in history.

Sherman Hines

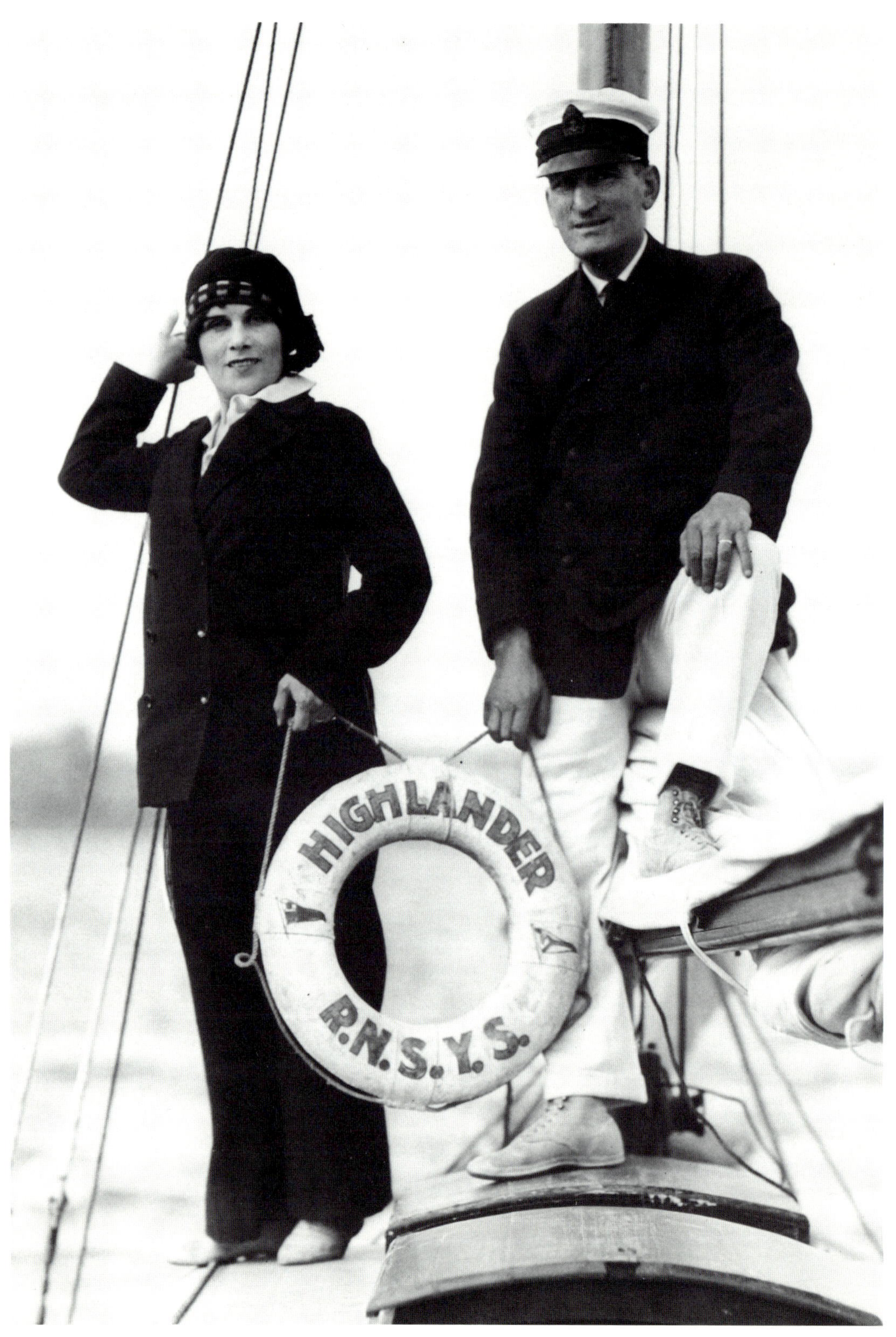

Elda and Wallace MacAskill aboard *Highlander*

Preface

I met Wallace MacAskill for the first time in 1951, although I had admired his work since 1937, when he published a collection of his marine photographs under the title *Out of Halifax.* A limited edition, it was quickly snapped up, but I managed to obtain a copy. In the spring of 1951 he gathered a second collection and asked me to write the picture captions and a foreword. I called at his little shop on Barrington Street in Halifax and noted in my diary: "He is a short stocky Cape Bretoner, speaks in a mild voice with a faintly Gaelic intonation, has a pale face, blue eyes, white hair, a jutting nose. Simple and pleasant in his ways and speech, a poet with the camera, fascinated all his life with the sea." The book was published that autumn under the title *Lure of the Sea,* again in a limited edition which sold quickly in Canada and the United States. Most of the copies had ordinary case-bound covers but a few presentation copies were bound in sail cloth, and he inscribed one to me. He was planning a third collection when he died in 1956.

MacAskill was born in Cape Breton in 1893, with a cherished Highland ancestry. An early interest in the camera took him to New York, where he studied portrait photography, and then came home to open a small studio in Sydney, N.S. But already his mind was drawn to ships and the sea. Shortly before World War I he moved to Halifax, where he could observe every kind of ship, large or small, sail or steam, and from there he ranged along the coast to visit the fishing people. Eventually he built his cottage "Brigadoon" on the edge of the high crag where York Redoubt, the most powerful of the Halifax forts, guarded the harbour entrance. From the curved window casements of "Brigadoon" one looked across the channel to the stony spit on McNab's Island called Hangman's Beach, where long ago the Royal Navy used to dangle the bodies of deserters and mutineers as a warning to every Jack Tar passing by. "Brigadoon" also looked seaward and in the other direction it had good views of the harbour and the port in general.

During World War II the channel was barred by anti-submarine booms and nets except where the gate vessels, one green, one red, gave admittance to the harbour, and so "Brigadoon" had an eagle's aerie view of all the war traffic, in and out. As a bustling naval base and assembly port for trans-Atlantic convoys Halifax became literally the crossroads of the world, especially in those dark days when Britain and the Commonwealth stood alone against Hitler's might. From the site of "Brigadoon" the MacAskills could watch the passage of all types of ships from the huge "Queens," *Mary* and *Elizabeth,* each carrying 15,000 troops, down to queer tall-funnelled spar-decked craft drawn hither from Oriental coasts and rivers. Here passed famous British

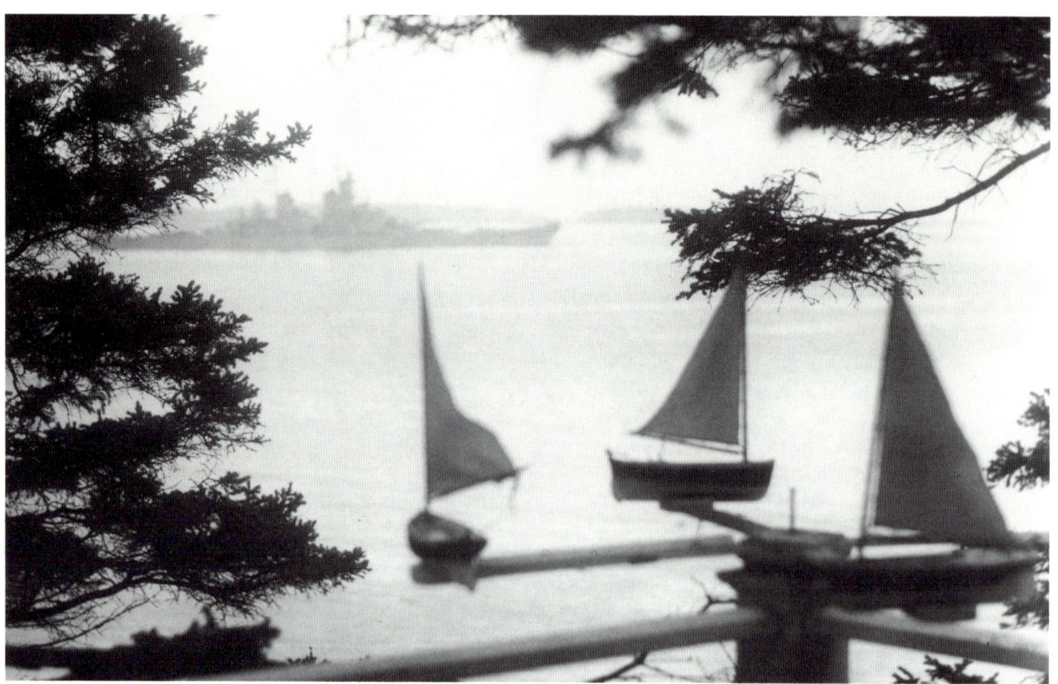

View of the entrance to Halifax harbour from "Brigadoon"

battleships, aircraft carriers, cruisers and armed merchant liners, as well as Canada's fast growing anti-submarine fleet of destroyers, frigates and corvettes.

In 1943 a German submarine laid mines of a new, intricate and highly dangerous type across the harbour entrance, and "Brigadoon" had a clear view of naval men carefully drawing one of them ashore on Hangman's Beach and with cool courage taking it apart piece by piece. The Germans never mined the Halifax entrance again (they had much more urgent use for their mines in Europe) but their submarines prowled outside until the war's end. On Christmas Eve 1944 the minesweeper *Clayoquot* was torpedoed and sunk within gunshot of York Redoubt, and in April 1945 so was the minesweeper *Esquimalt.*

Aside from its seaward views the interior of "Brigadoon" was fascinating in itself, its walls hung with interesting nautical bricabrac and photographs. Here Wallace and his wife Elda entertained their guests in the warm Cape Breton style. Yet MacAskill was no mere observer of the sea. In various craft but notably in his yacht *Highlander* he sailed on it, usually with a bagpiper in his crew to provide fair winds of the musical kind. He sailed very well, too. During his active life he won just about every racing trophy of the Royal Nova Scotia Yacht Squadron.

Meanwhile his nautical pictures were circulating about the world. In a single year they were shown in 27 countries, mostly in leading newspapers and magazines. Three years before his death the Photographic Association of America made 50 slides of his work, together with tapes telling exactly how the pictures were taken and with what. These too were studied around the world.

Wallace and Elda were born in a time when the wooden windjammer was sinking fast under the onslaught of iron and steam. Sail had a brief renaissance during the First World War, when losses by submarine warfare gave a sudden importance to anything that could float and carry a cargo. But it was a swansong. The last Nova Scotian to carry square sail, a barkentine built at Meteghan during the war, perished in a storm

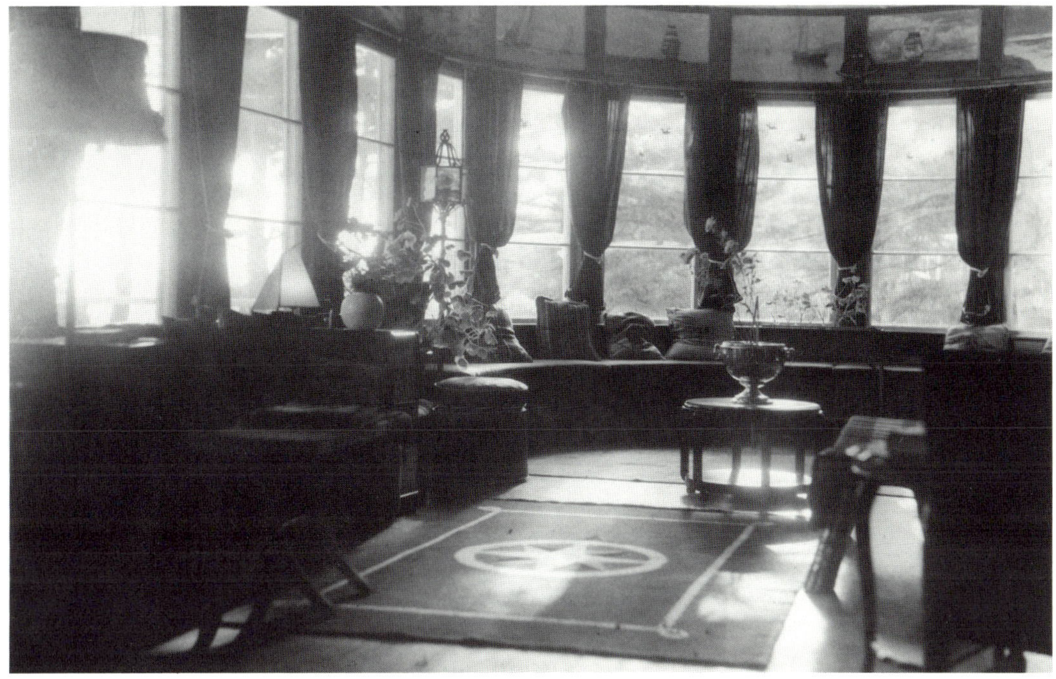

Interior of "Brigadoon"

off Bermuda in 1924. Fore-and-aft sail hung on for a few years in the bank fishing fleet and in stately tern schooners plying the fish and lumber trade with the West Indies, but after 1930 most of these were disrobed by the diesel engine.

Joseph Conrad once remarked, "The special call of an art which has passed away is never reproduced. It is as utterly gone out of the world as the song of a destroyed wild bird." That was Wallace MacAskill's sentiment as well. In recent times a few captious souls have pooh-poohed the sentiment, saying that he merely "romanticized" the dying age of sail. The truth is that in his time, and just in time, he managed to catch various aspects of what has been called "the most beautiful thing ever made by man for a purpose of utility" and in doing so preserved them for posterity.

Posterity is all the richer for it.

Thomas H. Raddall

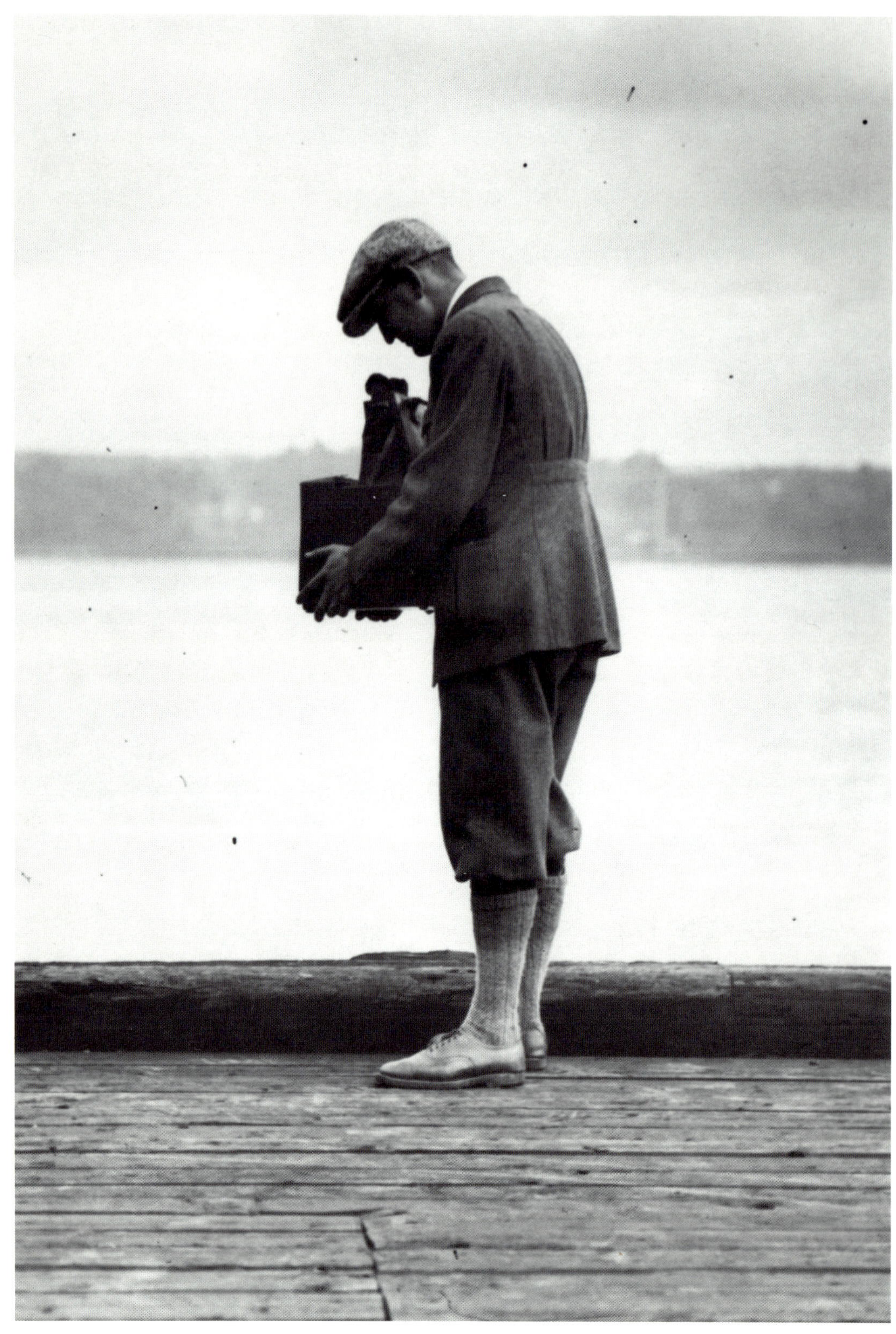

MacAskill photographing on the Halifax waterfront

W. R. MacAskill: The Man and His Time

In the 1920s and '30s, Wallace MacAskill was not only the world's best marine photographer, he was also an eccentric, hard-sailing, hard-drinking and death-defying lover of the sea. If "death-defying" sounds overwrought, consider his adventures at Peggy's Cove, N.S.

People come from around the world to see this tiny, quintessential North Atlantic fishing village; to admire its lighthouse and shacks, which may well have appeared in more amateur paintings than the bridges of Paris; and, above all, to shudder at the clean, murdering ocean as, again and again, she rises in curling green mountains and slugs rock with a force that could break every bone in a man's body. And has.

Over the years, the Atlantic swept so many visitors to a horrible death that the government mounted on the lighthouse a grim warning for the foolhardy: "Savour the sea from a distance." But long before this sign, and before the tourists, MacAskill took the photographs that would help make Peggy's Cove famous; and, in order to capture on film the lethal, white explosions of surf that forever fascinated him, he'd clamber down the rocks, carrying his big square camera, while a friend paid out a safety line.

"For 15 minutes or more," Phyllis R. Blakely wrote in *The Atlantic Advocate* (June 1960), "'Mac' would cling to his precarious perch, with the spray soaking his clothing, waiting for the right moment. After a successful shot, he scrambled back up the rocks with an infectious Scottish grin on his face."

MacAskill took similar risks at sea. When he shot *Starboard Lookout,* he was aboard the *Bluenose* as she raced home from the Banks with a full load of fish. She was clawing off Sable Island in heavy seas. The photograph shows a lone crewman down at the leeward rail, beneath taut, curving sails. The schooner has a sharp heel to starboard, and the man stands well forward. His back is to the camera. He seems to be outfacing the foaming wall of whiteness that the schooner's charging bow hurls aft, and the photograph honours his loneliness. Indeed, it honours the loneliness of all seafaring men.

It respects the ocean's awful power. It celebrates the beautiful gall of a great sailing vessel. *Starboard Lookout* is one reason why lovers of marine photography began to talk of "MacAskills," just as art collectors talk of, say, "Picassos." To get it, MacAskill persuaded the crew to lash him to the right spot on *Bluenose*'s soaking, slanting, pitching deck. With the sea in his face, one hand protecting his lens from the spray, his lens opening set at f/11 and his shutter speed at a mere one hundredth of a second, he waited for what he wanted. He got it. Then they untied him and took him below.

"You can learn portrait work in a school or studio so it gets to be routine and automatic," he once said. "But to get sea pictures, you have to wait until you get the light right, wait until you get the boat paused in her heaving. On slippery rocks you have to know the sea. Otherwise, it could be dangerous if you got caught in the backwash of a wave."

How good was he? Well, in 1924, he first exhibited his *Gray Dawn* at the Royal Photographic Society of Great Britain and, after that, this one photograph — it shows an old schooner ghosting out of port in dark air on calm, shimmering water — earned him more than a hundred awards. In 1928, the Nova Scotia seascapes he entered in an international competition won him a medal embossed with the royal arms of Spain. (It was one of the last medals that King Alphonso issued before he fled the political turbulence in Spain.)

In one year alone, no less than 74 MacAskills popped up in international exhibitions in 27 countries. In 1929, the Canadian government put one of his inimitable studies of *Bluenose* on a blue 50-cent stamp. The New Haven Philatelic Society declared this the world's most beautifully engraved stamp (and among Nova Scotian and New England schooner die-hards, it still is.)

He was not yet 40 and, so far as international recognition went, merely warming up. In 1937, The Derrydale Press of New York published *Out of Halifax, A Collection of Sea Pictures.* This was a limited edition of 100 MacAskills. The price was $15, steep for the Depression years, but MacAskill was in such demand they sold out in a few weeks. That same year, Canada put another MacAskill *Bluenose* on its 10-cent piece. It's still there, 49 years later, and the coin remains the most beloved in Canadian history.

In the early '50s he was, as Lyn Harrington put it in *Saturday Night,* "a giant among Canadian photographers and dean of marine portraitists." His work was so well known in Britain that no less a figure than John Masefield, the poet laureate, had urged him to shoot close-up photos of the rigging details aboard the last of the schooners. That way, Masefield figured, men of later times would be able to make accurate models and replicas.

Masefield was "the poet of the sea," and Thomas Raddall, Bluenose novelist of the sea, defined MacAskill as "the poet of the lens." When Princess Elizabeth and her sailor-husband Prince Philip attended a state dinner in Halifax in 1951, the Nova Scotia government could think of no more impressive gift for them than a boxed, canvas-bound edition of MacAskill's latest book, *Lure of the Sea.*

He was in his sixties. A heart attack had slowed him down, but the honours kept right on coming. In 1952, *Starboard Lookout* won the coveted Thunderbird Crest for marine photography. In 1953, a show of 50 MacAskills toured the United States. In 1954, he became one of the few Canadians elected as a Fellow of the Photographic Society of America. But two years later, this gentle romantic, this sea-obsessed Cape Breton Scot was gone.

He had called his beloved sloop *Highlander,* and each spring when he launched her from the Royal Nova Scotia Yacht Squadron, he would invite high-school bagpipe players to serenade her. Then he would take the youngsters out to sea to play some more. A dubious treat for the gulls and perhaps an unnerving experience for the crew of whatever fogbound vessels were nearby, those concerts may have been as close as MacAskill ever came to knowing heaven on earth.

Sometimes he wore the kilt himself. He drank only Drambuie and the finest Scotch. He named his ocean-front house "Brigadoon," and every New Year's Eve he asked his dinner guests to rise, put one foot up on a bench, and drink a toast to Bonnie Prince Charlie. Wallace R. MacAskill, 66, died on January 25, 1956, which happened to be the 197th anniversary of Robbie Burns' birthday.

He had been lucky. Not every man can spend his lifetime doing exactly what he wants to do. As a boy, two things entranced him: photography, which was still young but full of promise; and "the age of sail," which was still magnificent but full of doom. Sailing vessels would last just long enough to enable him to devote his life to photographing their eternal but fleeting grace, the men who sailed them, and the seas they roved. And to get paid for doing it.

He was born on Cape Breton Island, at St. Peter's, southern gateway to Bras d'Or Lake. It's a shimmering, inland sea, full of islands, wooded points and silent inlets. In summer, the yachting in Bras d'Or is still as good as you'll find anywhere and, around the turn of the century, that's where young Wally learned to sail. At 11, he knew the little sailboat he wanted but feared his father wouldn't let him have her. He saved money he earned from odd jobs, bought her on the sly and mastered her during secret solo voyages in nearby coves. One day his father, a general merchant, had an appointment down the coast but no transportation. It was a chance for Wally to come clean. He announced he had a boat, knew how to sail her, and would gladly take his dad wherever he wanted to go. Fine, said Mr. MacAskill, and off they went. After that, Wally sailed openly and honourably.

Photography soon hooked him as surely as sailing had and, in hindsight, his life seems to have been charted. It's uncertain how he got his own camera at the age of 12 but, according to one story, his instant zeal for photography so impressed an American tourist at St. Peter's that the man sold him a good one for next to nothing.

MacAskill fans will not be surprised to hear that, even when he was still in short pants, his favourite photographic targets were fishing vessels, fishermen at their nets, waves abusing rock, and a white lighthouse on a far point. He was nothing if not consistent. On the day after he died, more than half a century after he'd snapped his first photograph, the *Halifax Chronicle-Herald* described his oldest passions:

> He knew, as few others, the Atlantic in all its moods. He portrayed the strength of the waters as they broke on the rocks of lonely coves, their stillness in the great harbours; he knew, too, the men of the sea and the vessels they manned, the last of the square-riggers, the humblest of fishing craft, the deep-water men and the schoonermen and the dorymen.

MacAskill made framed photographs of sea and sail so familiar it's easy to forget he was a pioneer, that photographers once earned their living only in the portrait and news businesses. Indeed, it was to study portrait photography that, at 16, he went to the Wade School of Photography in New York. One of his photos quickly won a contest and appeared in a New York newspaper. It was a portrait — sure, a portrait of the sea.

He returned to St. Peter's; set up a studio with two brothers; moved to Glace Bay, Cape Breton, and ran a photography business there; and then, just before World War I, settled in Halifax as a commercial and sometimes newspaper photographer. But on his vacations he took the kind of pictures he wanted and, pretty soon, his pleasure became his business. By the Roaring Twenties, he was already in his prime. (So, of course, was the *Bluenose*.) He was deadly serious about his work, and this was at no time more apparent than during a cruise from Halifax to his beloved Cape Breton aboard the yacht *Restless*. Phyllis R. Blakely wrote:

> On this cruise, his fellow yachtsmen learned that he did not obtain his photographs by merely clicking a shutter. MacAskill would get up at five, row ashore, climb halfway up a mountain carrying his heavy press camera, and wait patiently for the sun to reach a certain spot. Often he returned to the *Restless* without taking a photo. MacAskill was a ruthless critic, and destroyed 99 out of 100 of his negatives. He considered it lucky when he obtained three pictures on this cruise which were fine enough to print and sell, and later to appear in living rooms across Canada and the United States.

He knew how to wait for the right moment, the split second when a bow wave co-operated with the glittering ocean surface to give him what he wanted, or surf on rock perfectly completed a scene of lighthouse, clouds, gulls. He had no colour film and used glass negatives for many of his earlier photos. He had no automatic light meters or range-finders, no motor-driven film advance, none of the built-in gadgetry that now makes it possible for the rankest amateur to take a memorable photograph.

He worked with a few filters, slow films and assorted cameras that, by today's standards, were primitive: a Rolleiflex, a Graflex and that Model T of news photography, a Press Graflex. Jack Wilcox, who spent his boyhood at Peggy's Cove, remembers:

> There would sometimes arrive at the cove a man with a huge bellows camera, a tripod of beautifully stained wood and polished brass, a photographer's hood, and boxes of equipment that, today, would require a van. This was Wallace MacAskill. He was there on the rocks more often in the mist and rain and the exploding surf than on sunny days. We agreed that this was a funny thing for a man to do. As he went about his work, he was without question the focal point of the fishermen. And they, in turn, became the focal point of his lens.

If he loved any activity more than photographing the sea, it was sailing his 12-metre-long sloop *Highlander.* "That's all he lived for," his friend Don Wilson recalls. "He'd put her away in the fall, and he'd just wait till spring to go out again. When he was racing, he was out for blood all the time. He was never satisfied unless he could put more sail on her . . . Water just poured over her. He was one of the earliest around here to have a spinnaker . . . In a race, everyone else worked for him like a slave. But he had good judgment as well. He was one of the best the Royal Nova Scotia Yacht Squadron ever had." Often he carried so much sail his mast broke, and after one of these minor disasters, a friend asked, "Why did you do that, Mac?" MacAskill said, "Ah, but it was lovely to see her go." In the 1930s, *Highlander* won every Halifax racing trophy for which she was eligible.

He was an odd man in some respects, a tweedy, plaid-shirted, brown-fingered spendthrift. He insisted on developing his prints himself, and the chemicals stained his fingers. Wilson says the darkroom above the studio on Barrington Street was "as cold as charity." Unless clothing had a vaguely Scottish look, it meant nothing to MacAskill. He rarely wore a dress shirt and tie, and some say he looked like a bum.

For most of his life, he refused to own or drive a car. He used taxis. As he grew older, his eyesight deteriorated till he could scarcely see, but he hated wearing glasses. They were somehow an insult, and besides, every dousing from *Highlander's* bowspray spattered them with salt stains. He was incompetent with money. He never knew how much he had, how much he spent. He gave money away as new fathers give away cigars. "All he wanted," a friend recalls, "was enough for groceries and a bit of Scotch."

"A bit" may be a polite understatement. Sharp at noon, he'd step out on the deck of his house (*Brigadoon*) overlooking the approaches to Halifax harbour, and strike a brass bell. Time for a drink of the Scotch he loved so well, while looking at the sea he also loved so well.

Brigadoon looked like a ship's bridge, and clung to a cliffside at Ferguson's Cove. It had big, curving windows that faced salt water, and MacAskill and his wife (born Elda Abriel) filled it with nautical artifacts. *Brigadoon* was both a showplace and an elaborate expression of their mutual feeling for the sea. "To my wife," he dedicated one book, "whose love of the sea is as great as my own." Mrs. MacAskill worked with him in the studio — her job was to tint his work to make colour prints — but, when the weather was right, they closed the shop, rounded up friends and cruised down to Herring Cove, Ketch Harbour and points beyond. MacAskill, of course, took a camera along.

In search of photos, he sailed aboard schooners to the fishing banks, to the Newfoundland seal hunt, down to New England ports. But he had no interest in travel for its own sake. Like an inshore fisherman, he found what he wanted mostly in familiar waters — off Halifax, up in Cape Breton, in the glory that was Lunenburg. Along the coast of Nova Scotia, infinite combinations of sea, sail, rock and weather offered enough scenes to occupy him for 10 lifetimes.

His monument is his work. In his last years, no respectable Halifax office failed to hang at least one MacAskill. Brewer Victor DeB. Oland, the late lieutenant-governor of Nova Scotia and sturdy champion of Bluenose schooner traditions, once said that if you were a businessman, "you had your desk here, your typewriter and secretary here, your adding machine here, and, up there, you had your MacAskill."

MacAskills still hang on tens of thousands of living-room walls, not only in Atlantic Canada, not only in New England, but also in the dry heart of the continent and, indeed, here and there throughout the world. For homesick expatriates of the northeastern seaboard of North America, they still "keep the salt in the blood." Despite technical breakthroughs that have revolutionized photography in recent years, despite the availability of gorgeous, full-colour, flawlessly executed seascapes by MacAskill's successors, Halifax shops still do a brisk trade in his work.

Some of his old — and merely black-and-white — photos appear so fuzzy you can scarcely tell what's going on, so out-of-focus a modern photographer might wonder how MacAskill ever earned his fabulous reputation. And yet, they exude romance. It's not just that he recorded the last fling of the age of sail and held it for us against what photography-essayist Susan Sontag has called "time's relentless melt."

The patina of age does give his work a sad charm, but there's something else: these photos somehow smell of the sea, sound of the sea, breathe of the sea. Exactly how he caught this effect so much better than other photographers is something that perhaps even he could never quite explain. It had something to do with his forever going out to meet the sea, but that's not the whole answer. The mystery proves again that, sometimes anyway, one picture really is worth more than ten thousand words. Even if, amazingly, the man who shot it hasn't been around for 30 years.

Harry Bruce

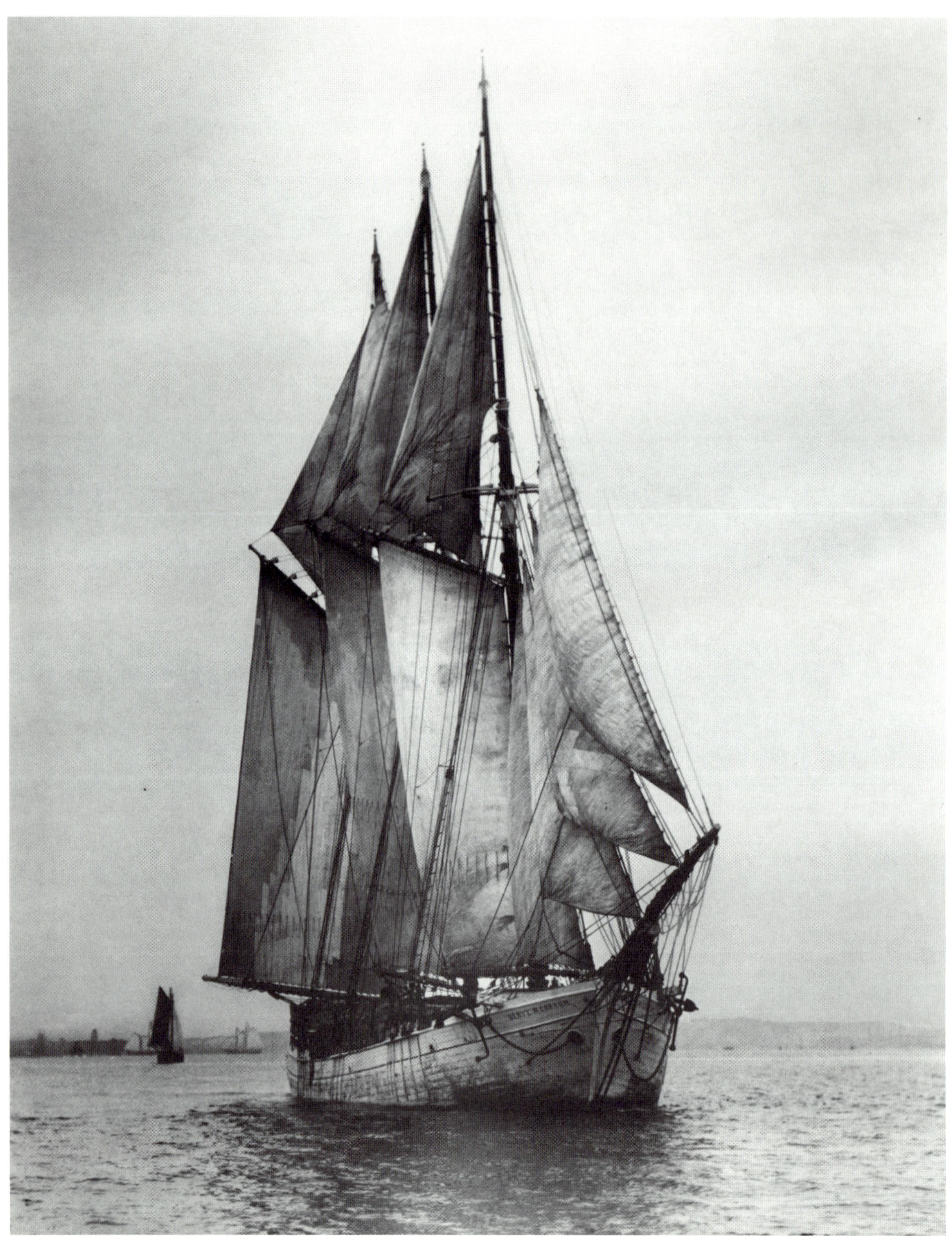

Laden with cargo, *Beryl M. Corkum* sails out of Halifax harbour

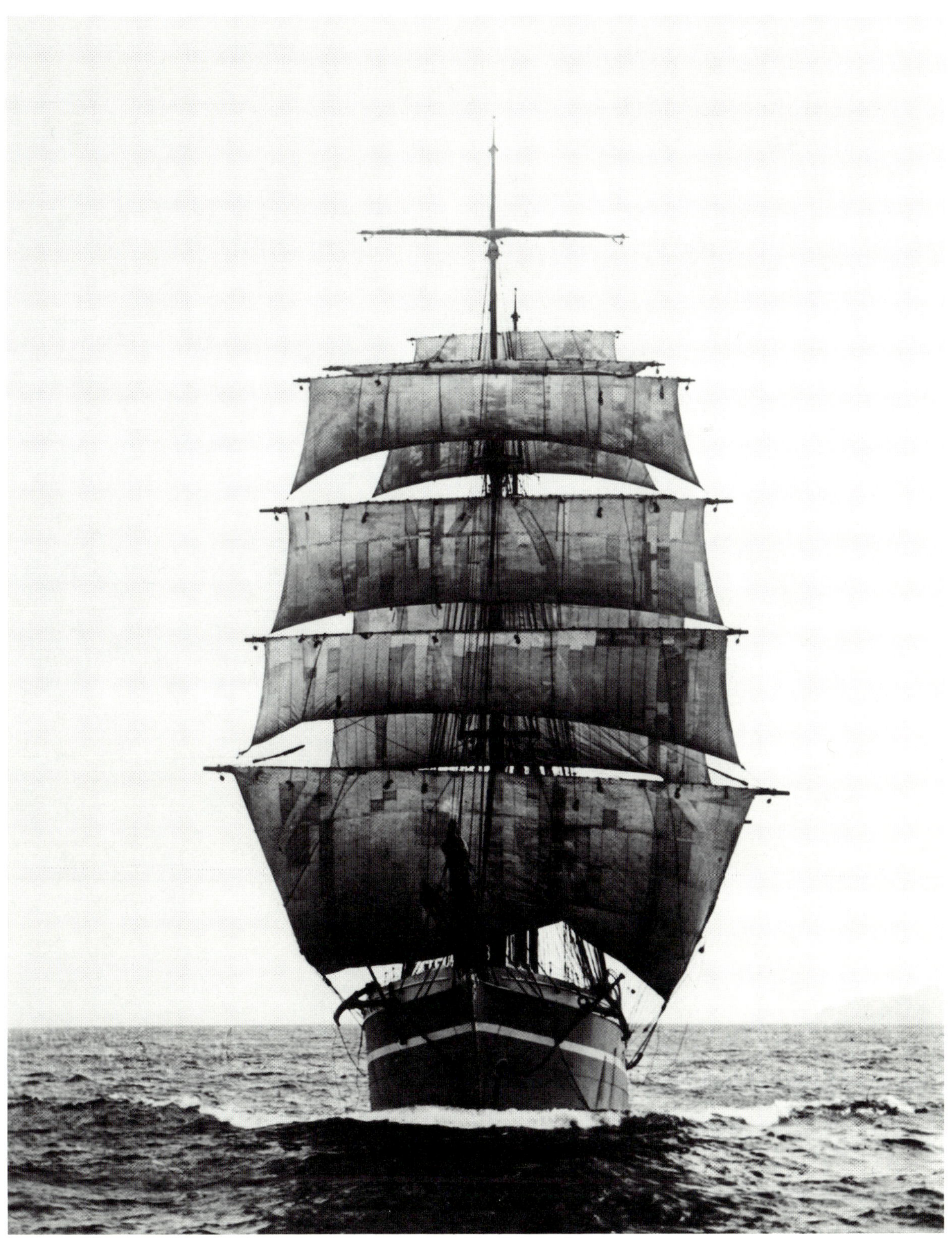

Three-masted barque sails into Halifax harbour

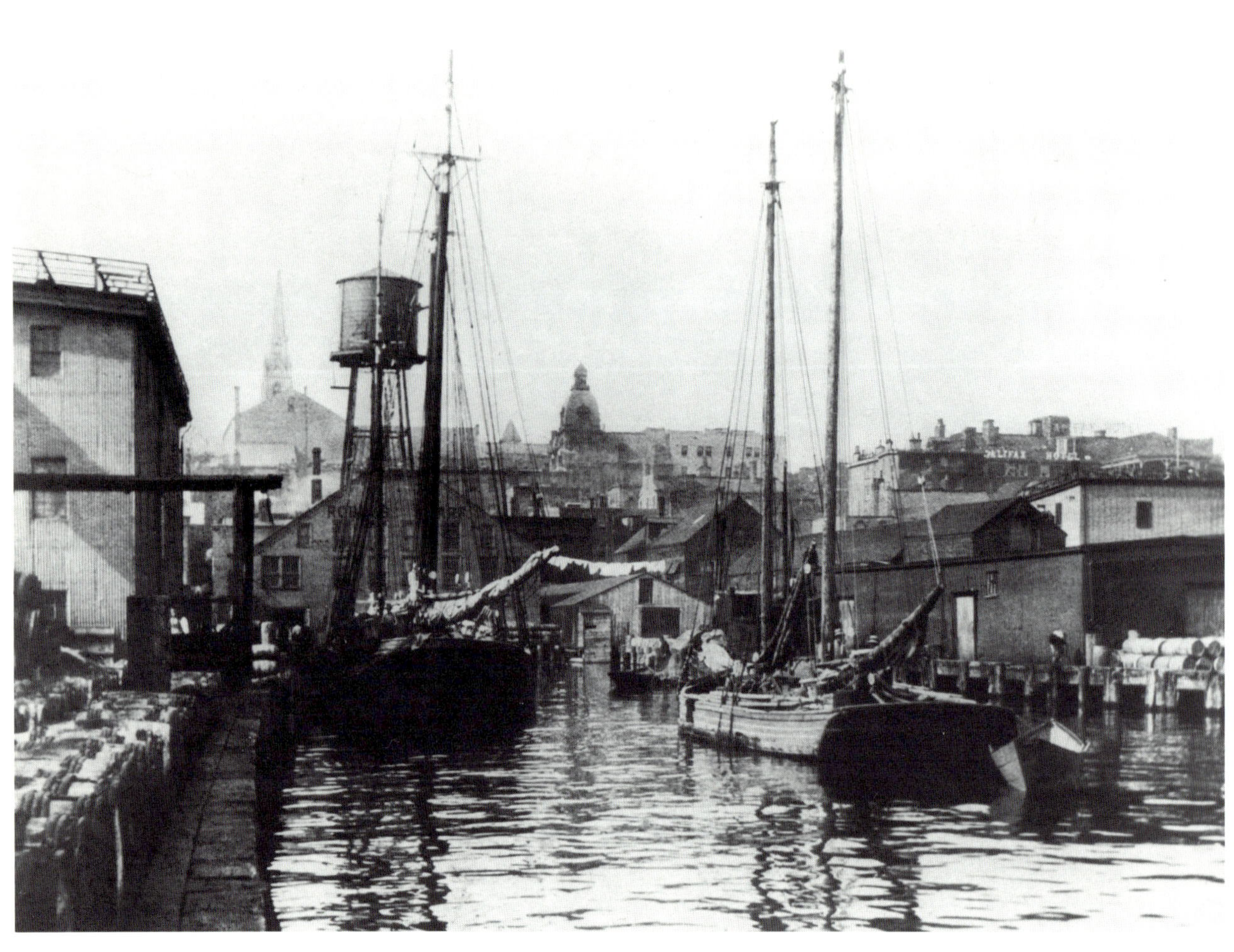

Schooners berthed on the Halifax waterfront

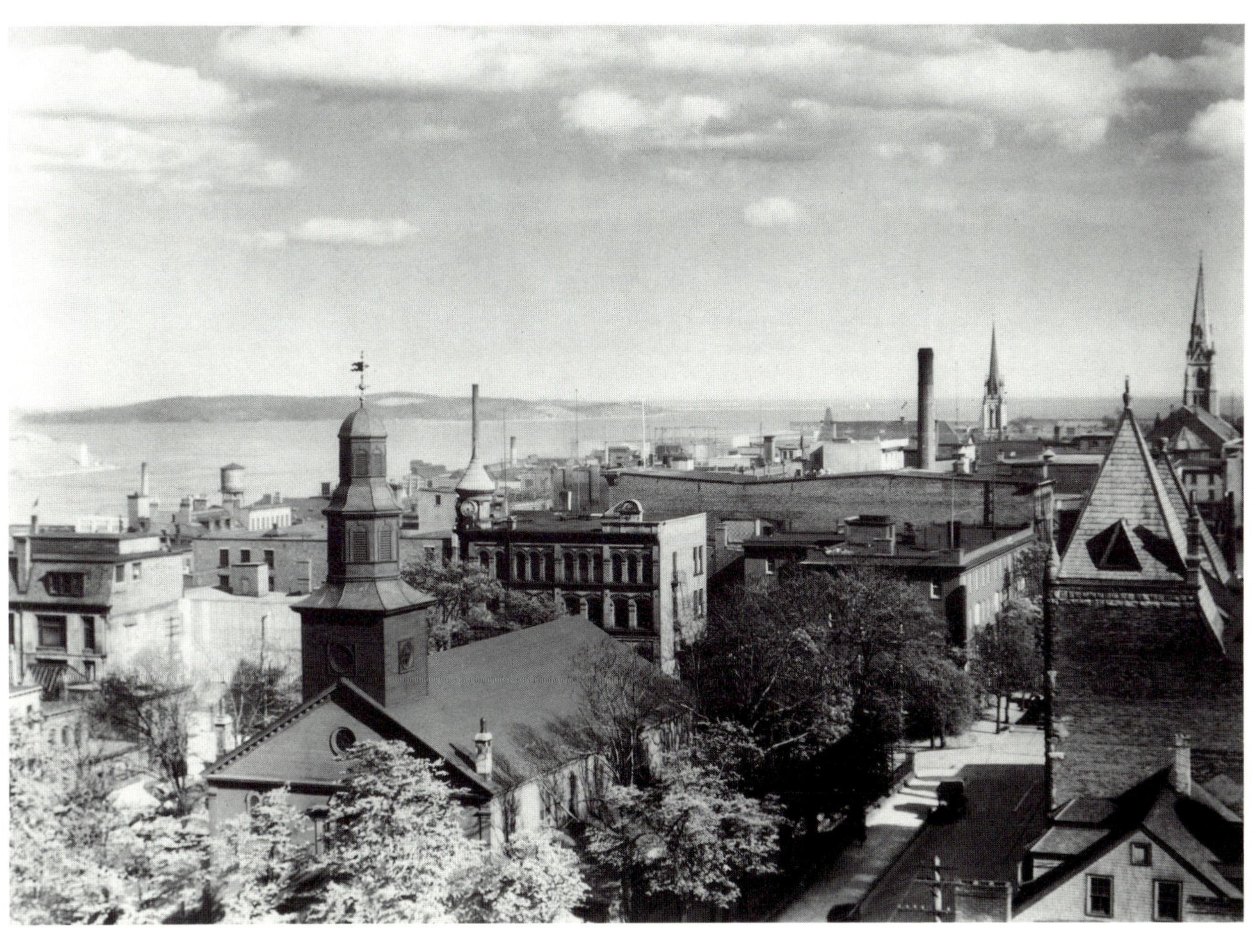

St. Paul's church with downtown Halifax and McNab's Island in the background

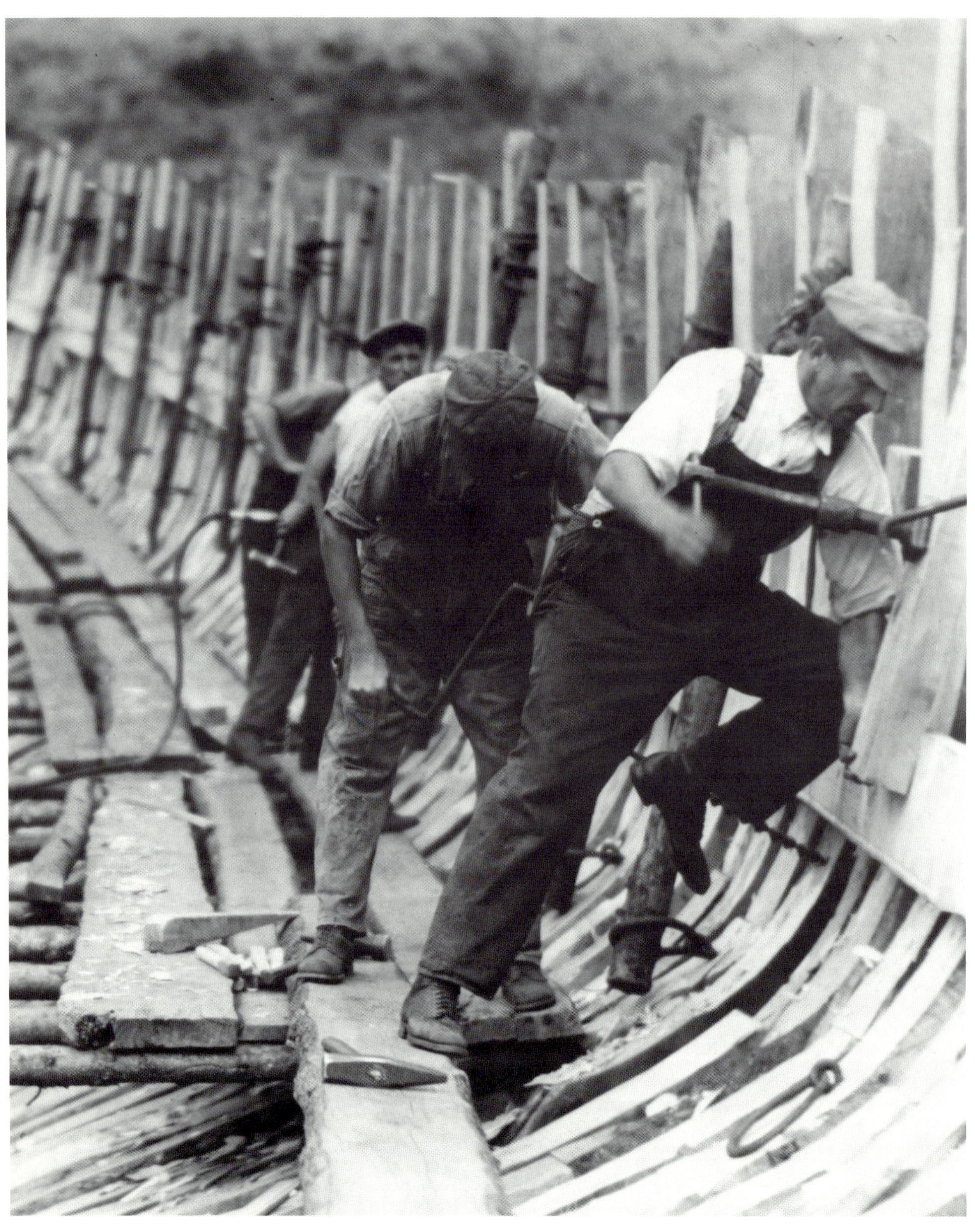

Shipwrights setting up the frames for a schooner

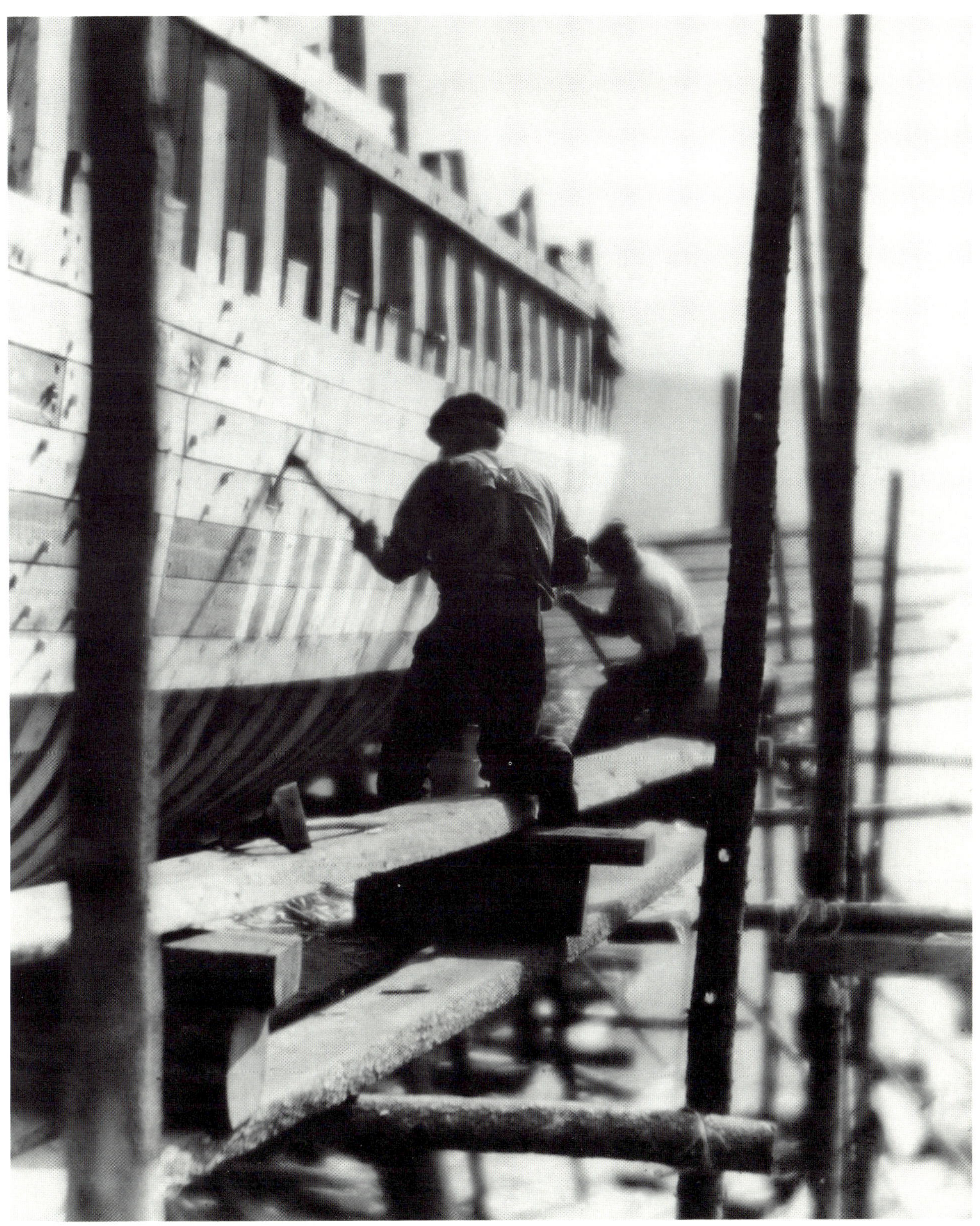

Shipwrights trimming treenails on a schooner's planking

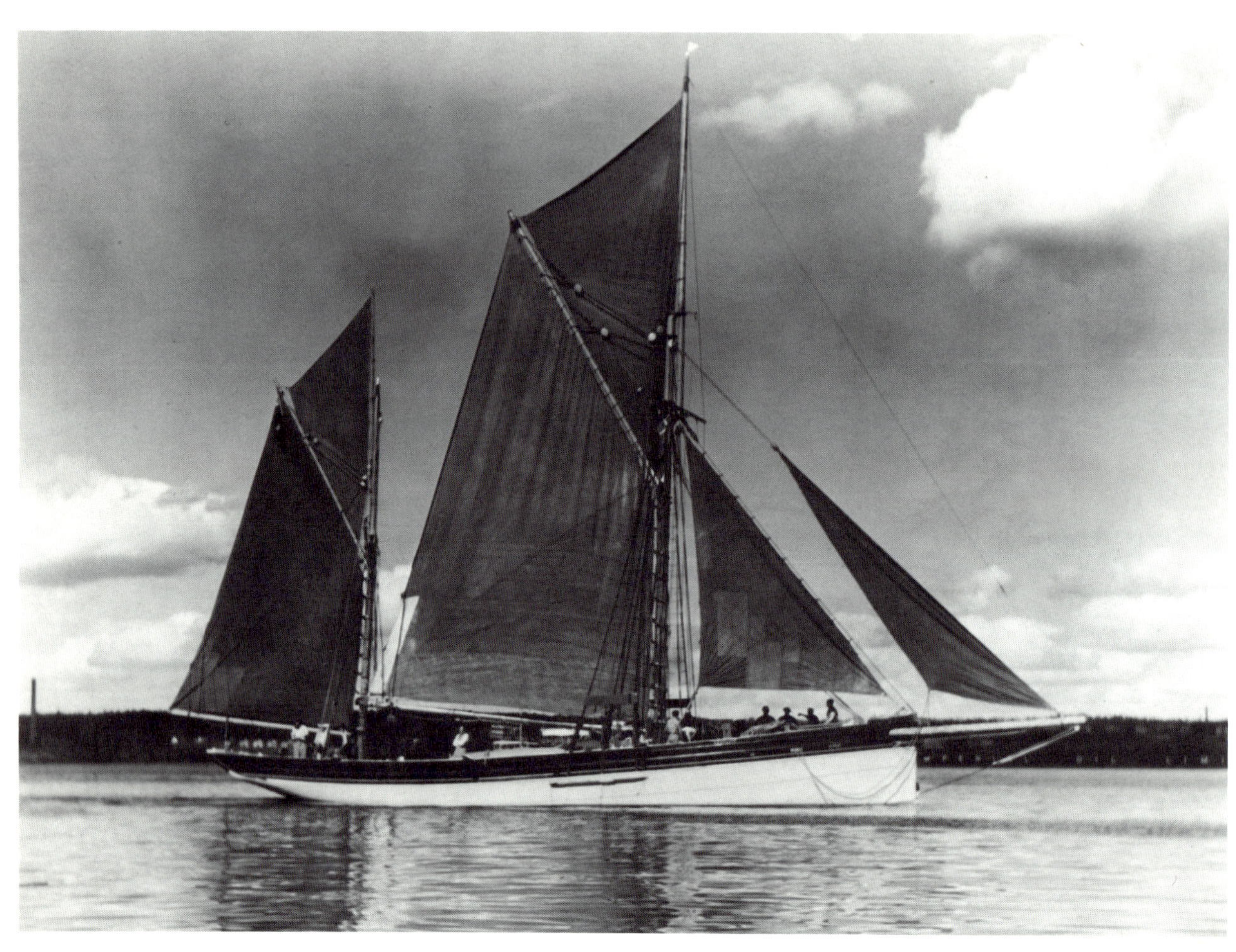

British-built ketch sailing in Halifax harbour

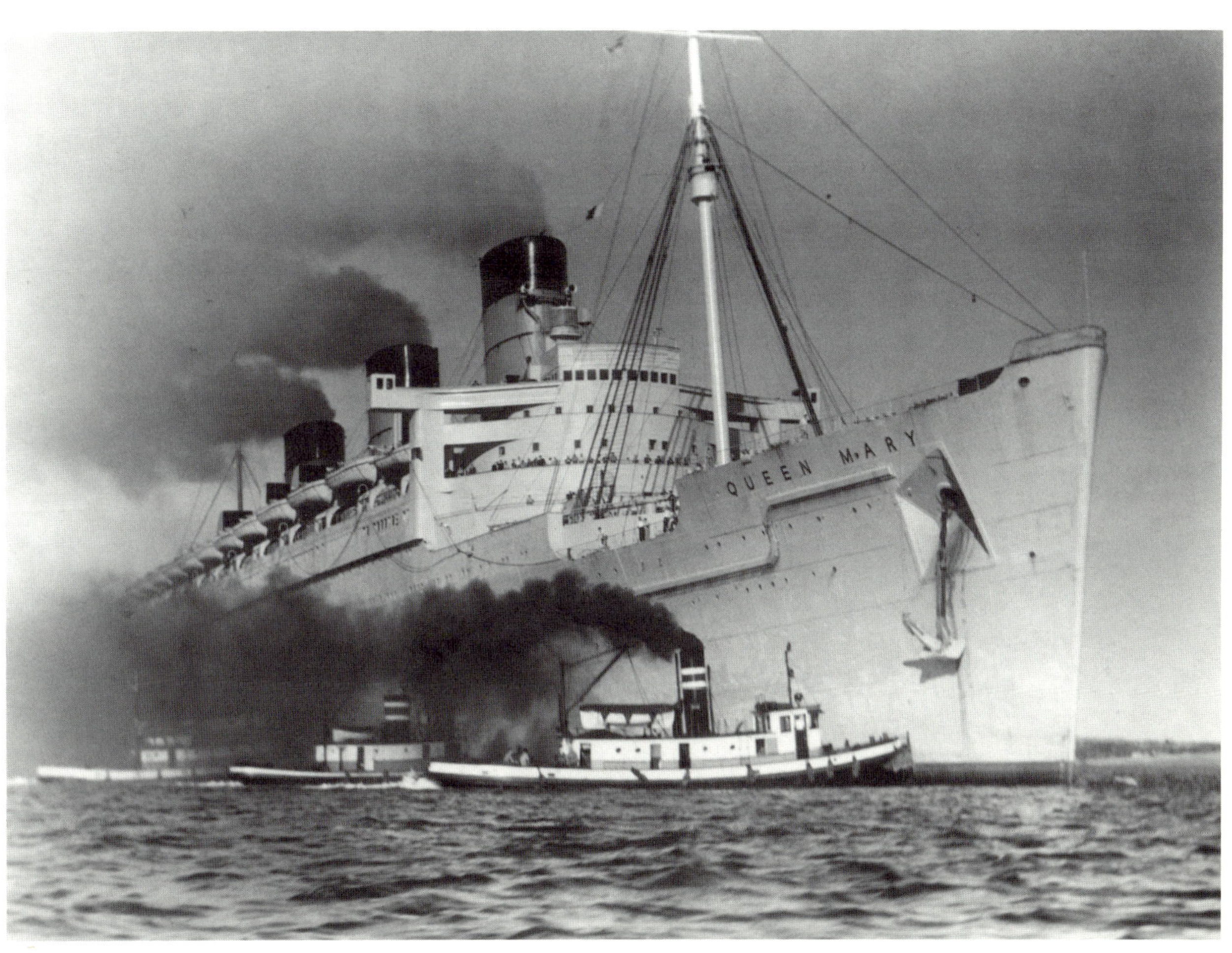

Aided by tugboats, the *Queen Mary* leaves Halifax harbour

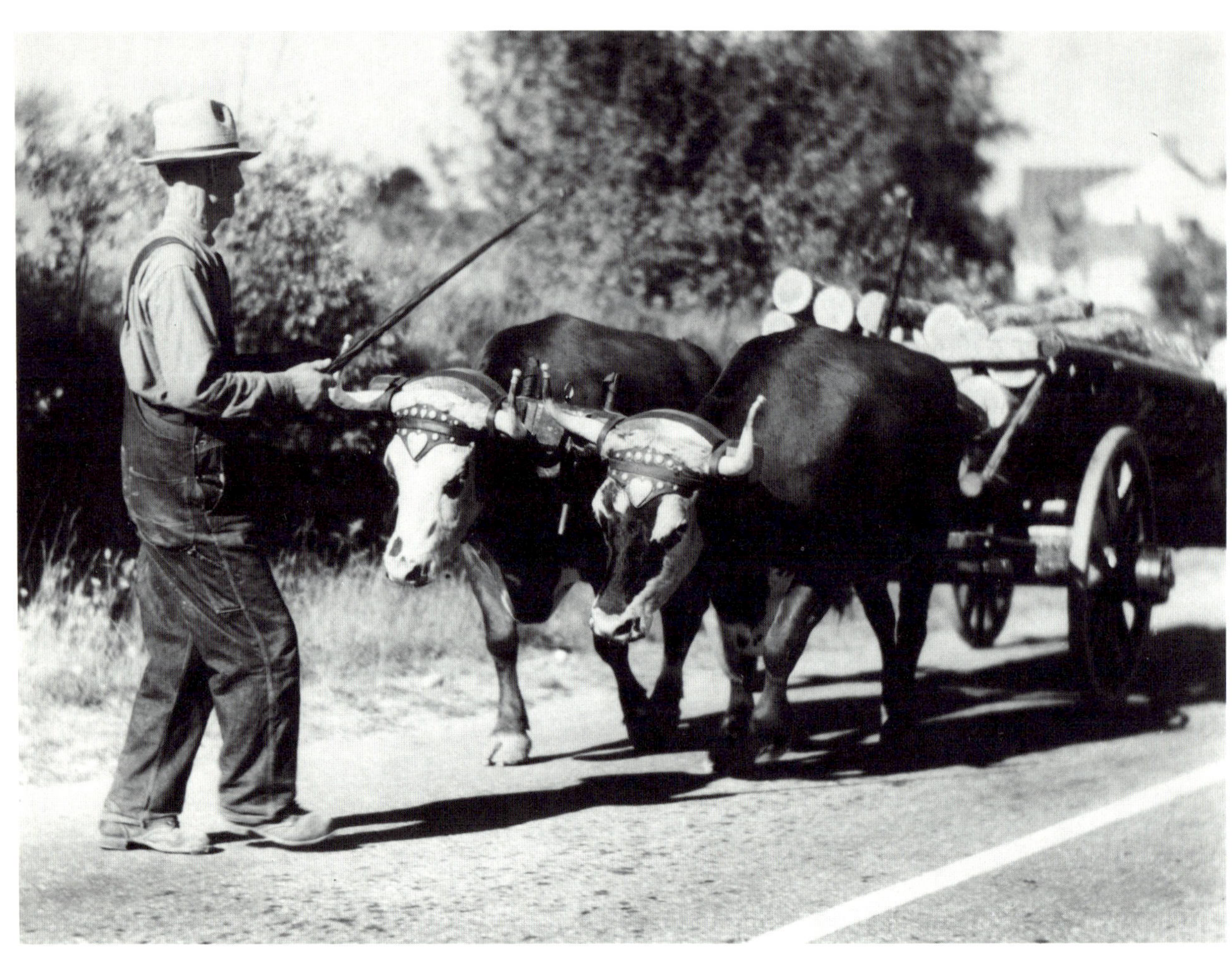

Teamster with a pair of oxen

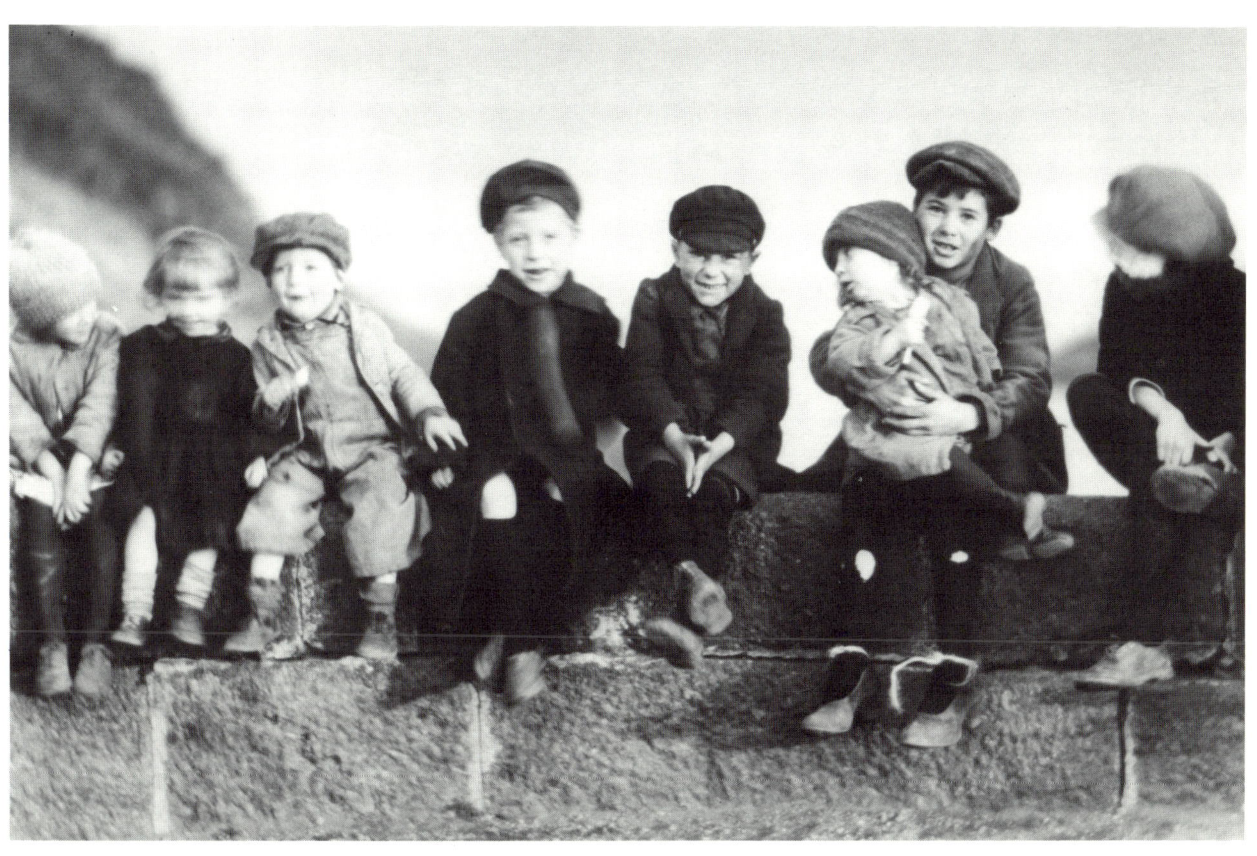

Children, St. John's, Newfoundland

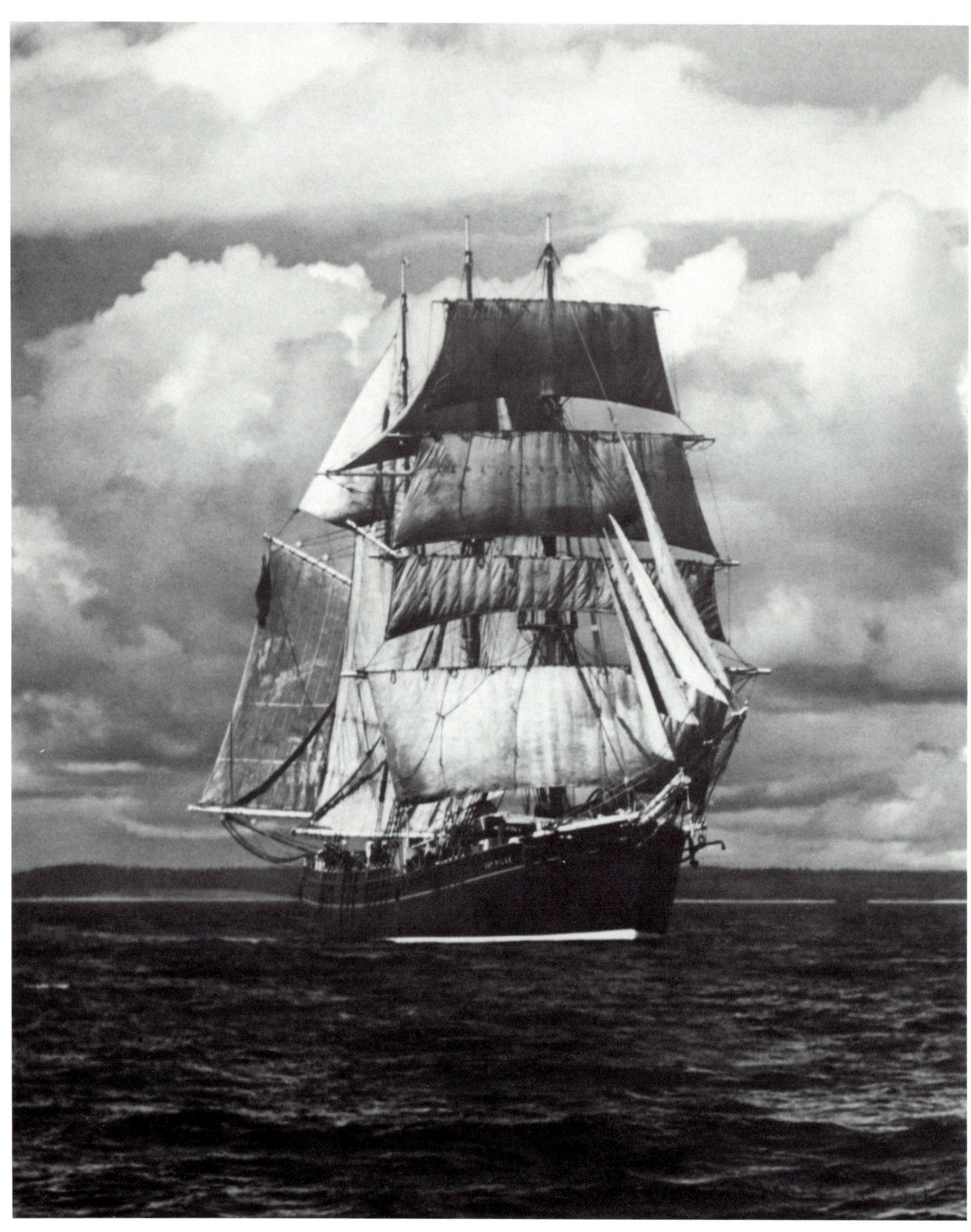

Barquentine *Cap Pilar* sails out of Halifax harbour

Favourite Images

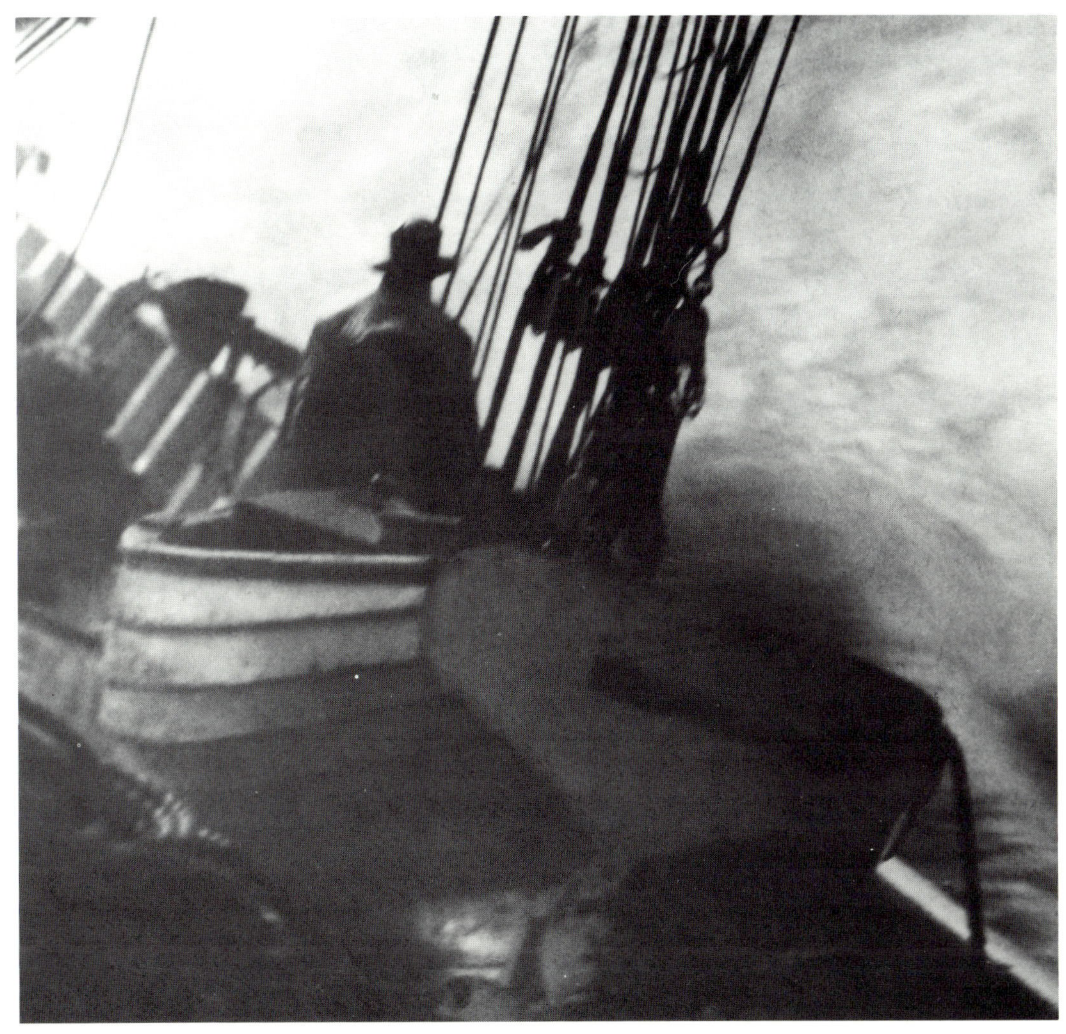

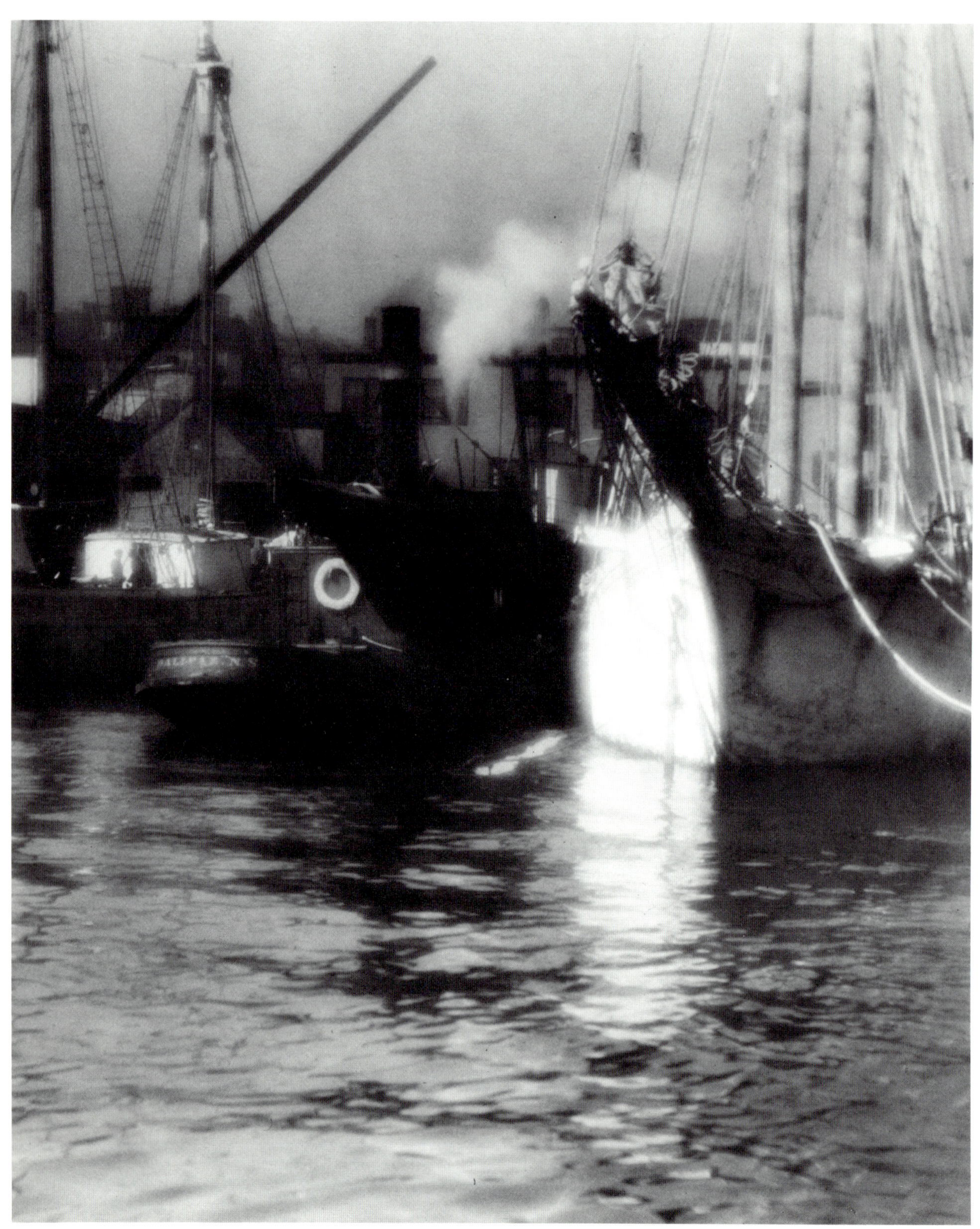

Along the Waterfront, 1924

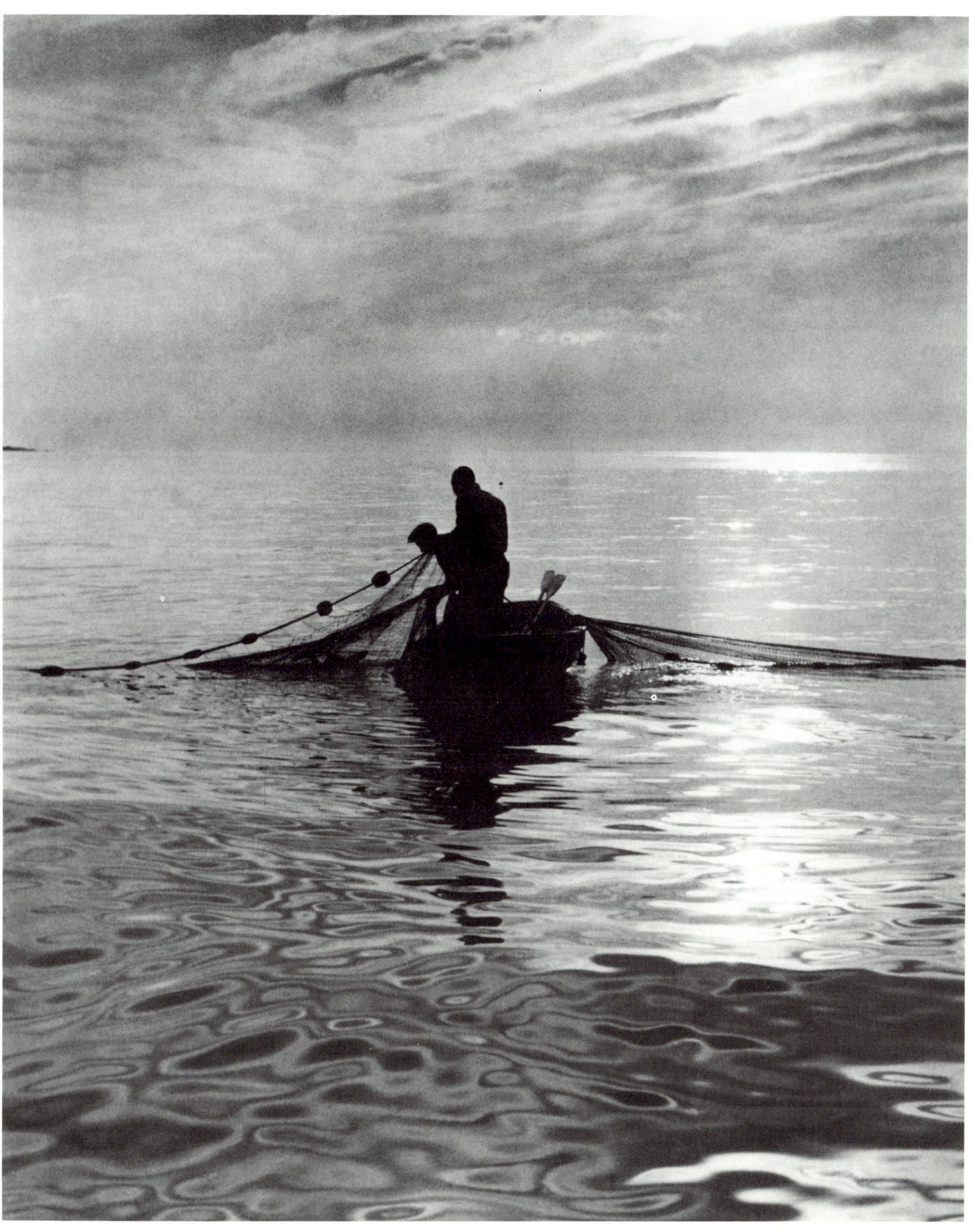

Toilers of the Sea, 1928

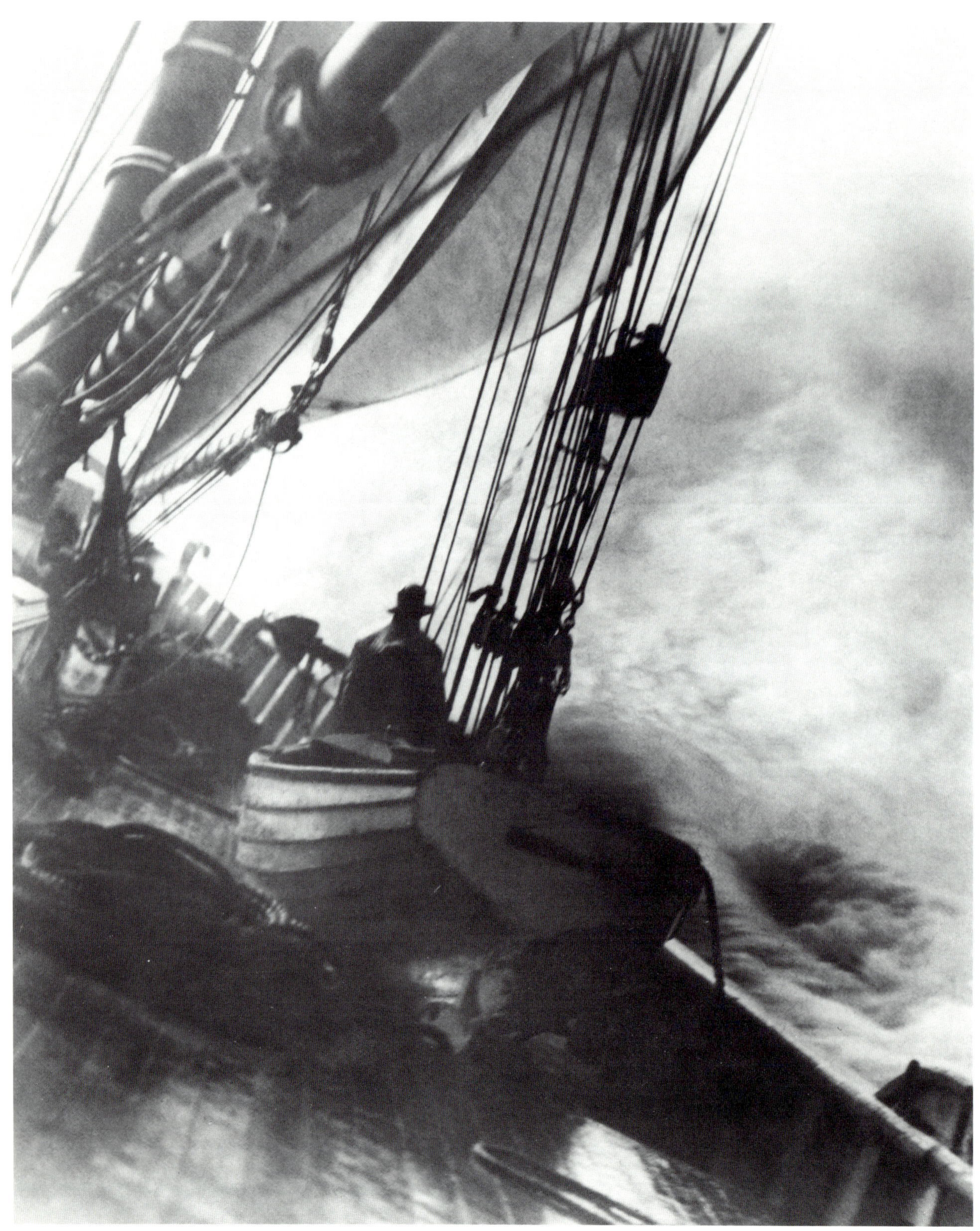

Starboard Lookout, 1933

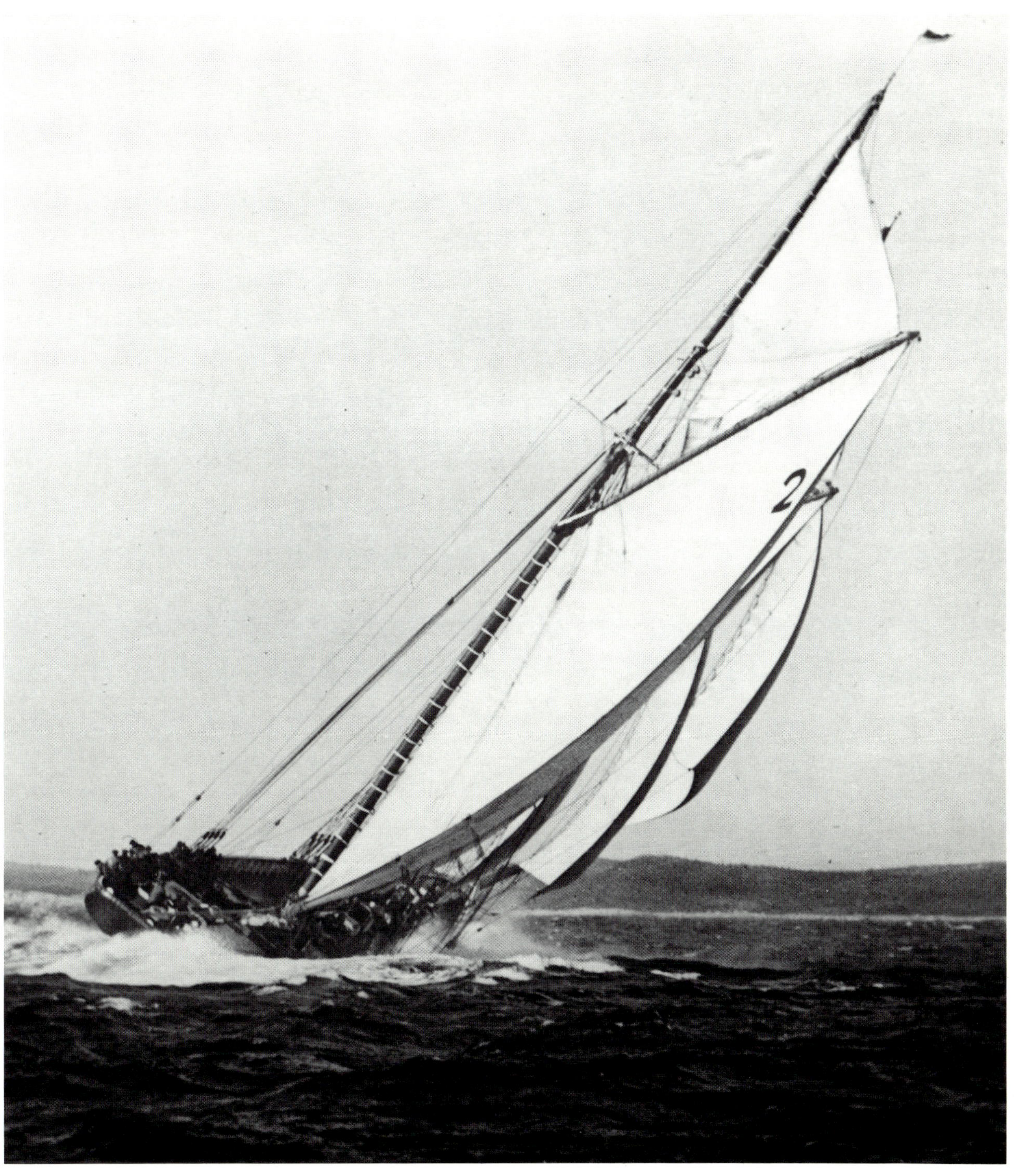

Bluenose, Heeling Under a Squall, 1921

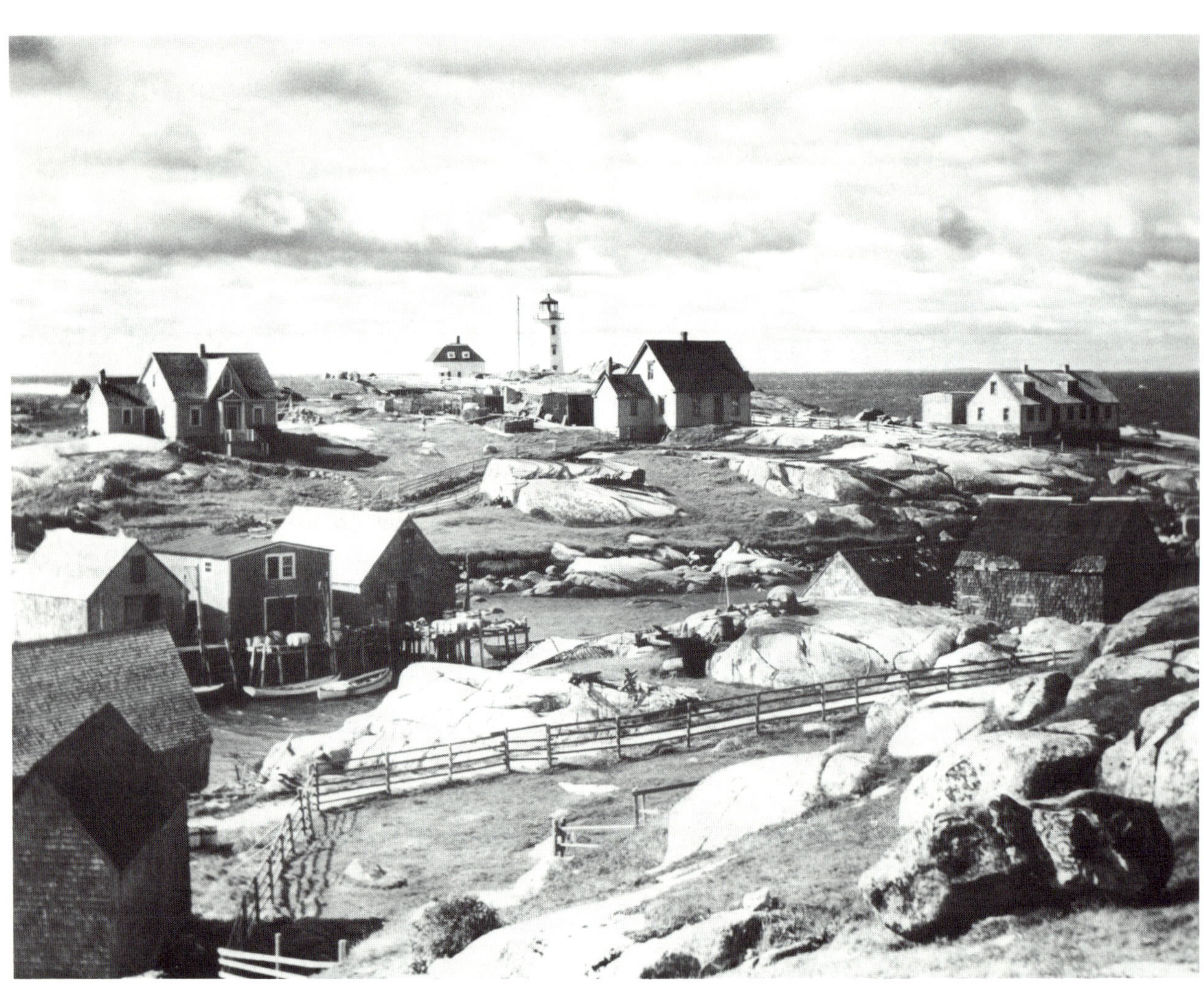

Peggy's Cove, 1926

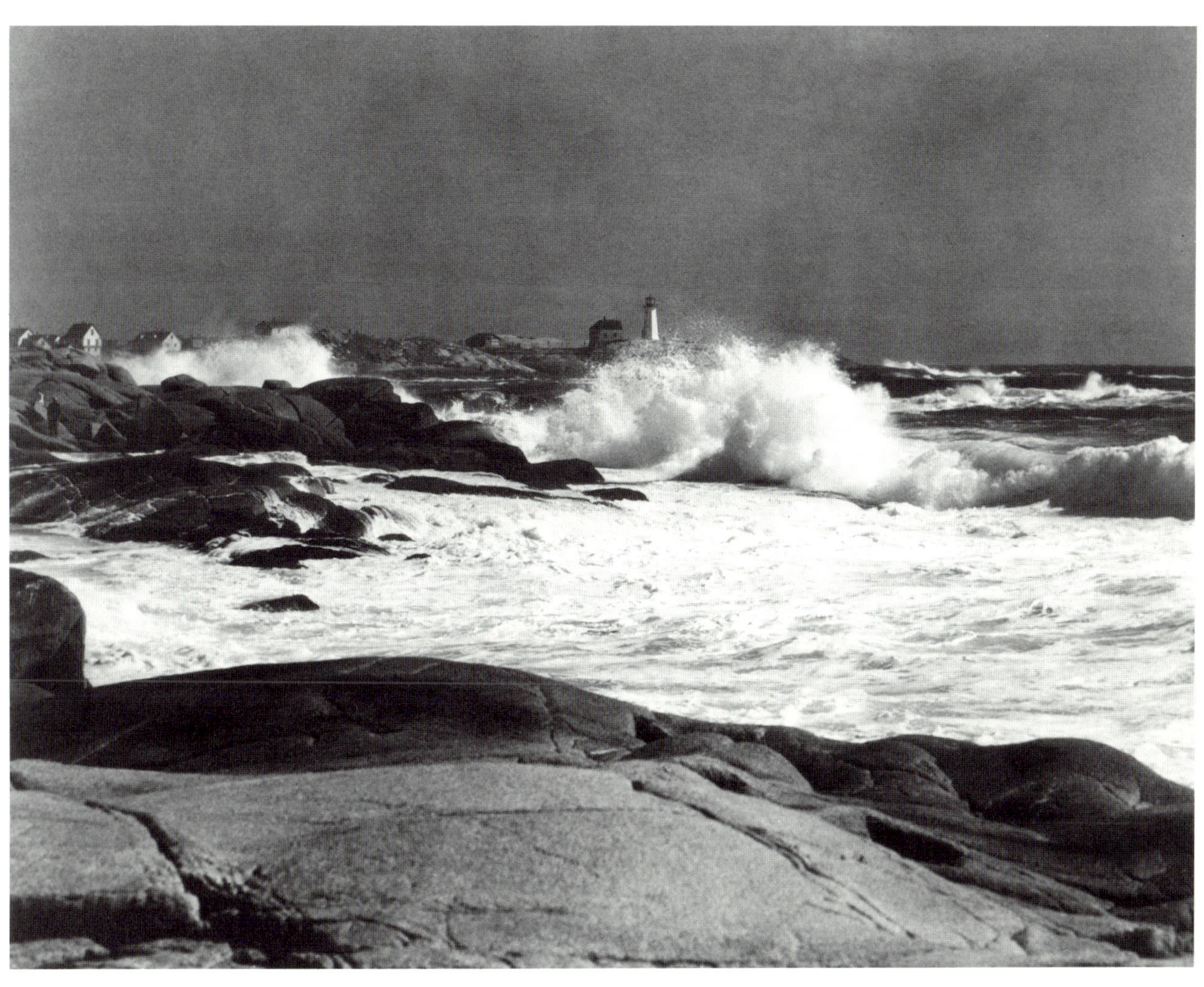

Surf at Peggy's Cove, 1938

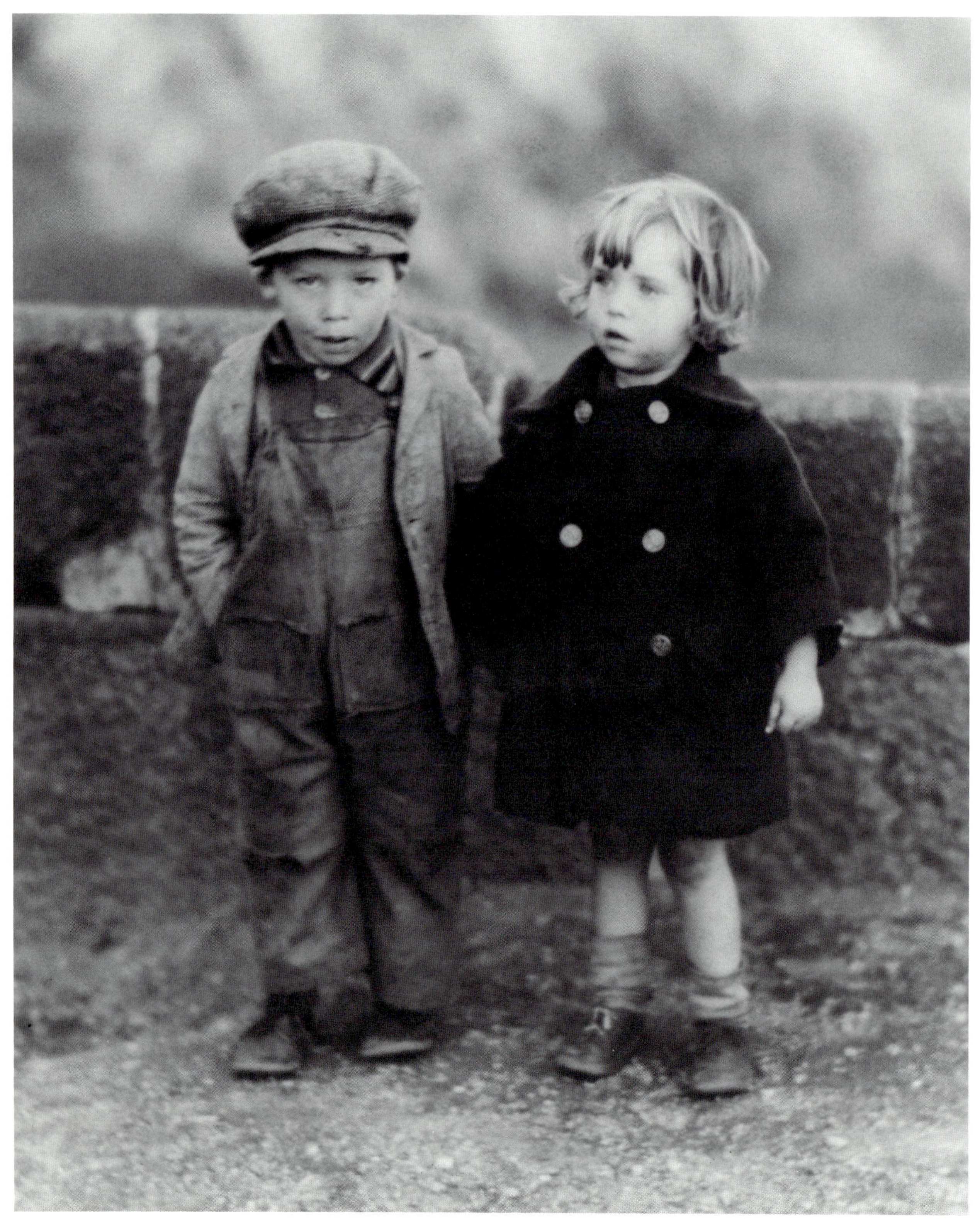

Young Folk, 1924

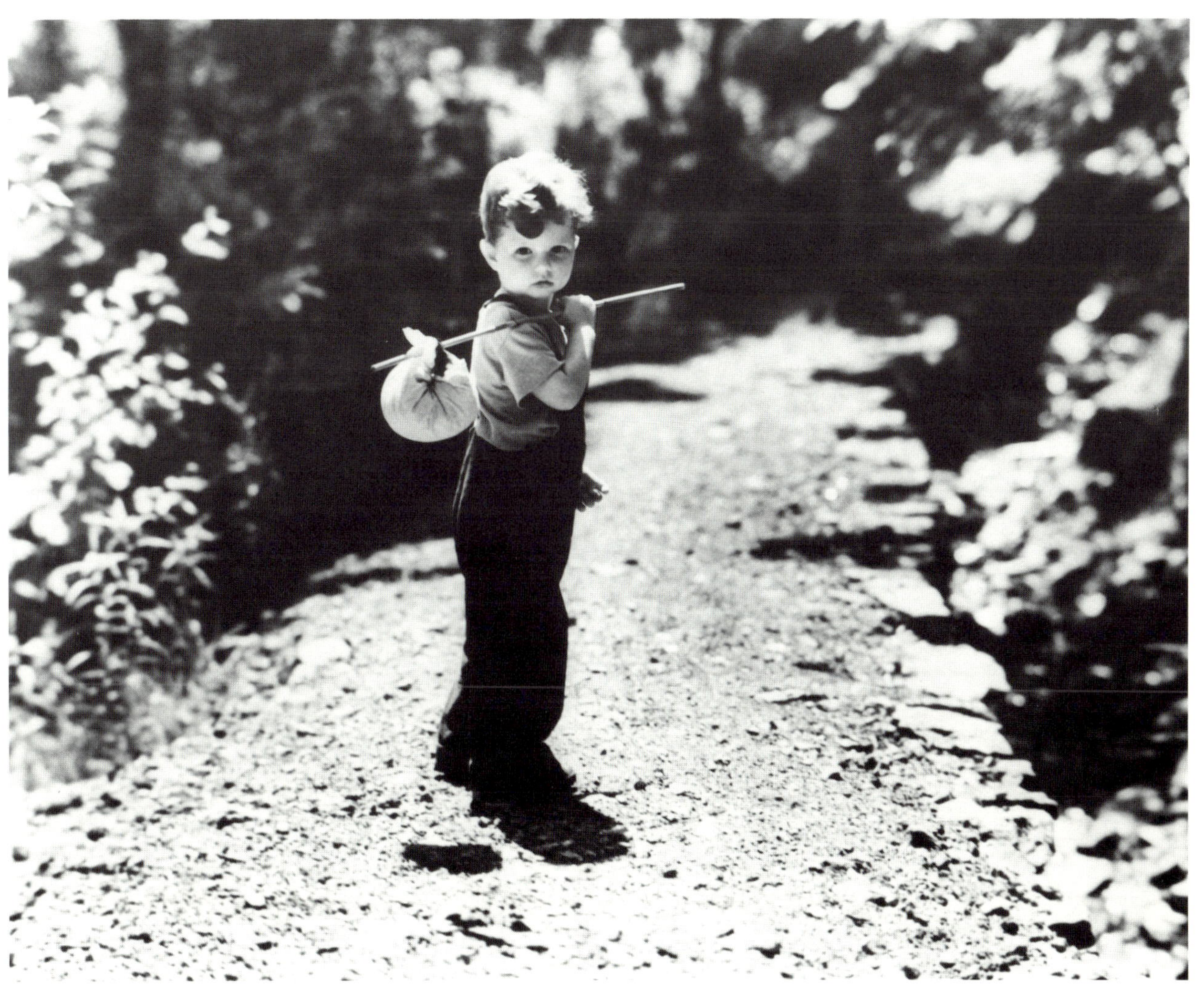

Wanderlust, 1926

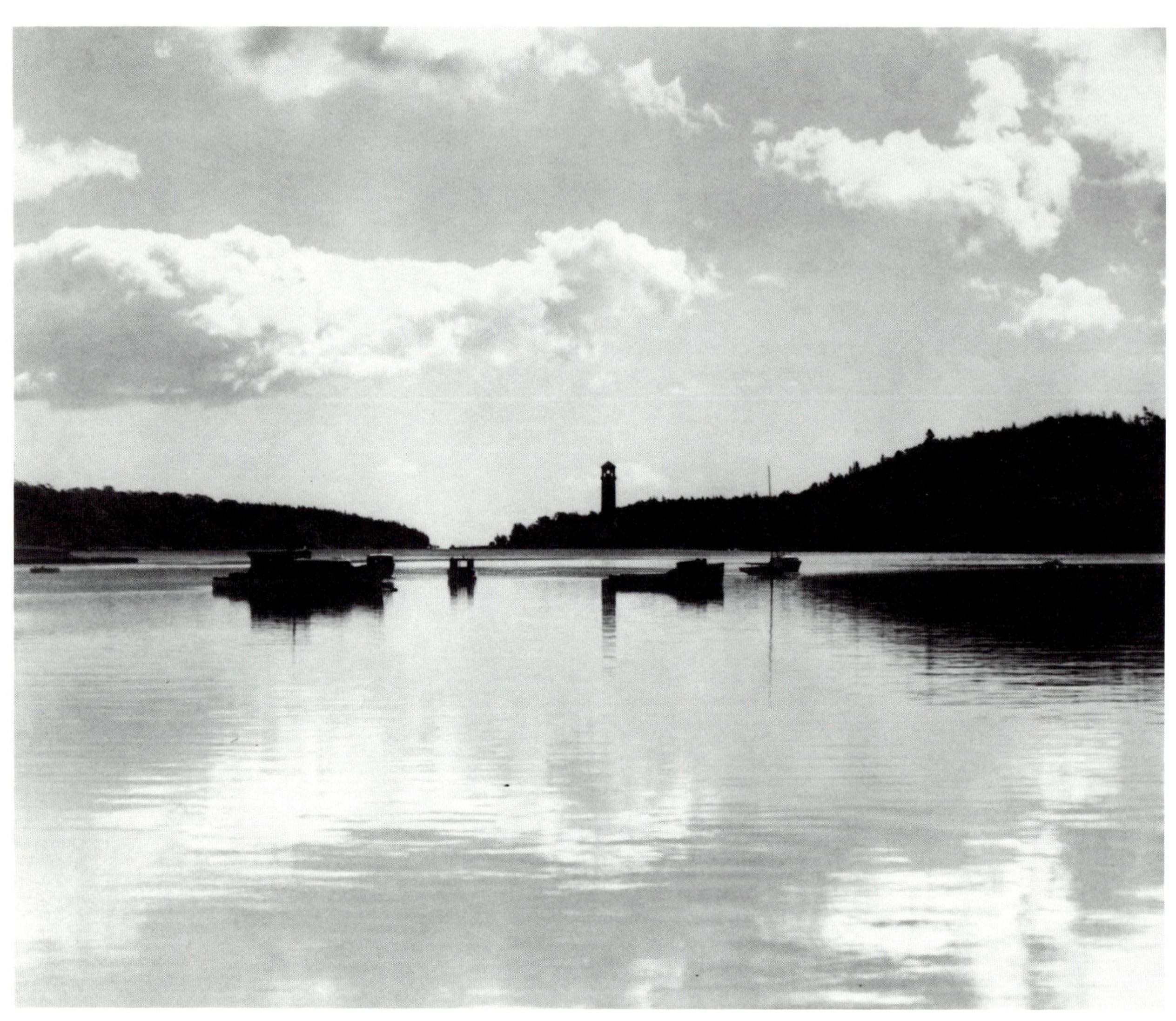

North West Arm, 1927

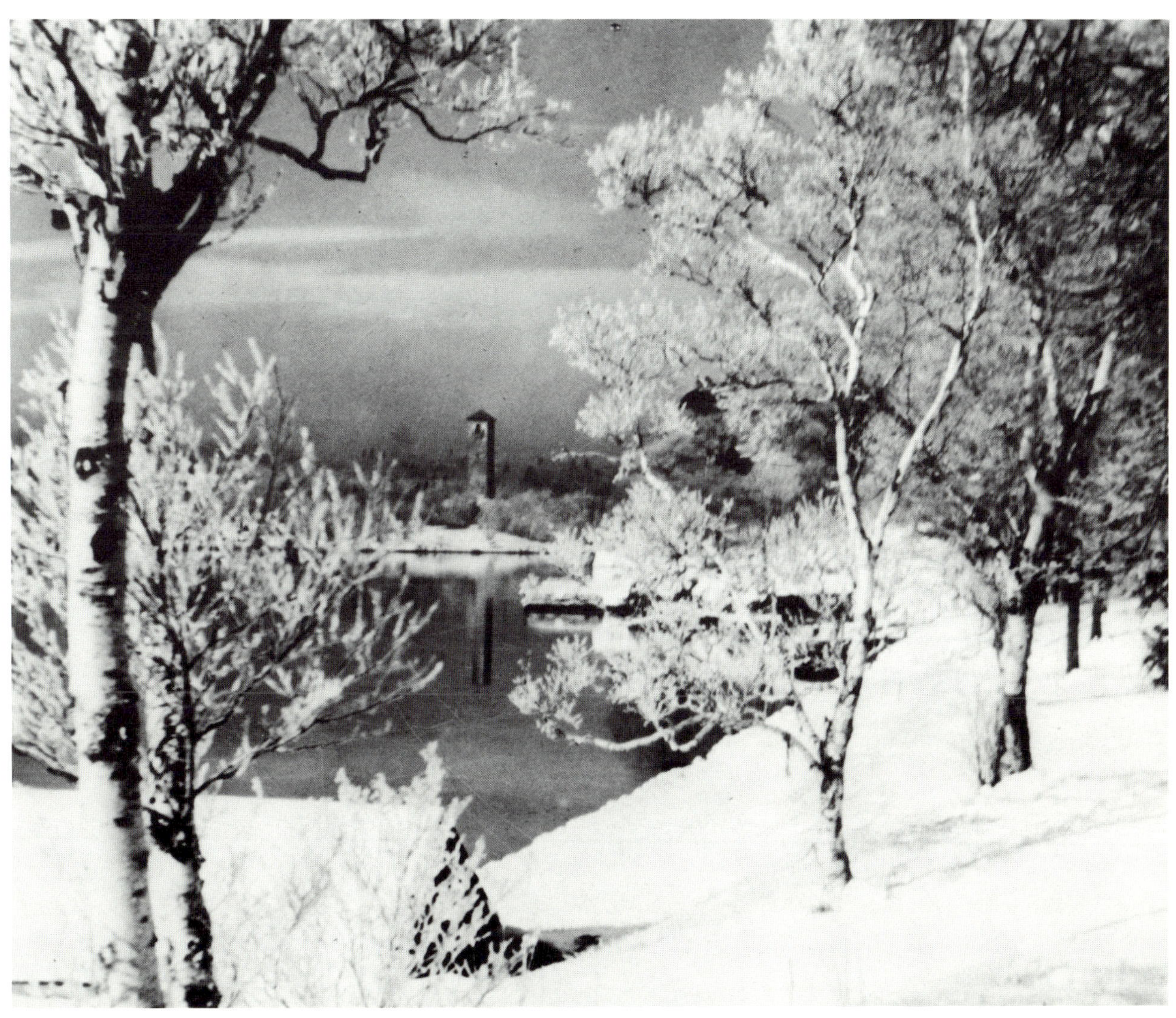

Winter, North West Arm, 1931

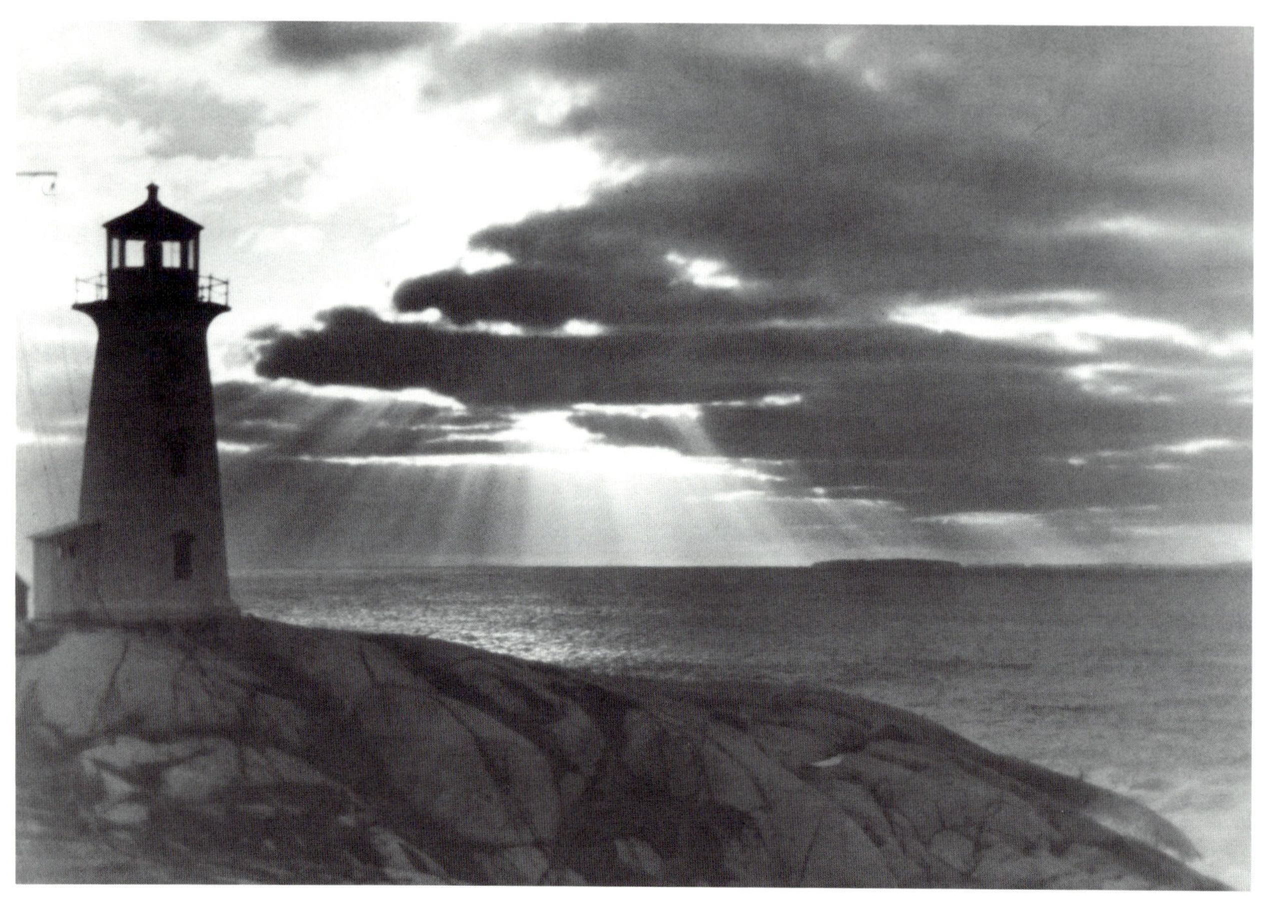

Twilight, Peggy's Cove, 1938

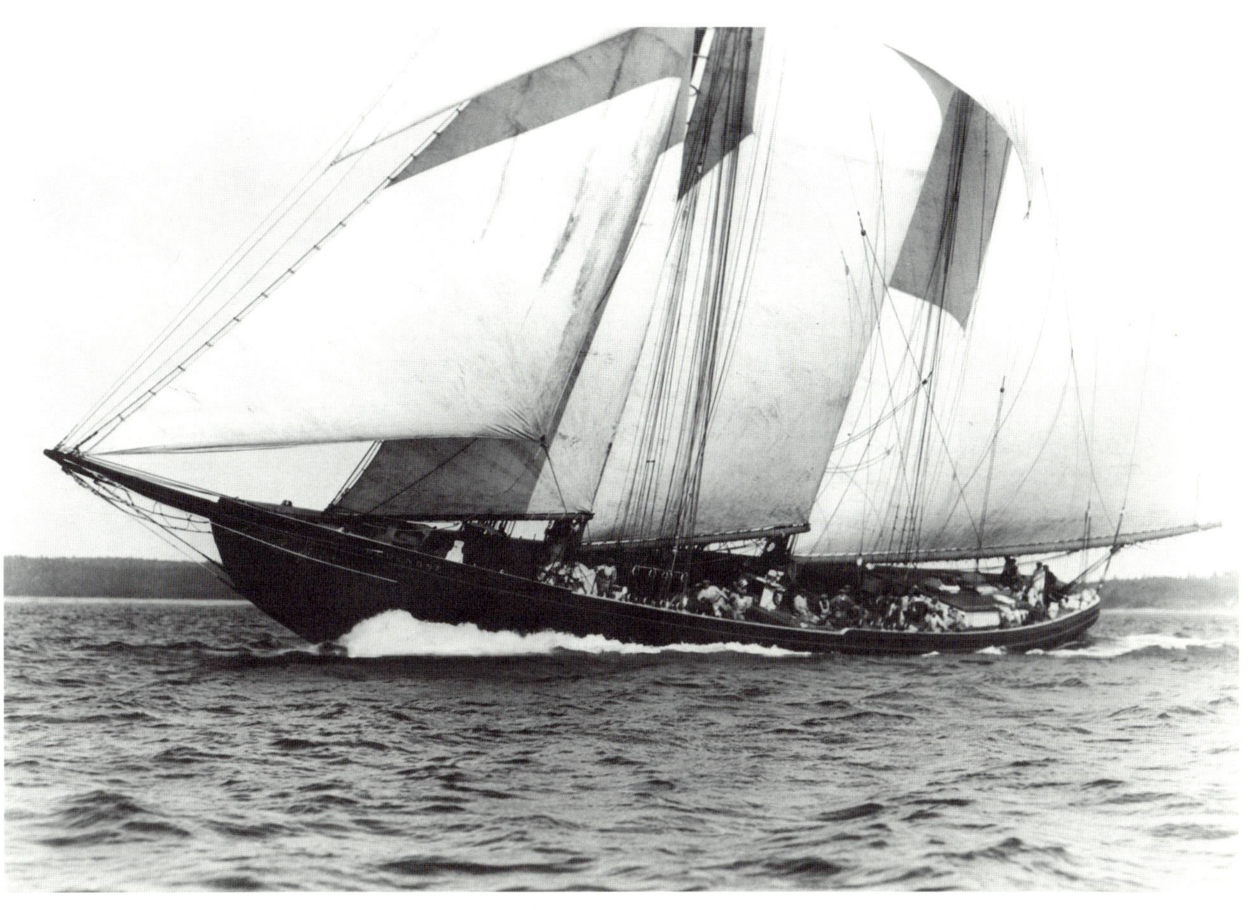

Bluenose, 1931

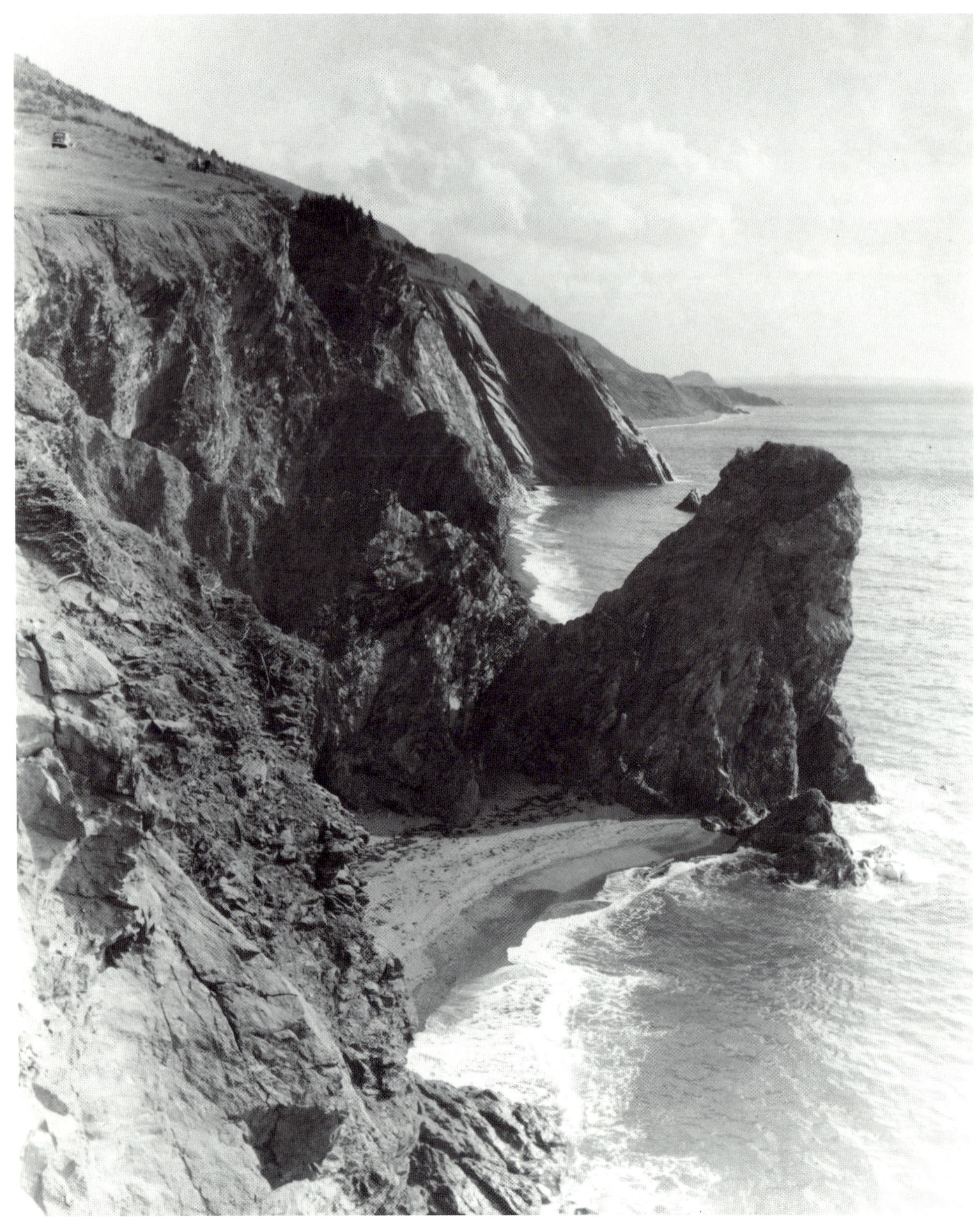

Rocky Coast, Cabot Trail, 1929

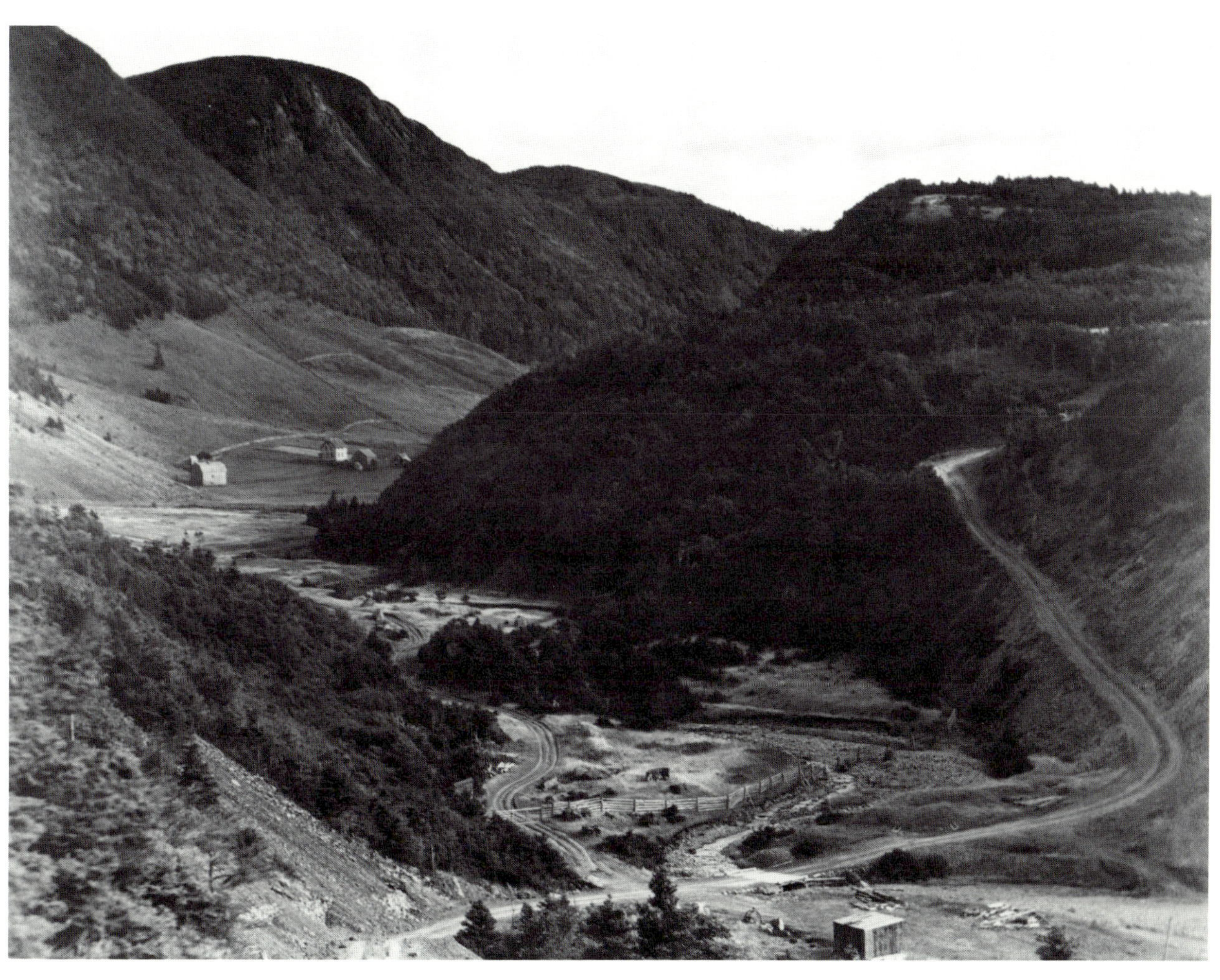

Cabot Trail, 1938

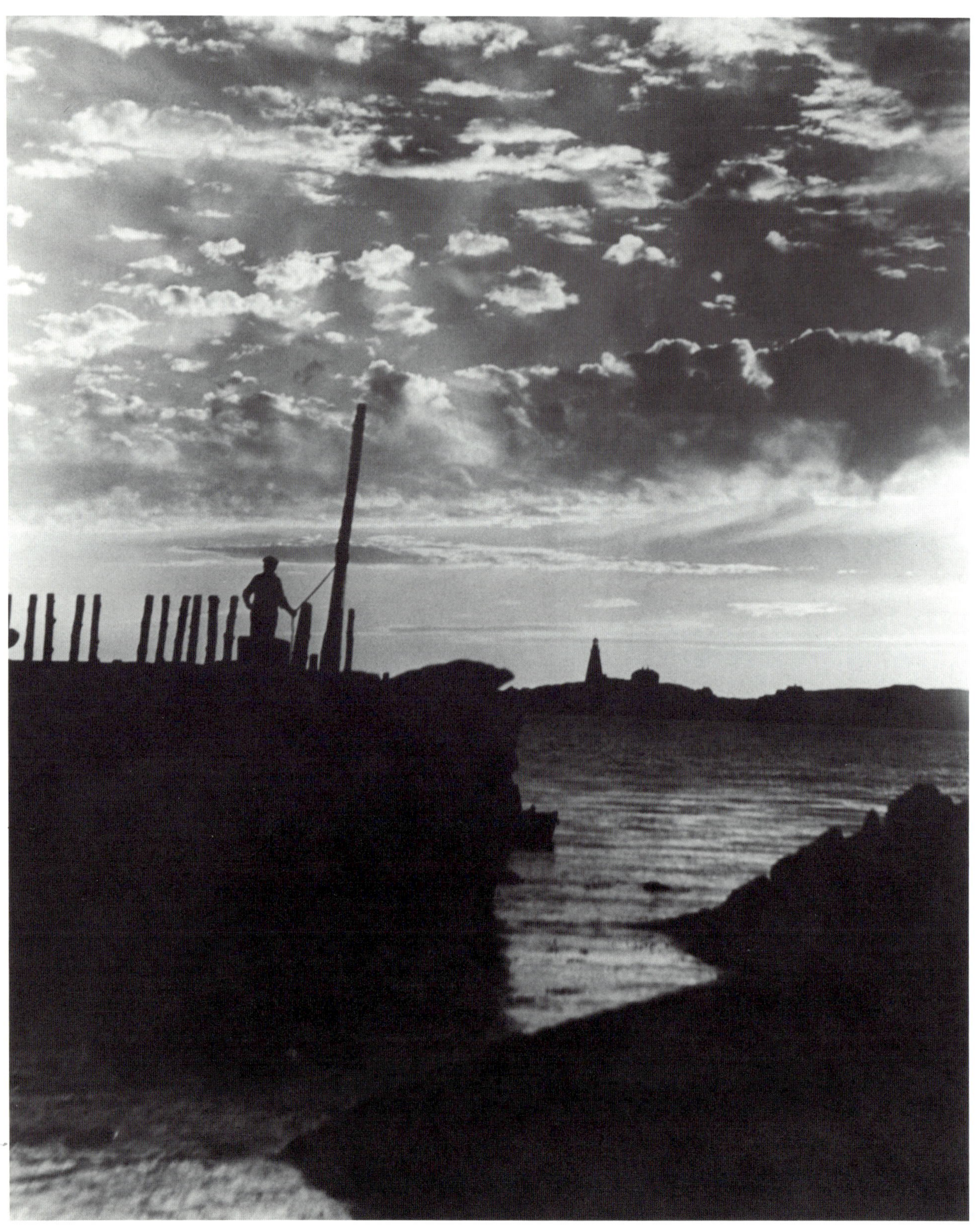

Yarmouth Light, 1931

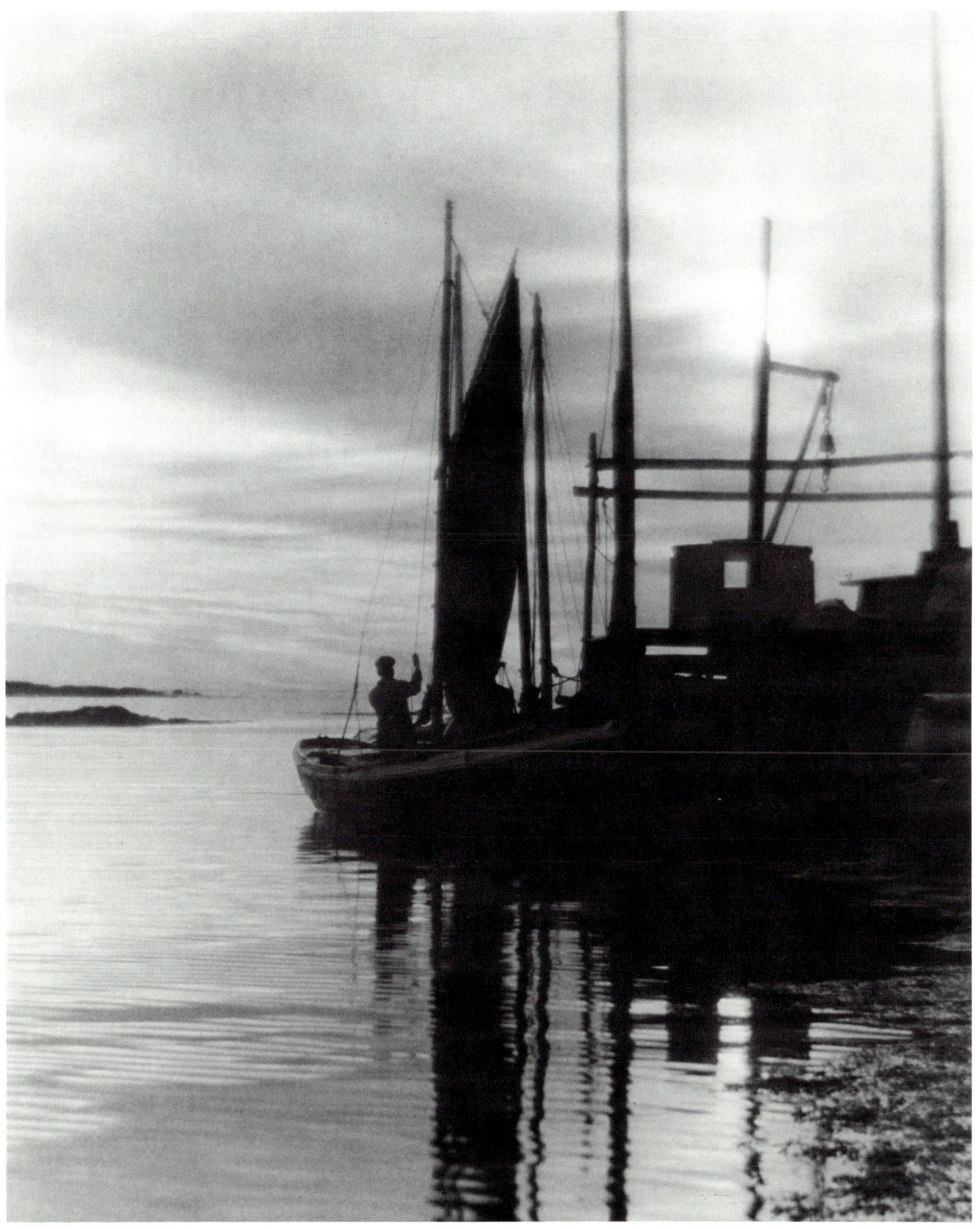

Fisherman's Return, 1935

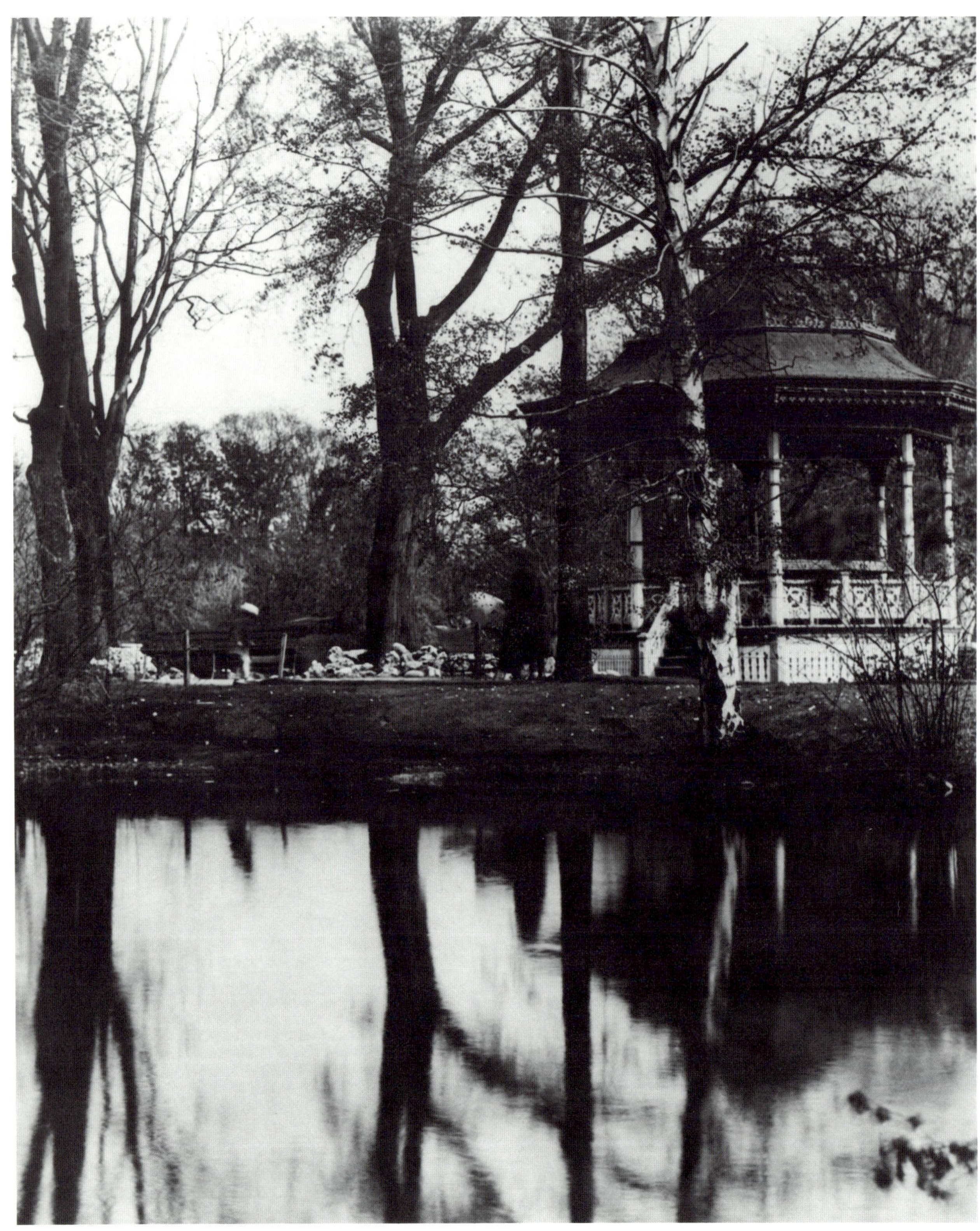

Halifax Public Gardens, 1927

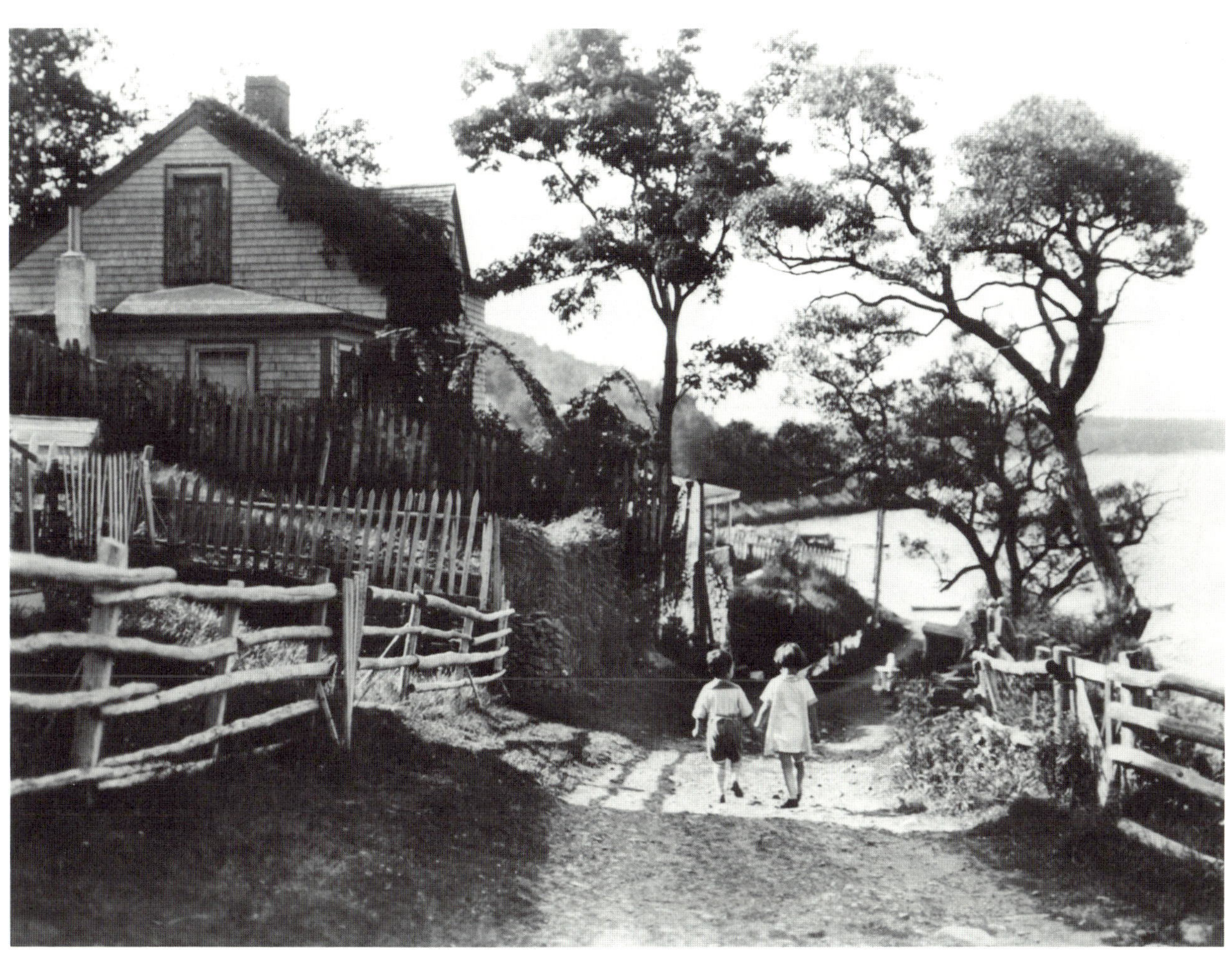

Kingdom by the Sea, 1923

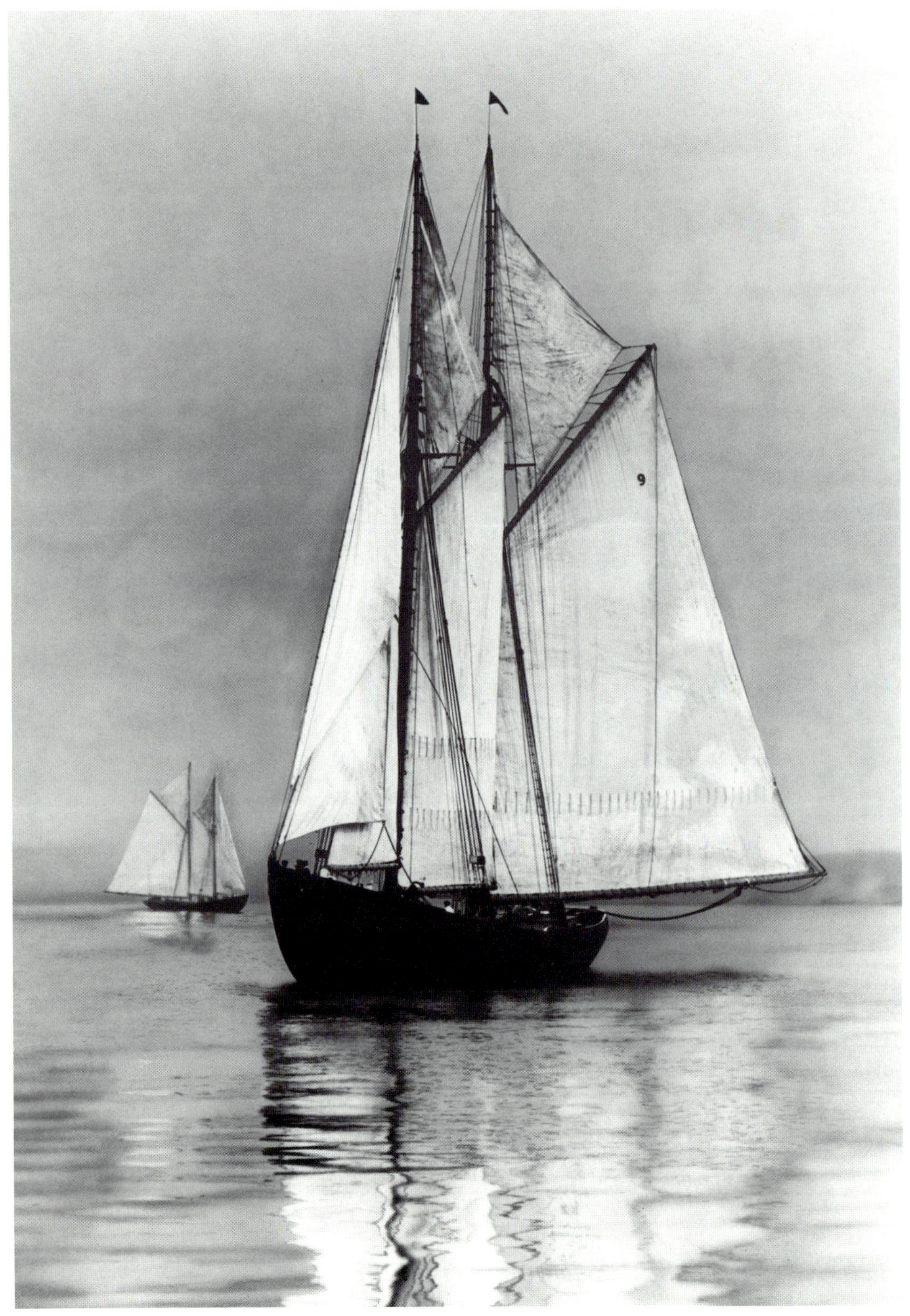

Reflections, 1921

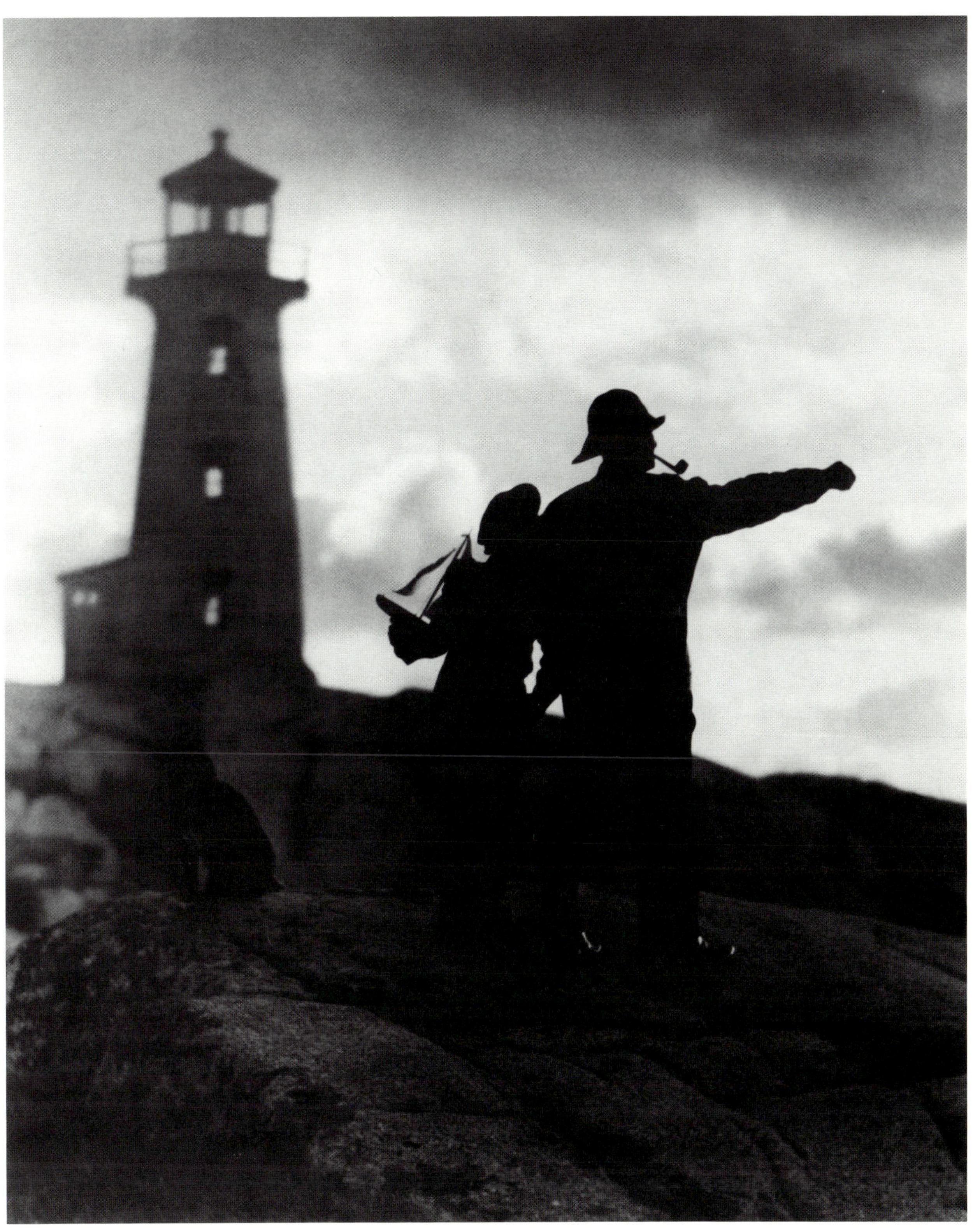

Saga of the Sea, 1936

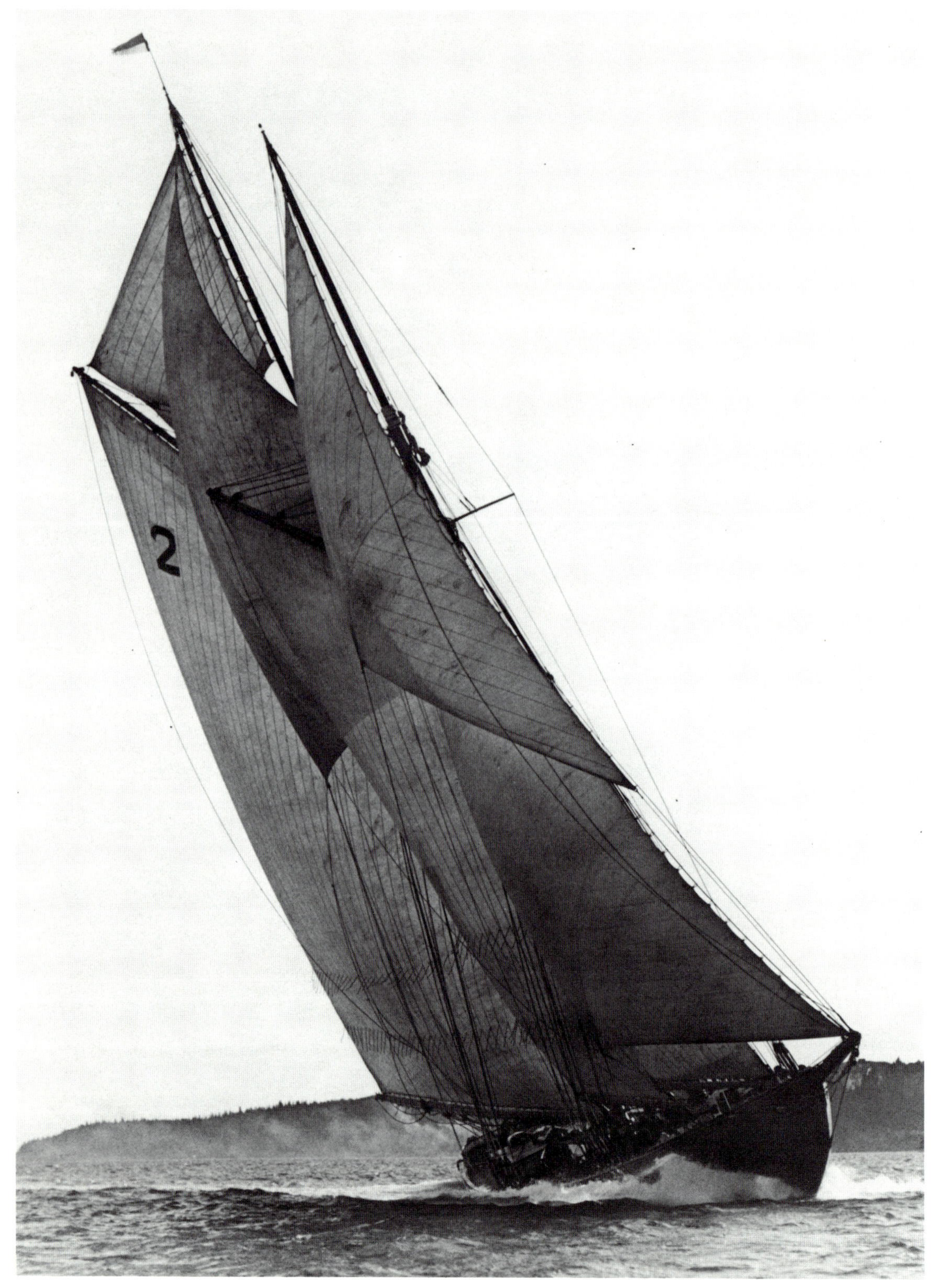

Bluenose, Close-hauled, 1931

Seascapes

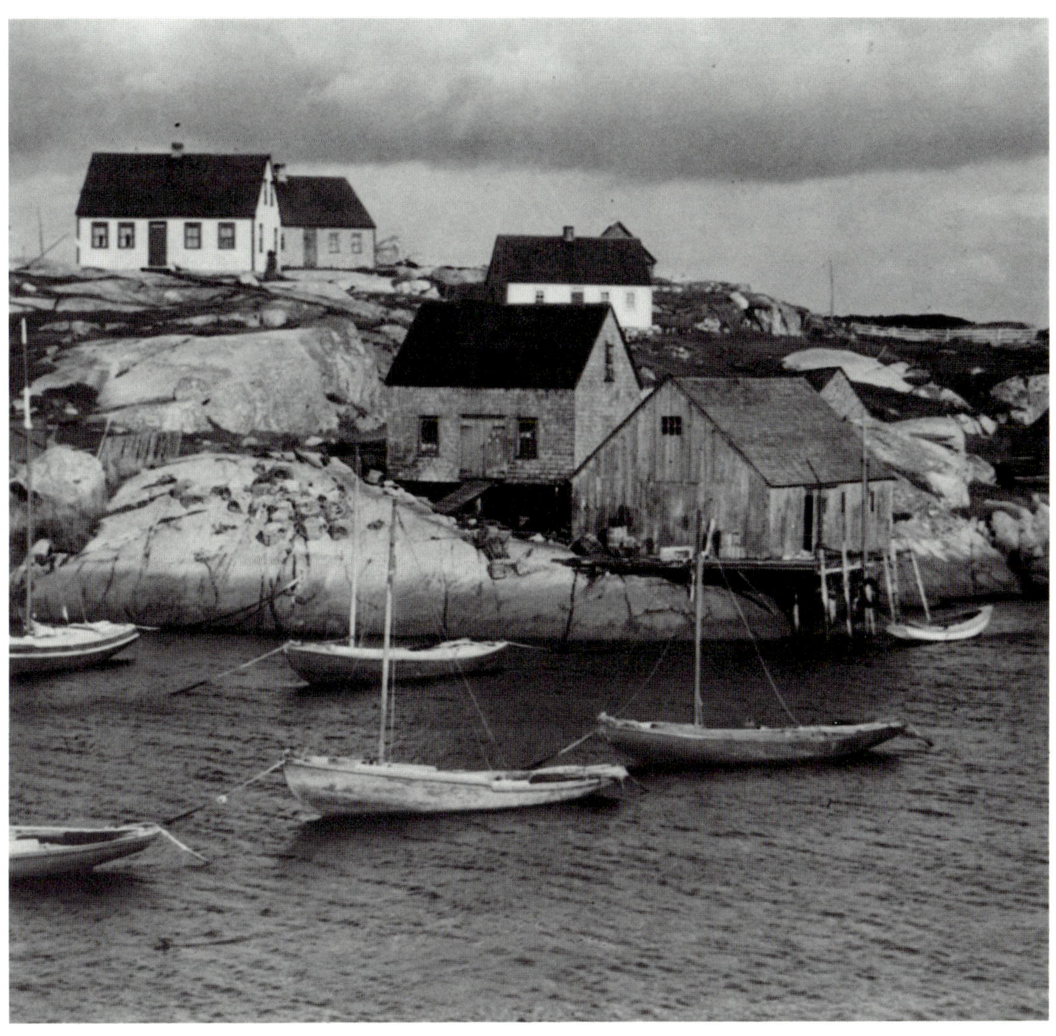

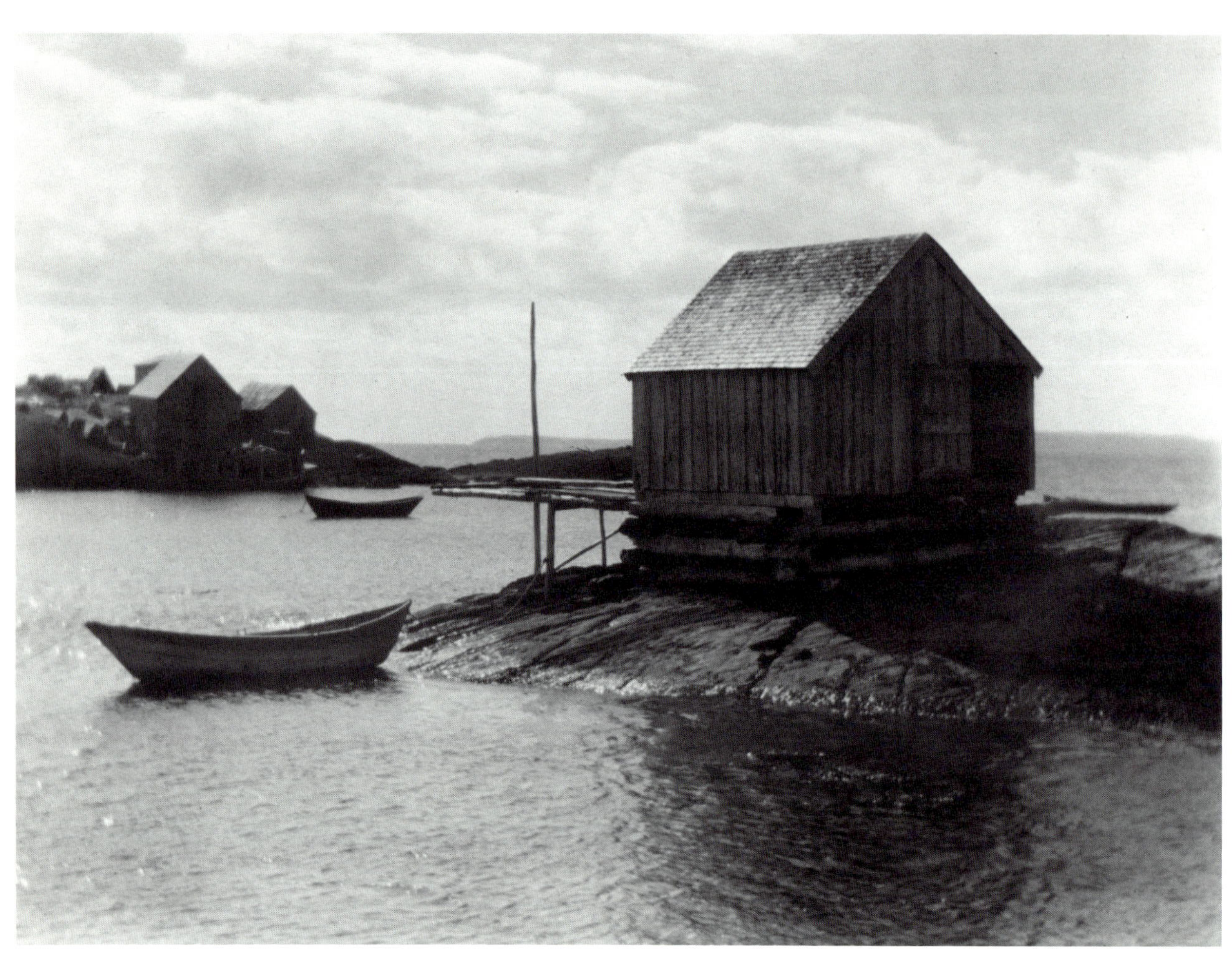

Blue Rocks

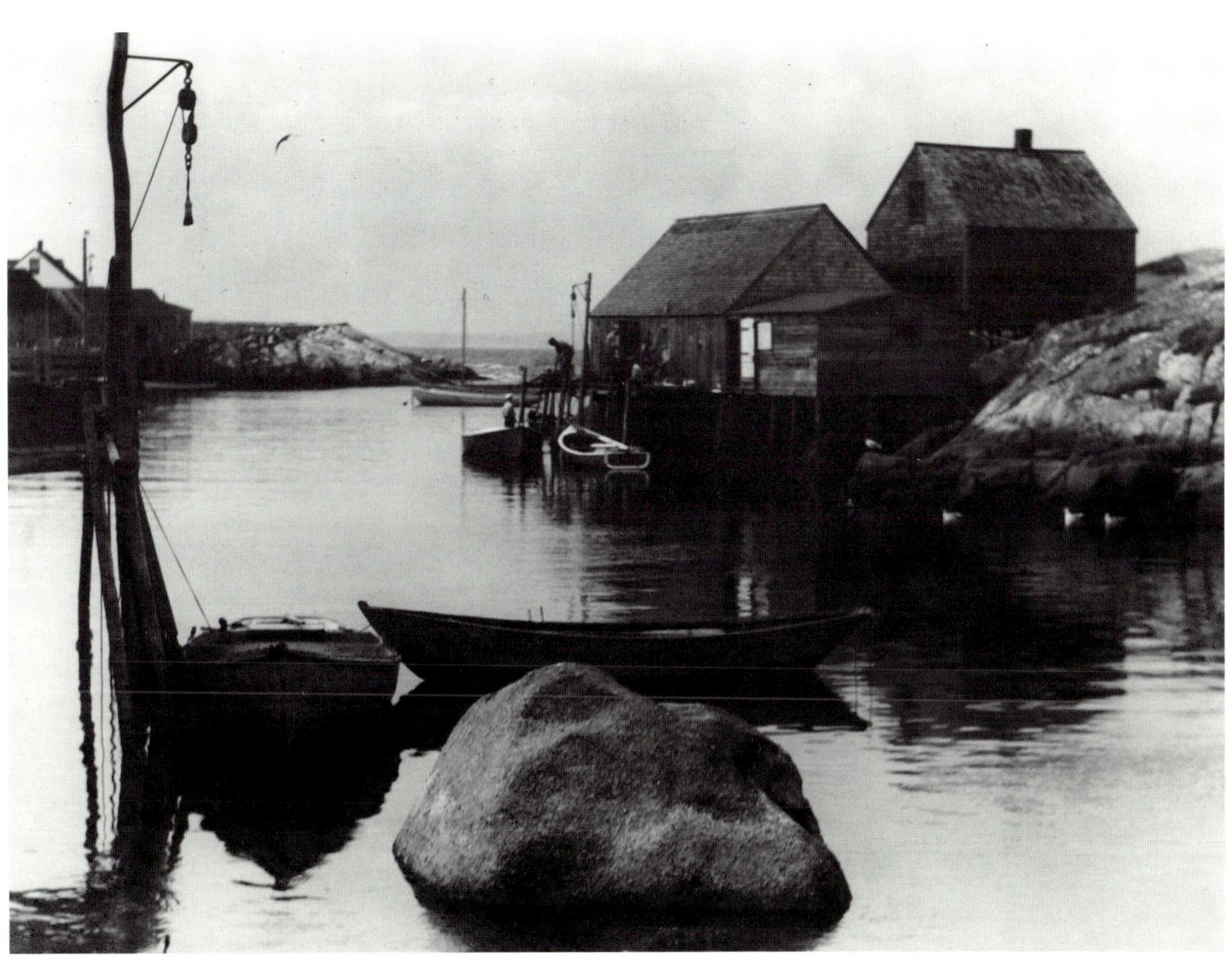

Peggy's Cove

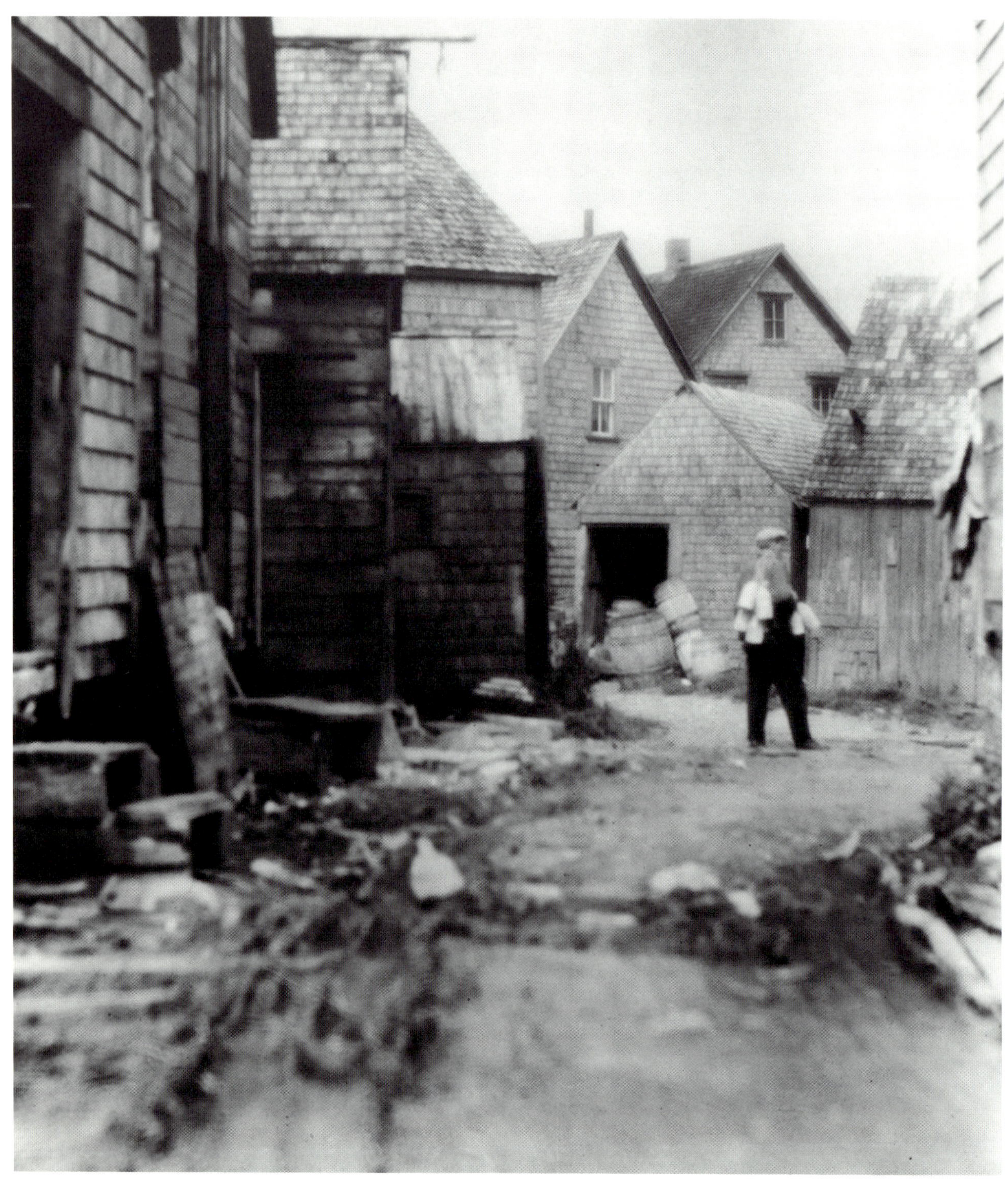

A village of fish stores

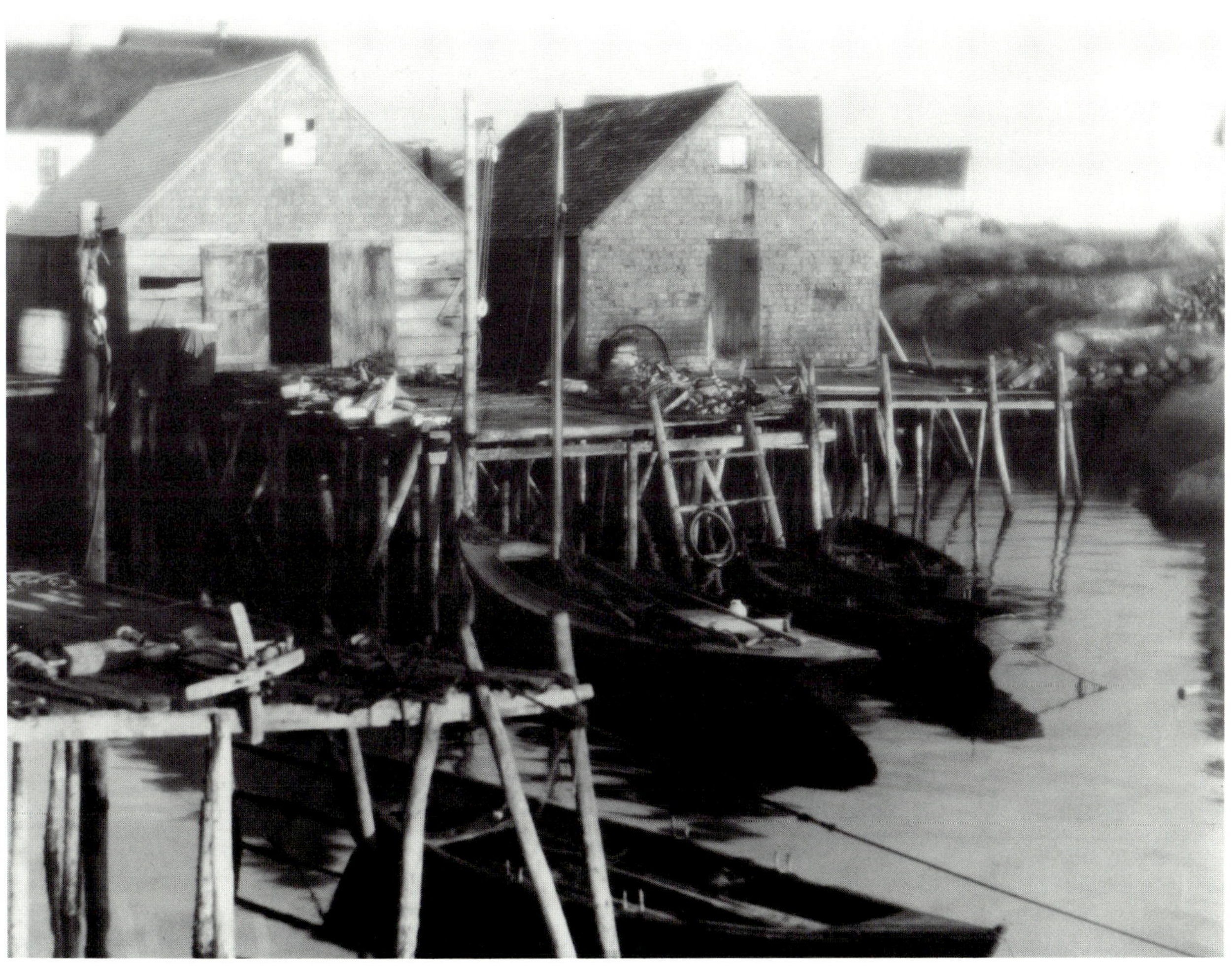

Fishing shacks

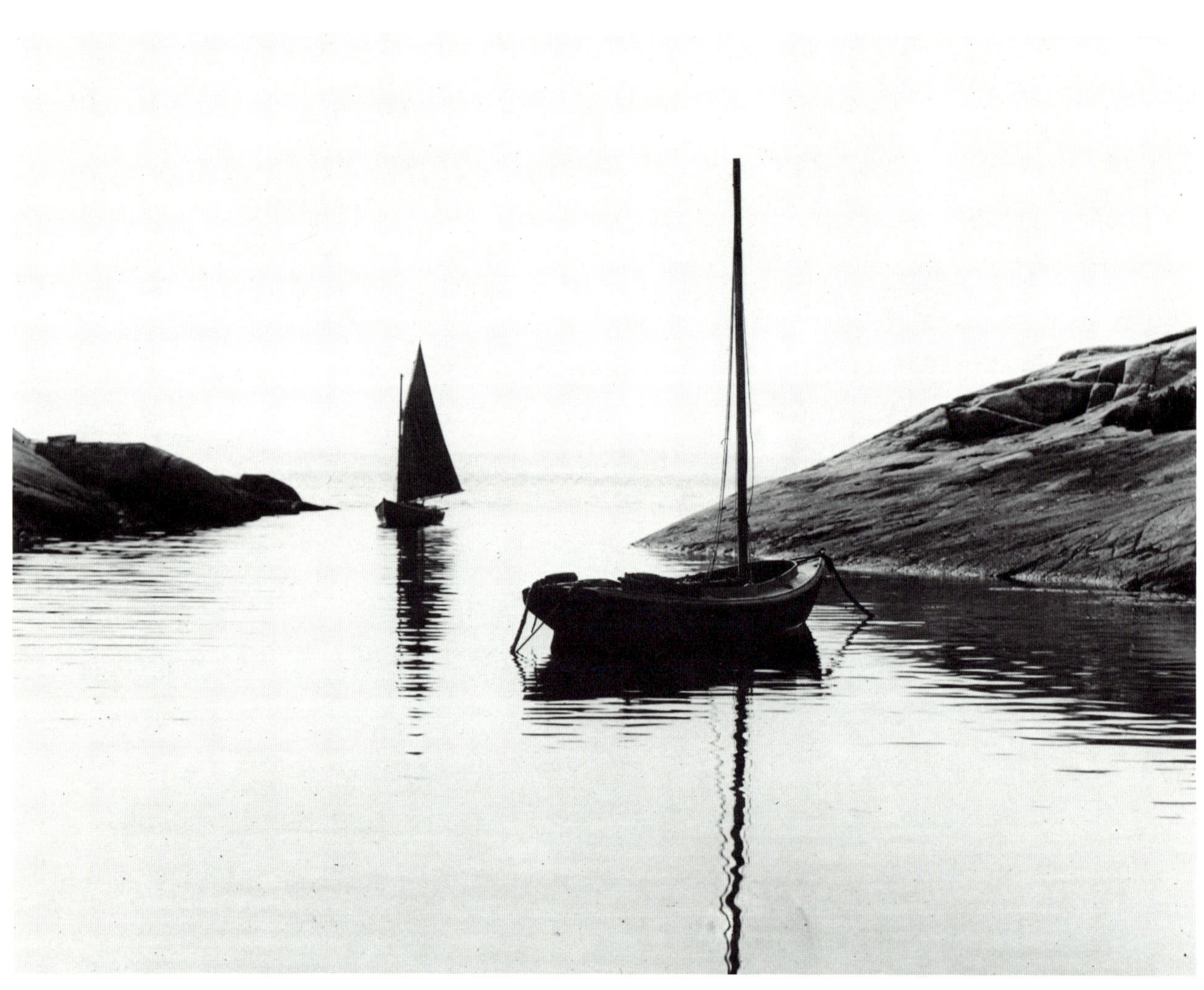

Peggy's Cove

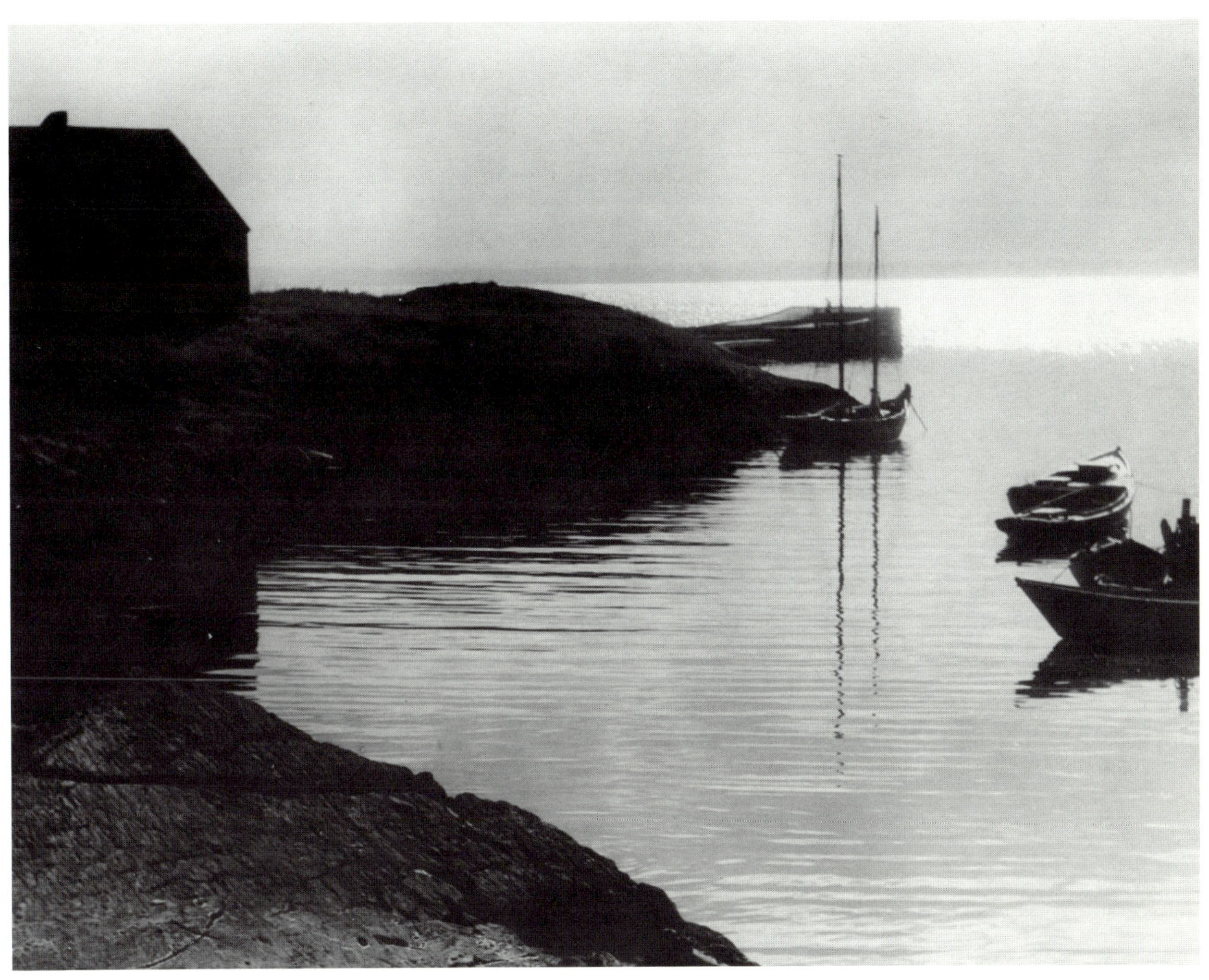

Blue Rocks

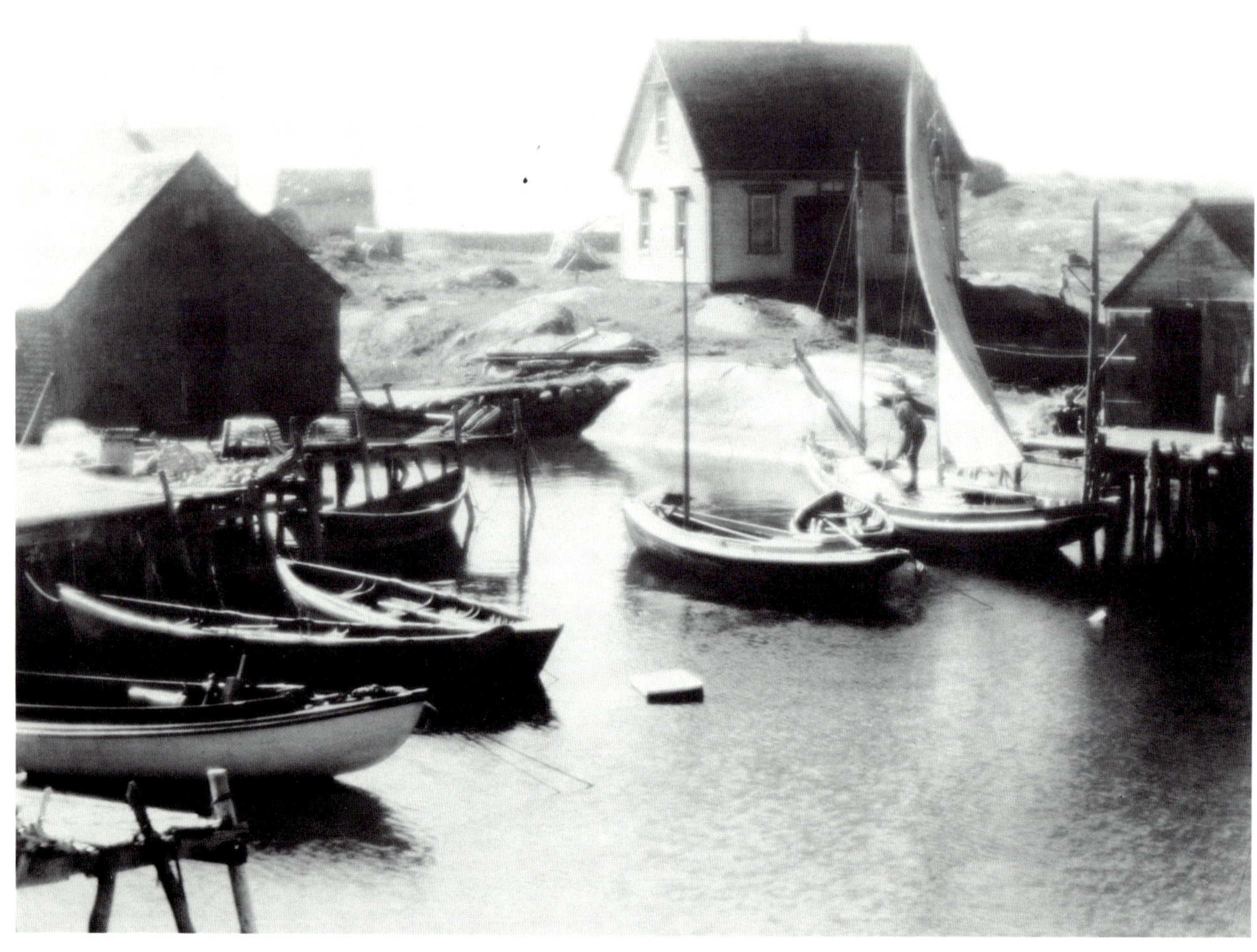

Peggy's Cove

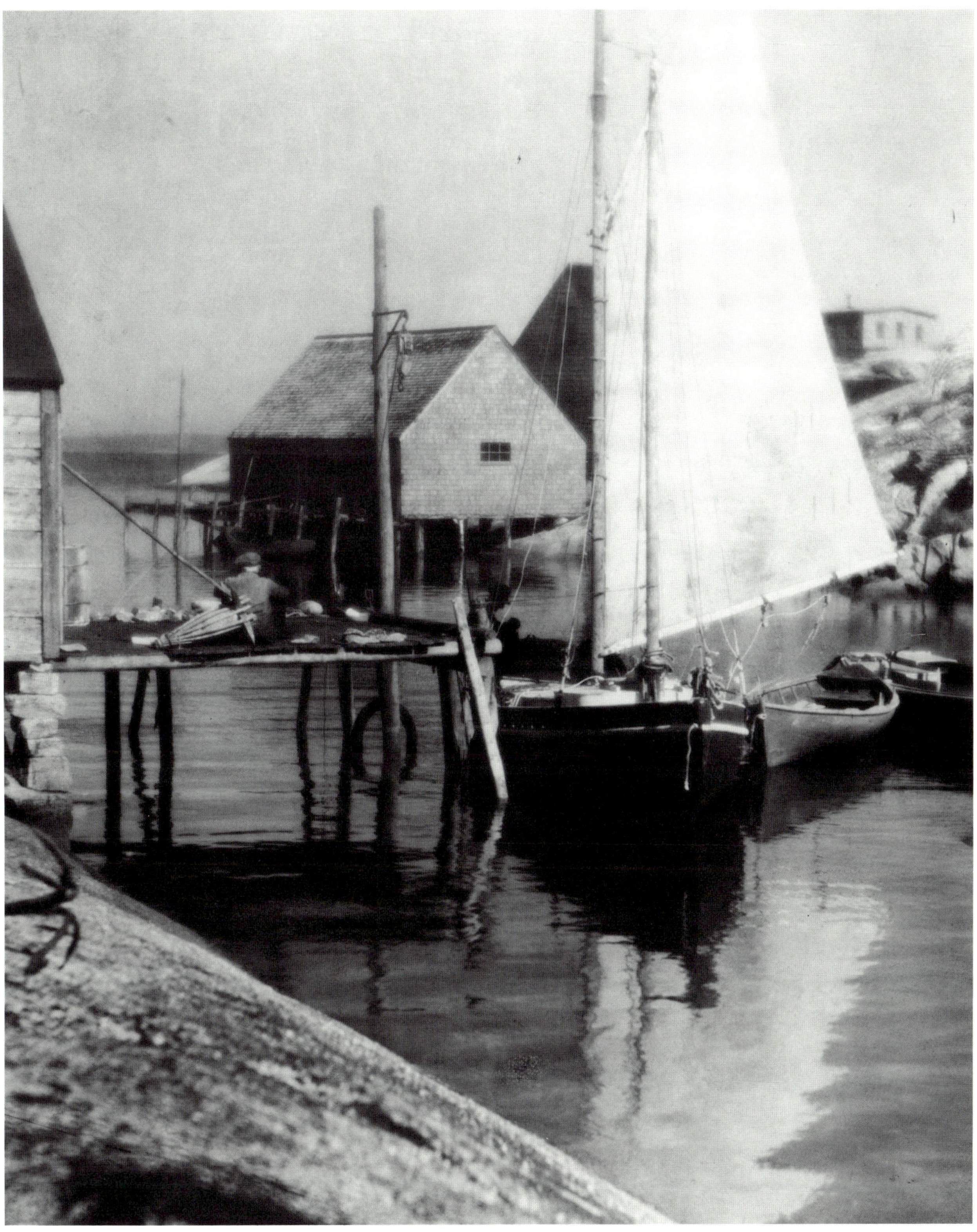

Peggy's Cove

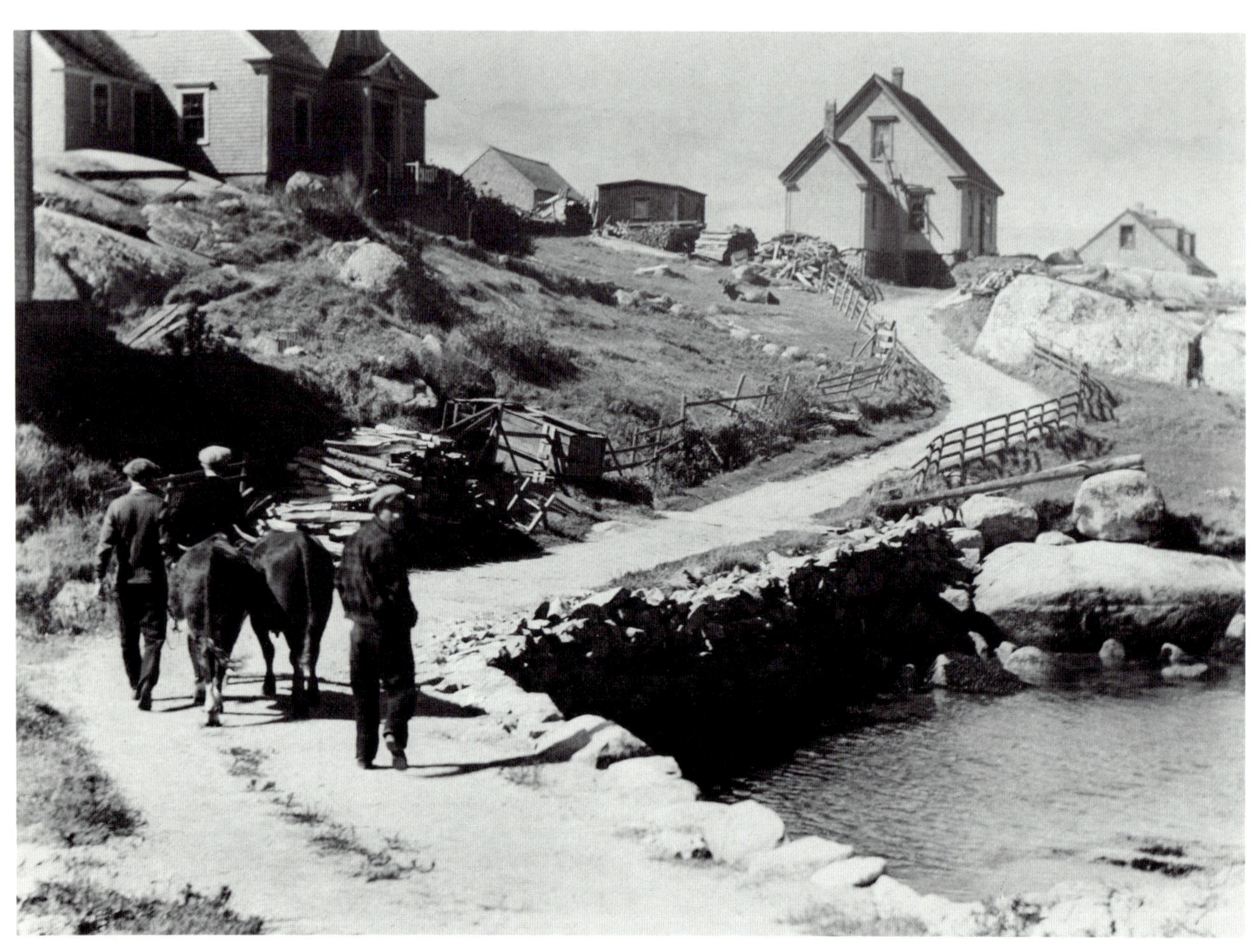

Peggy's Cove

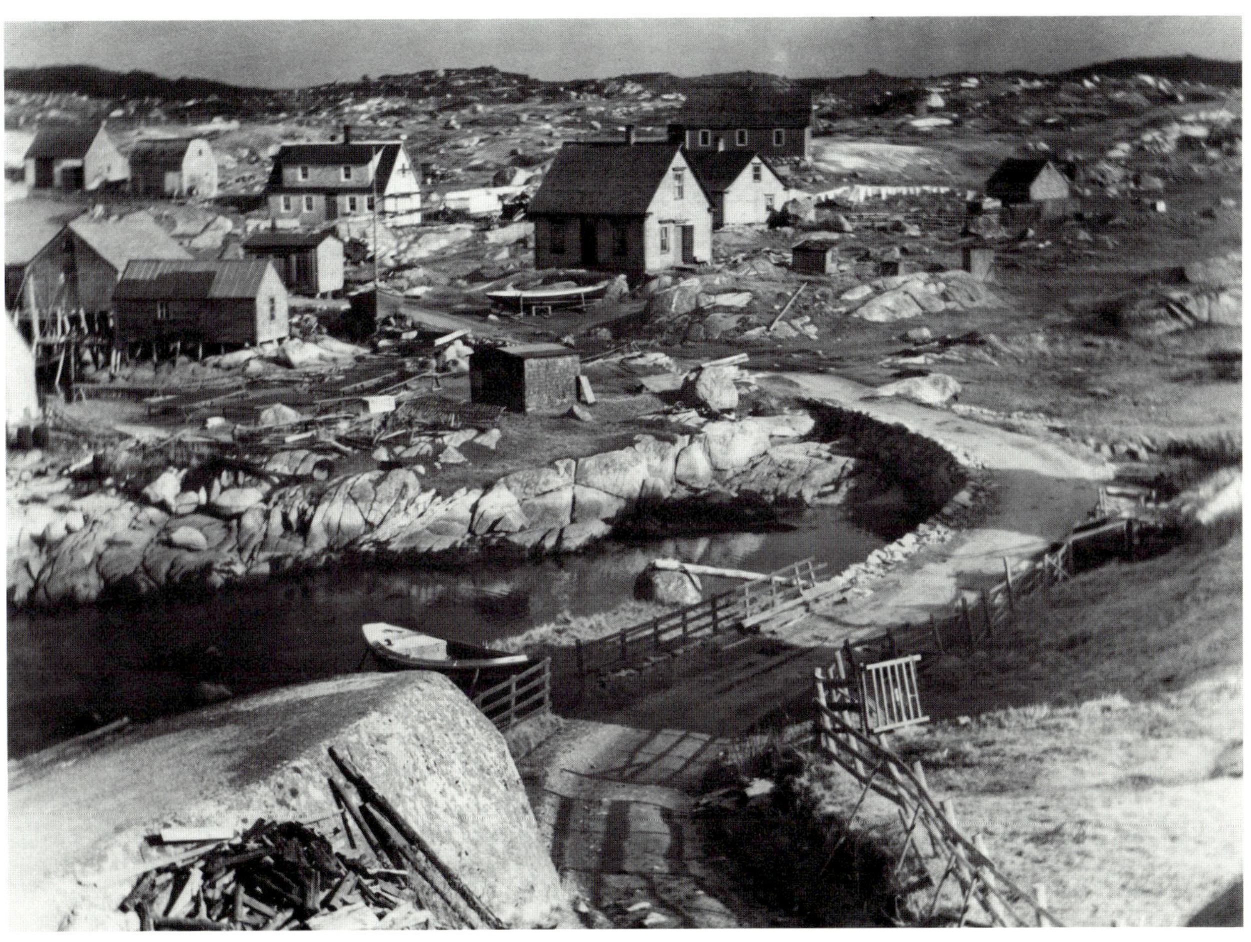

Peggy's Cove

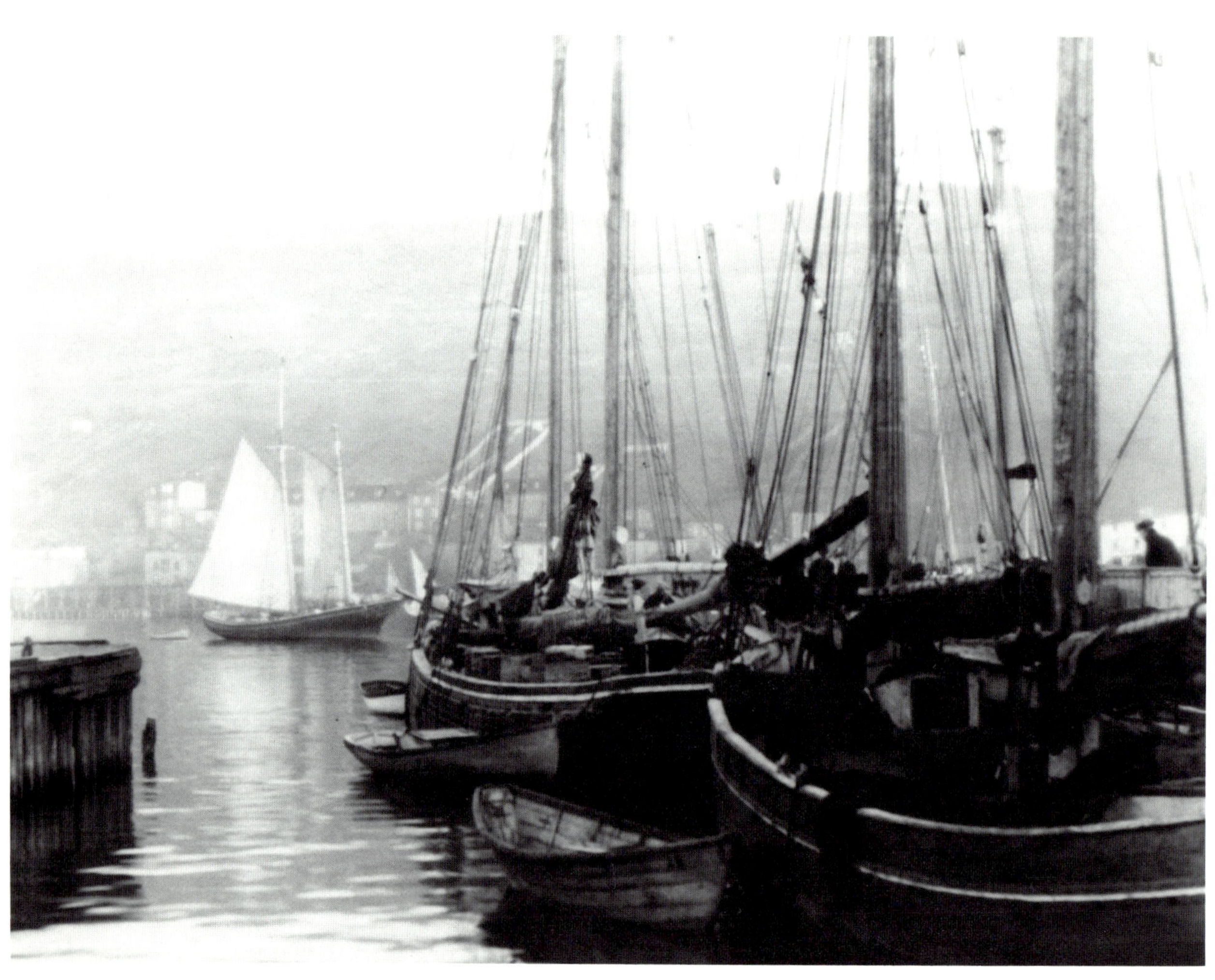

Schooner sailing into a Newfoundland harbour

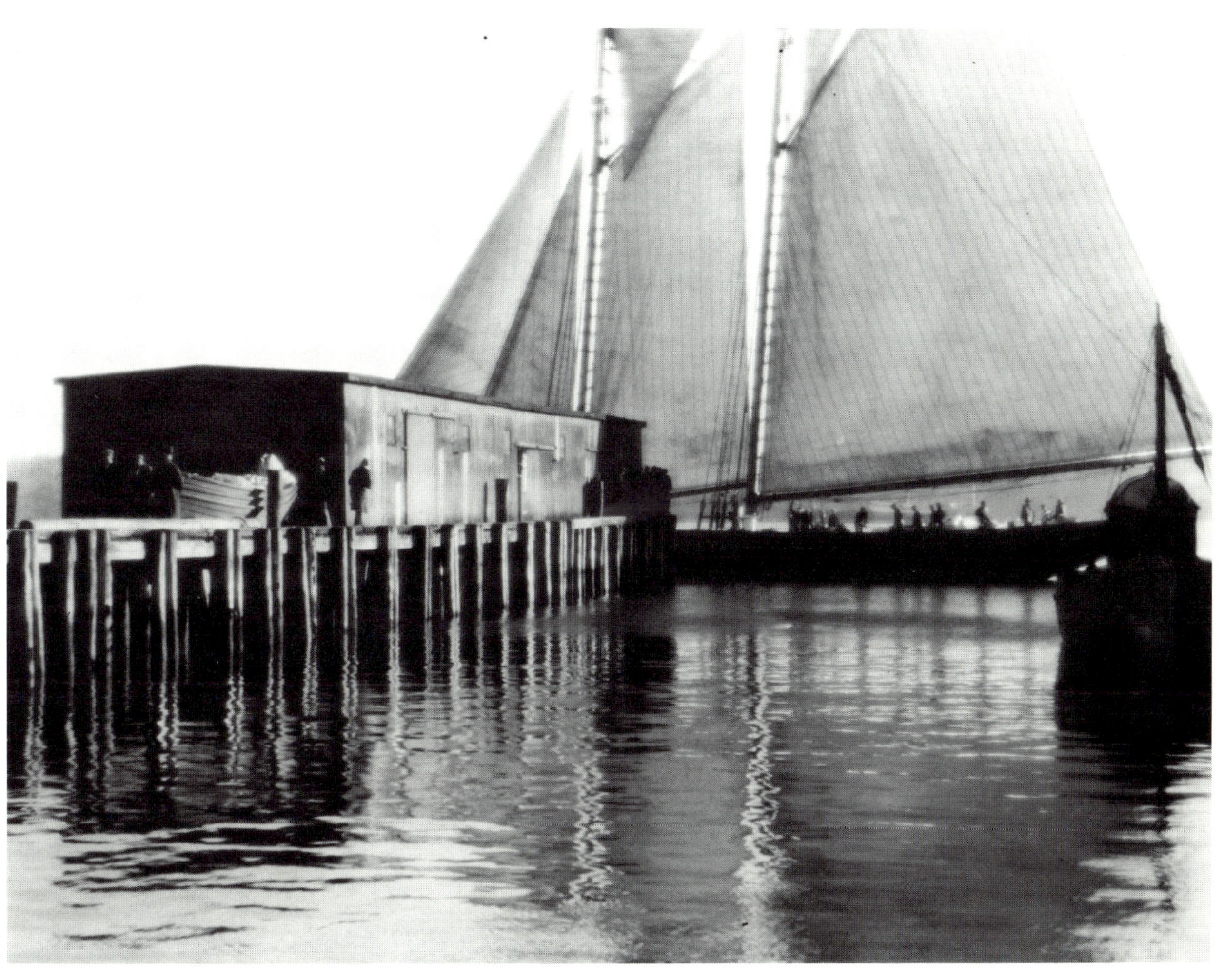

Schooner sailing into Halifax harbour

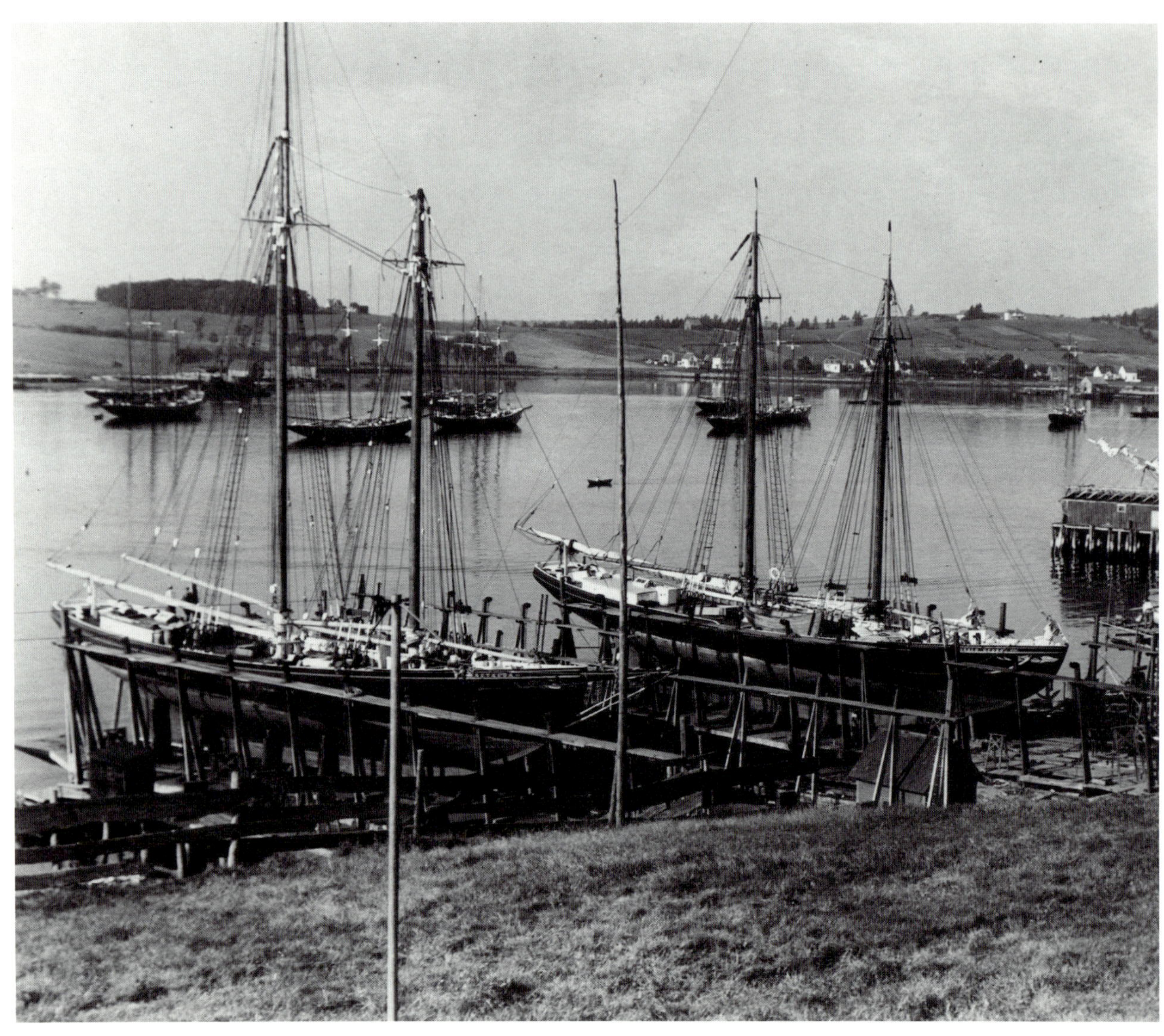

Schooners on the slip and in the harbour, Lunenburg

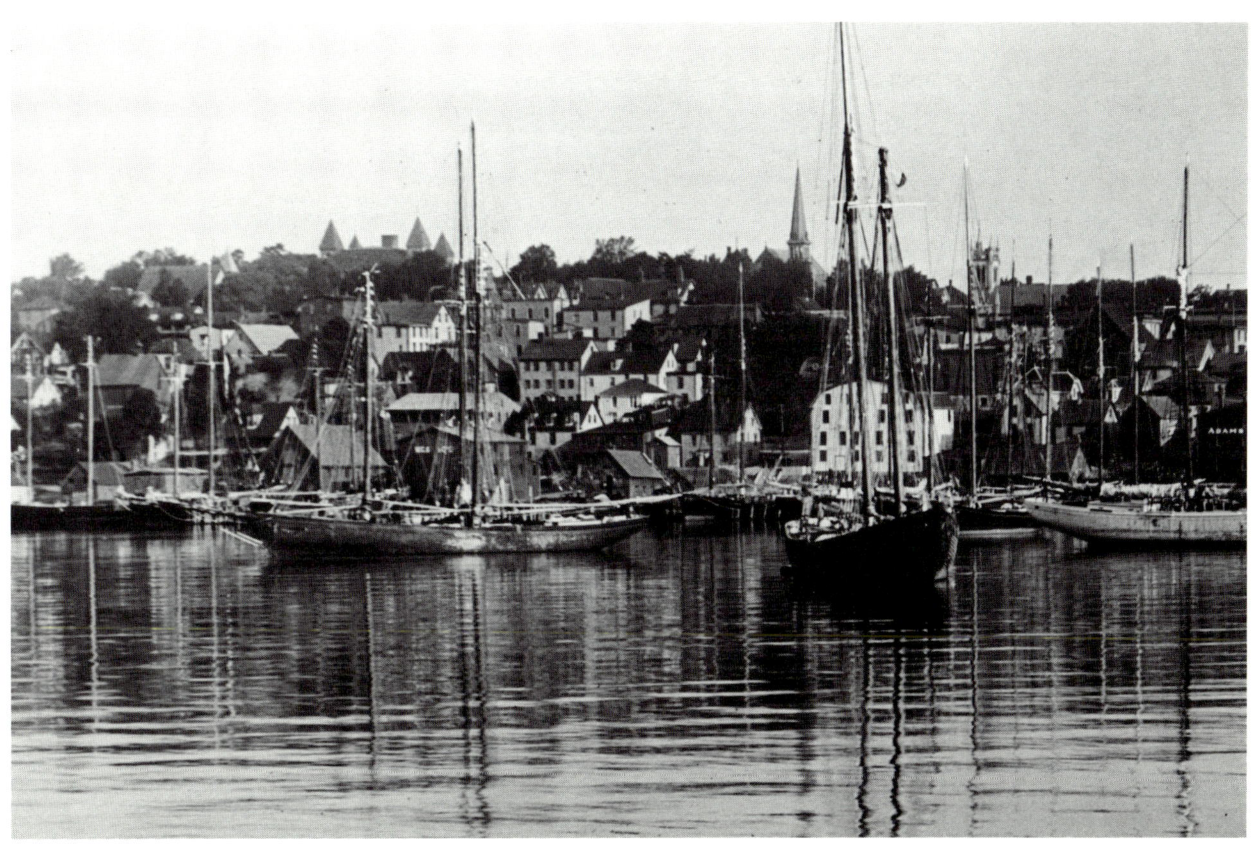

Schooners in Lunenburg harbour

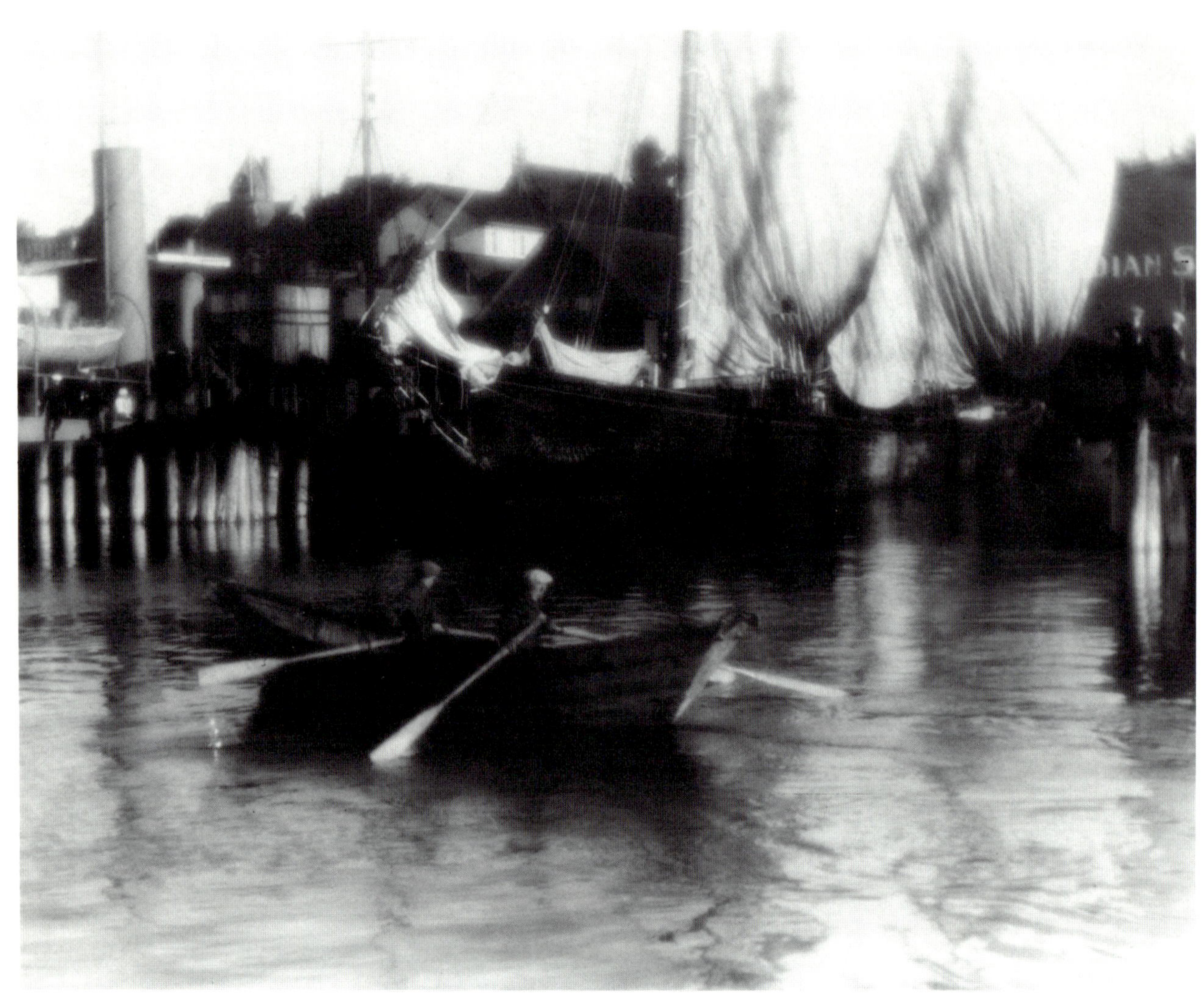

Lunenburg waterfront

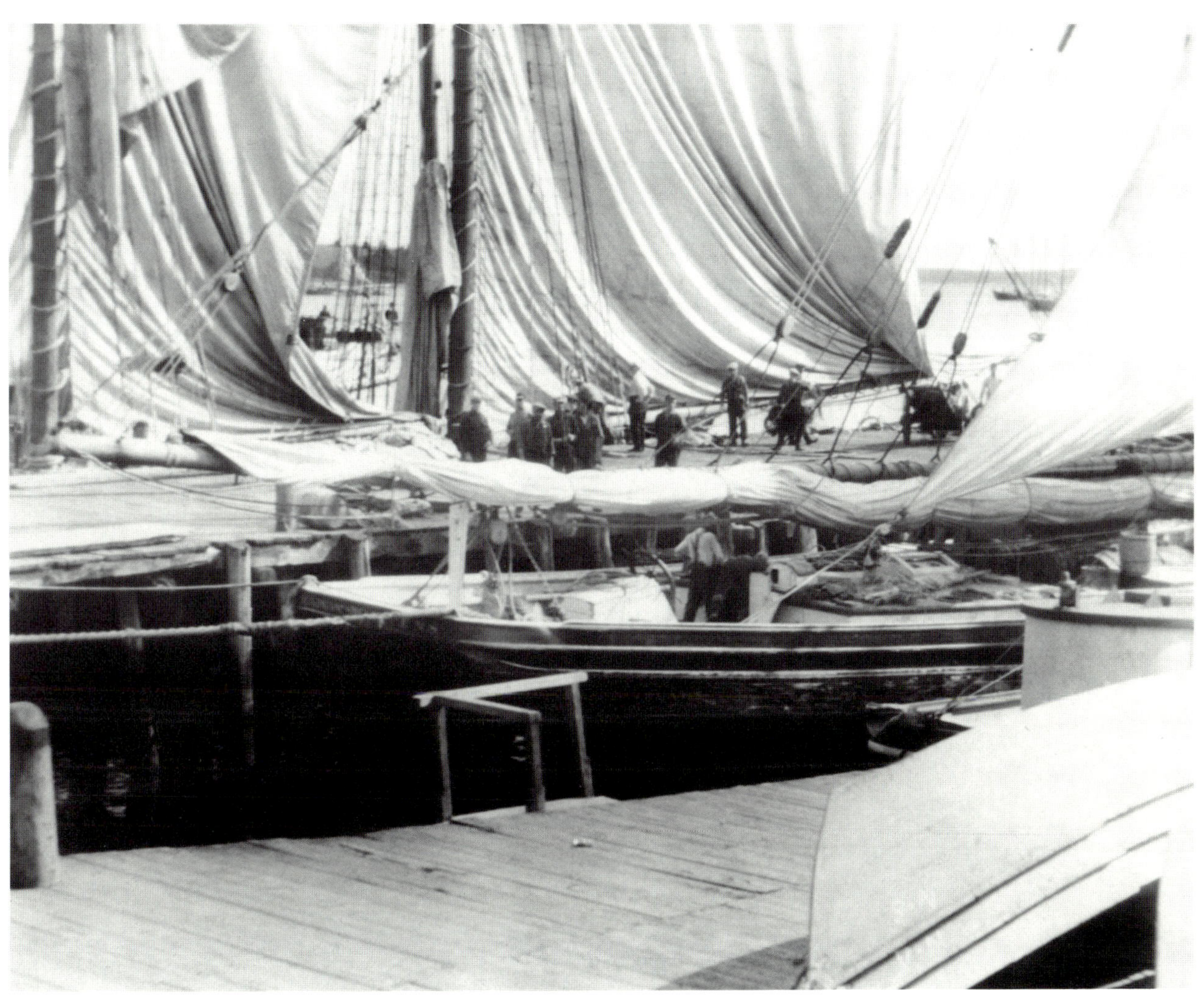

Drying sails, Lunenburg

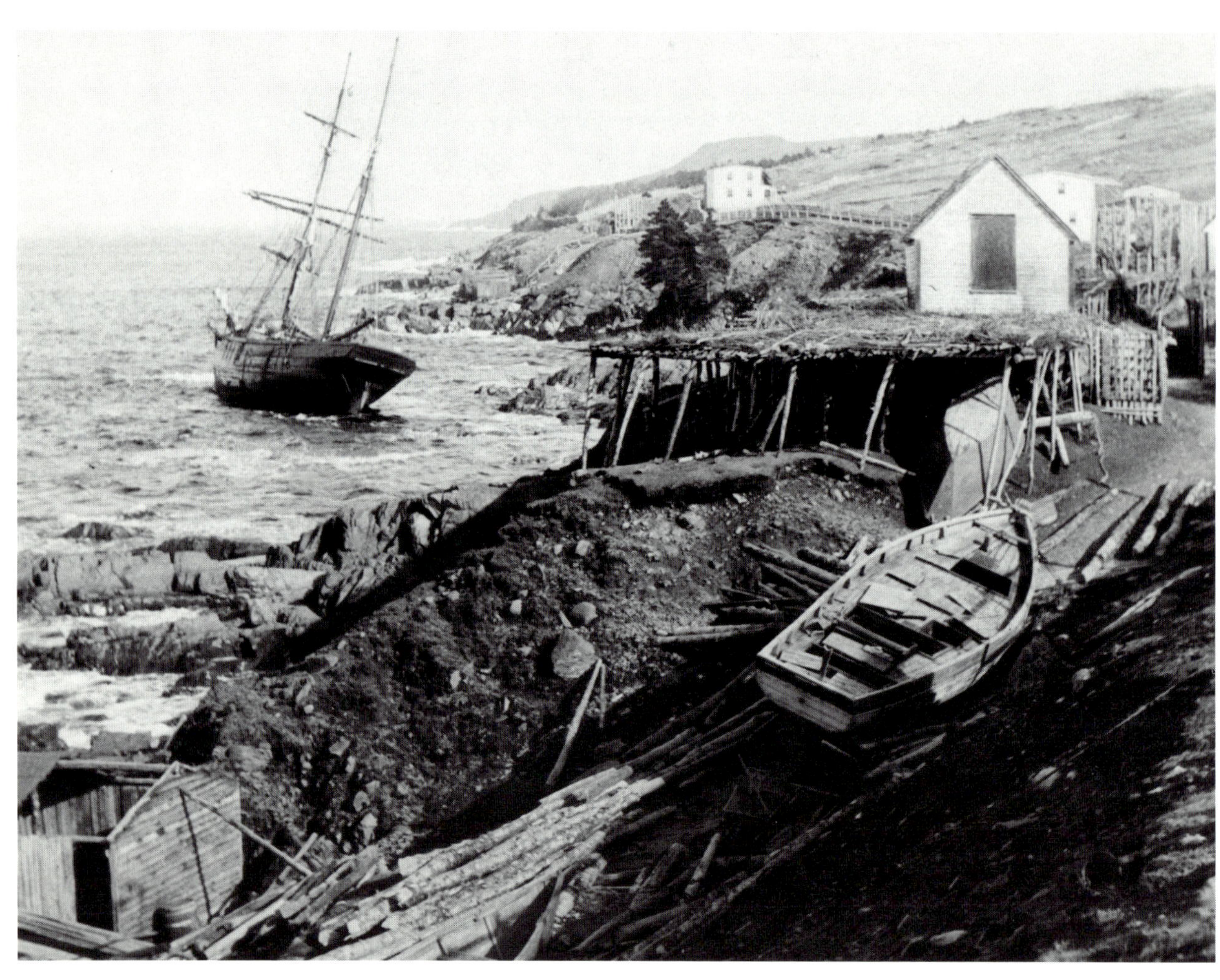

Shipwreck on the Newfoundland coast

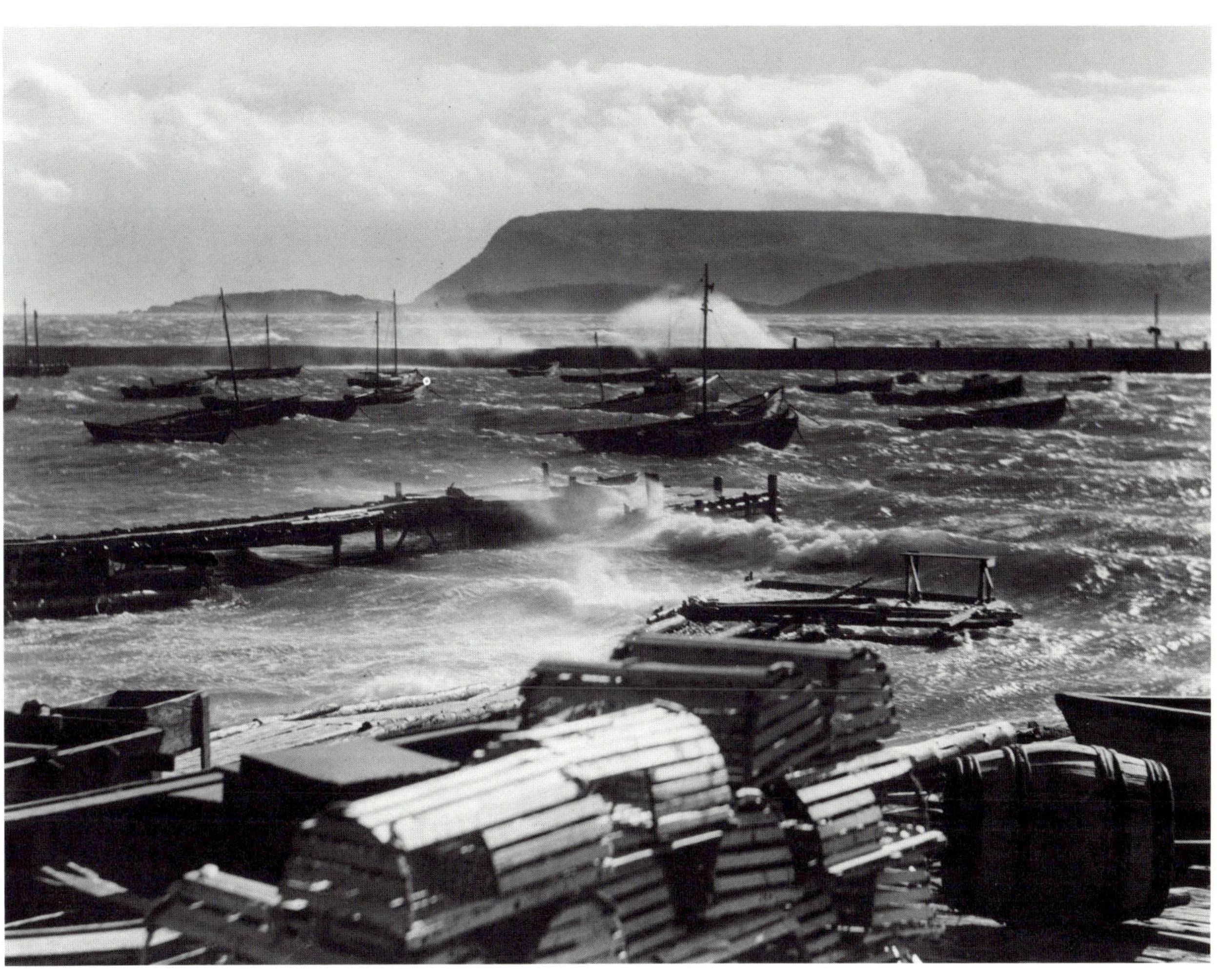

Storm at Ingonish

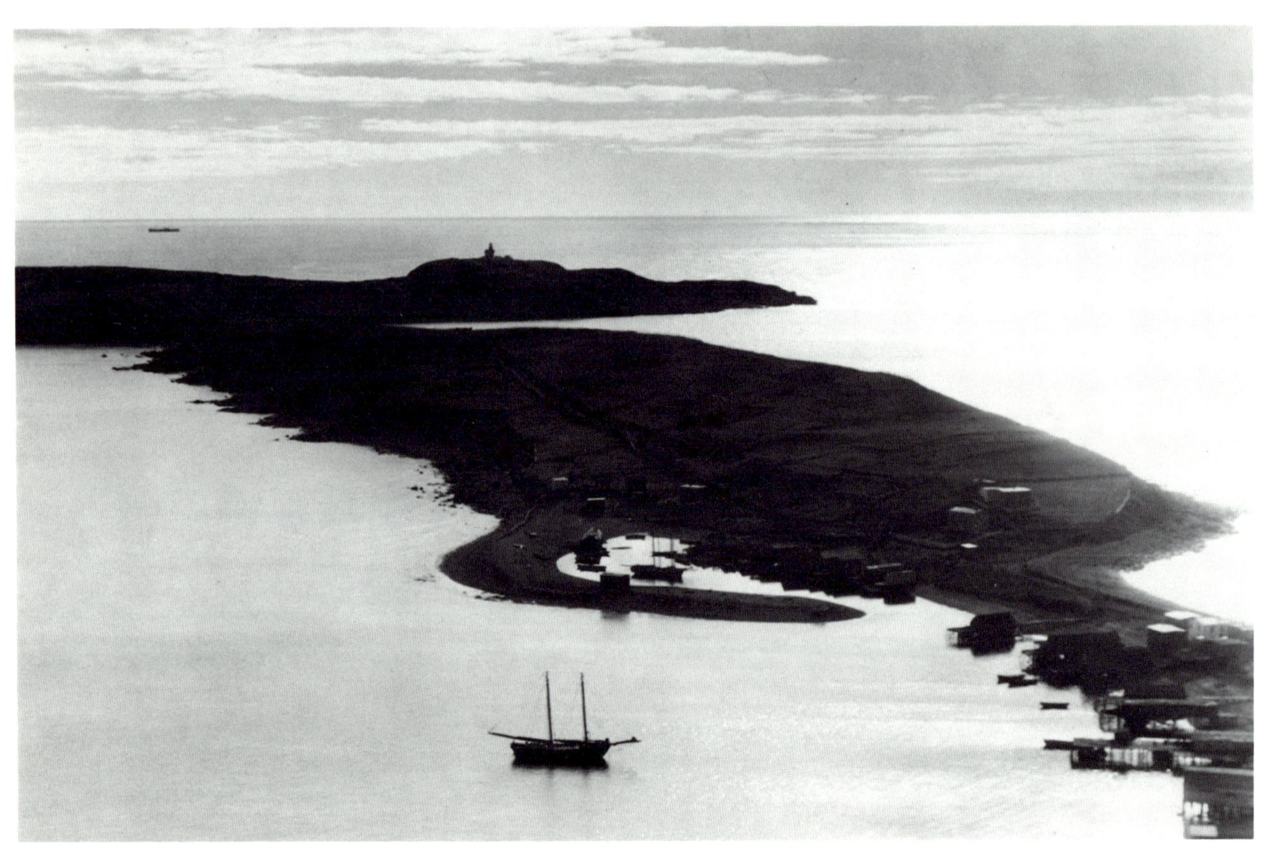

Coastal village, Newfoundland

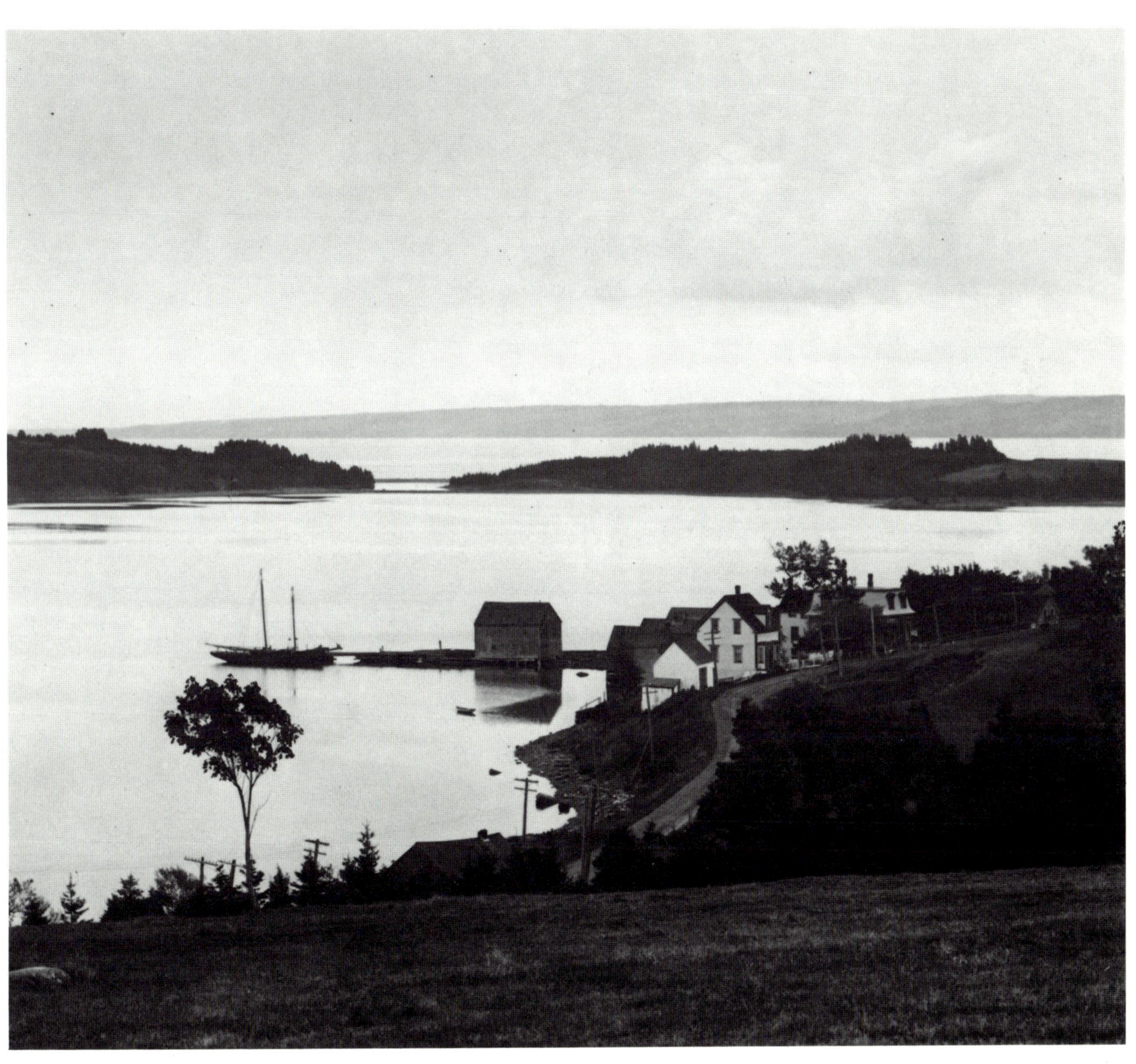

Coastal village, Nova Scotia

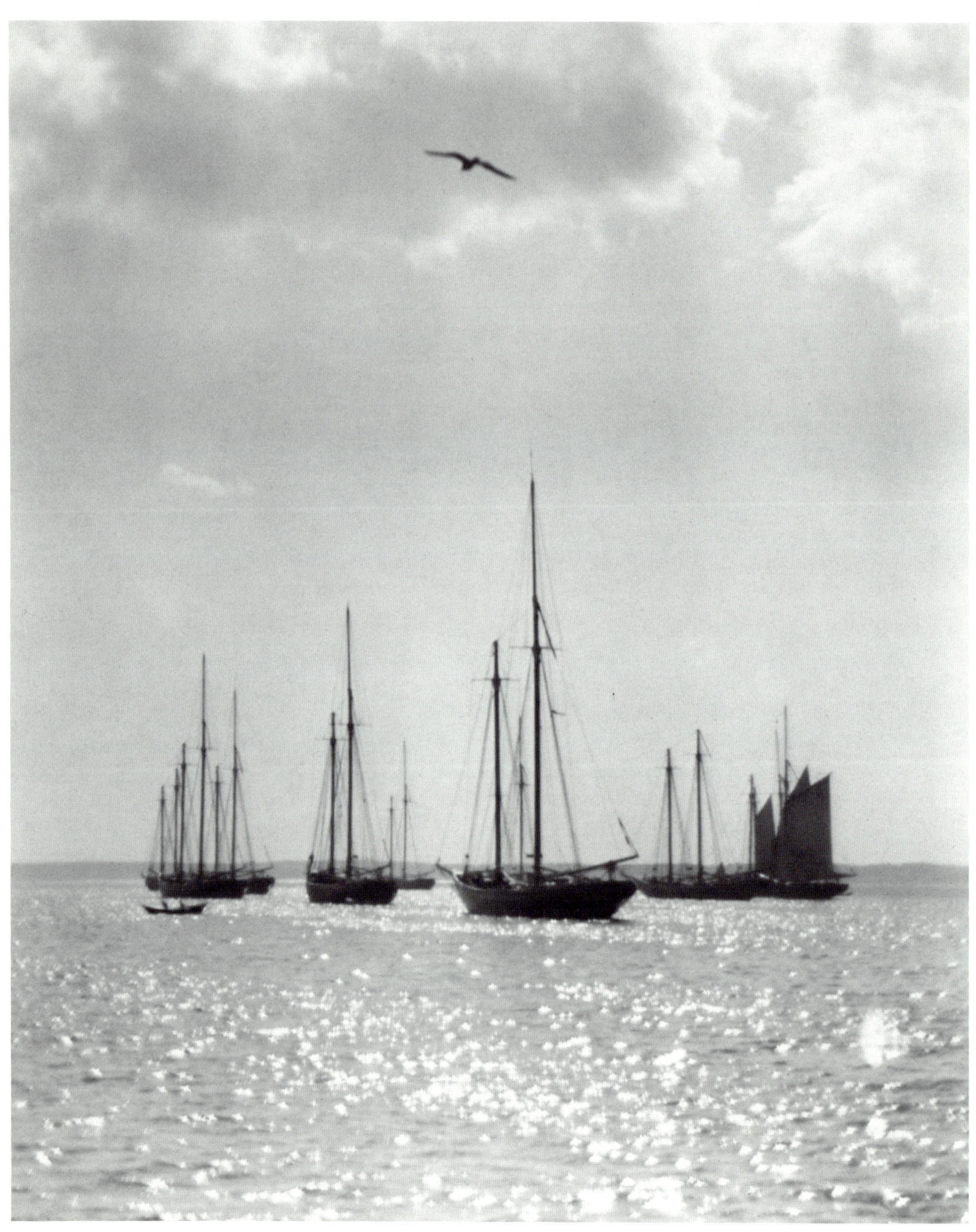

Schooners ready for the spring trip, Lunenburg

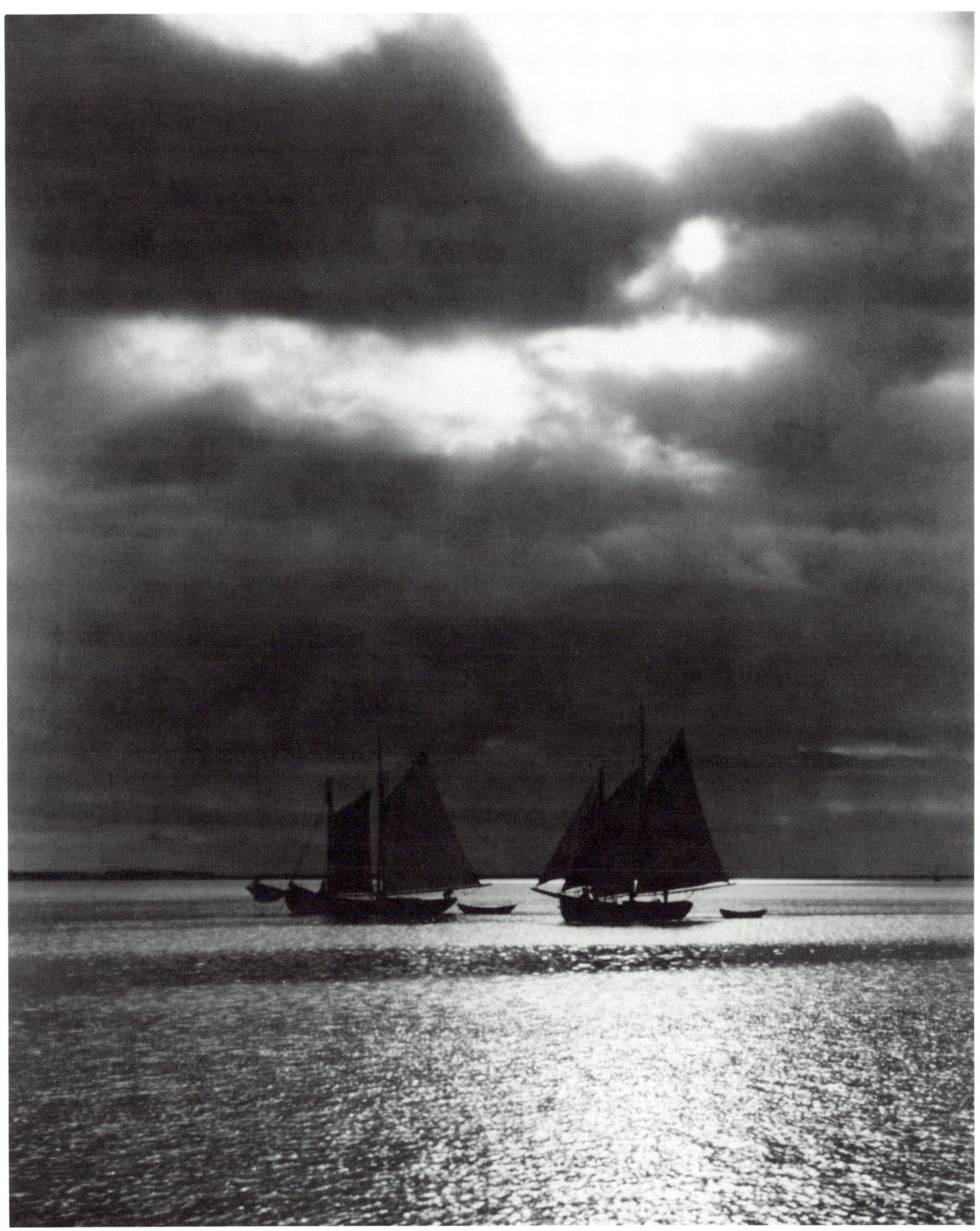

Inshore fishing schooners

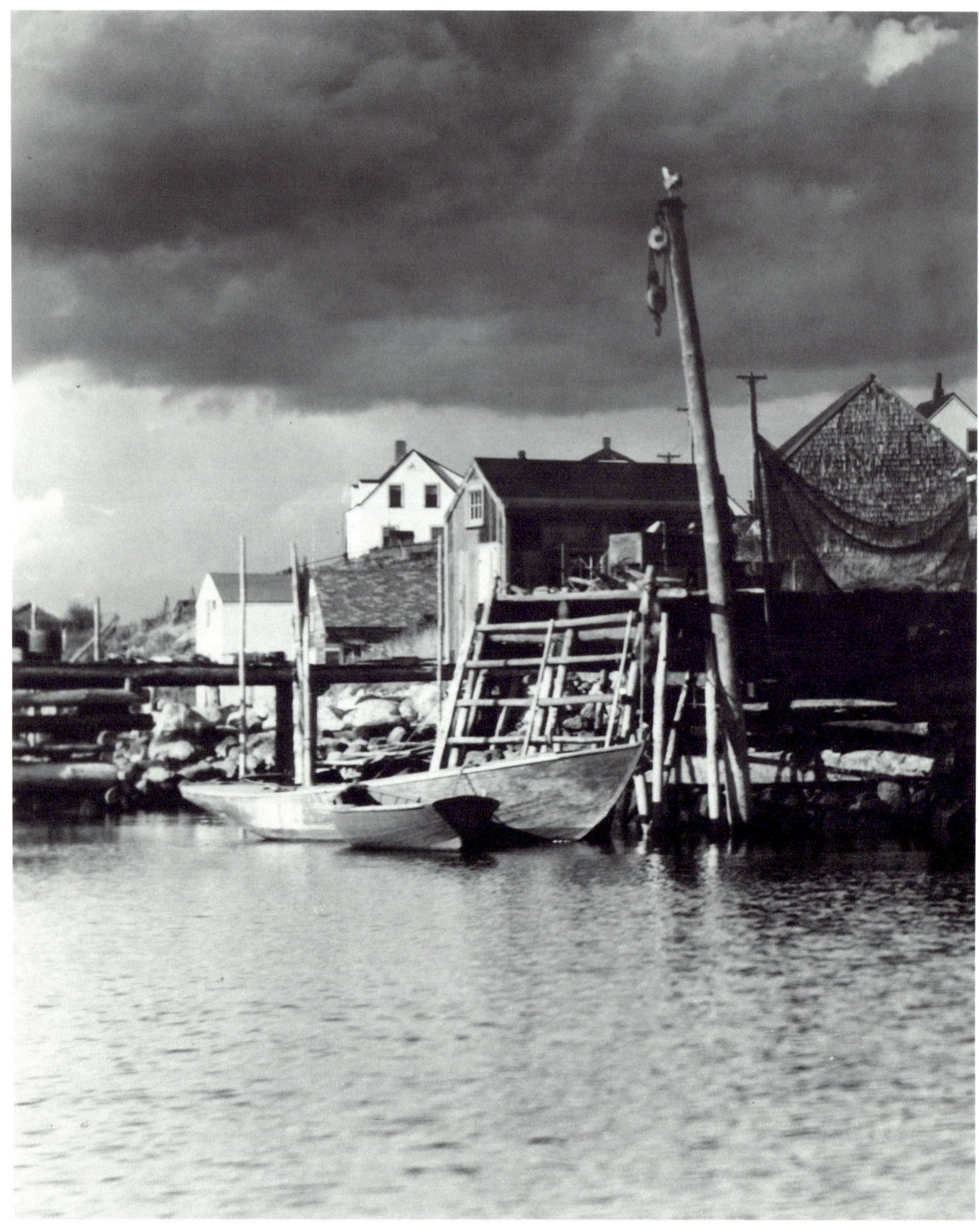

Herring Cove

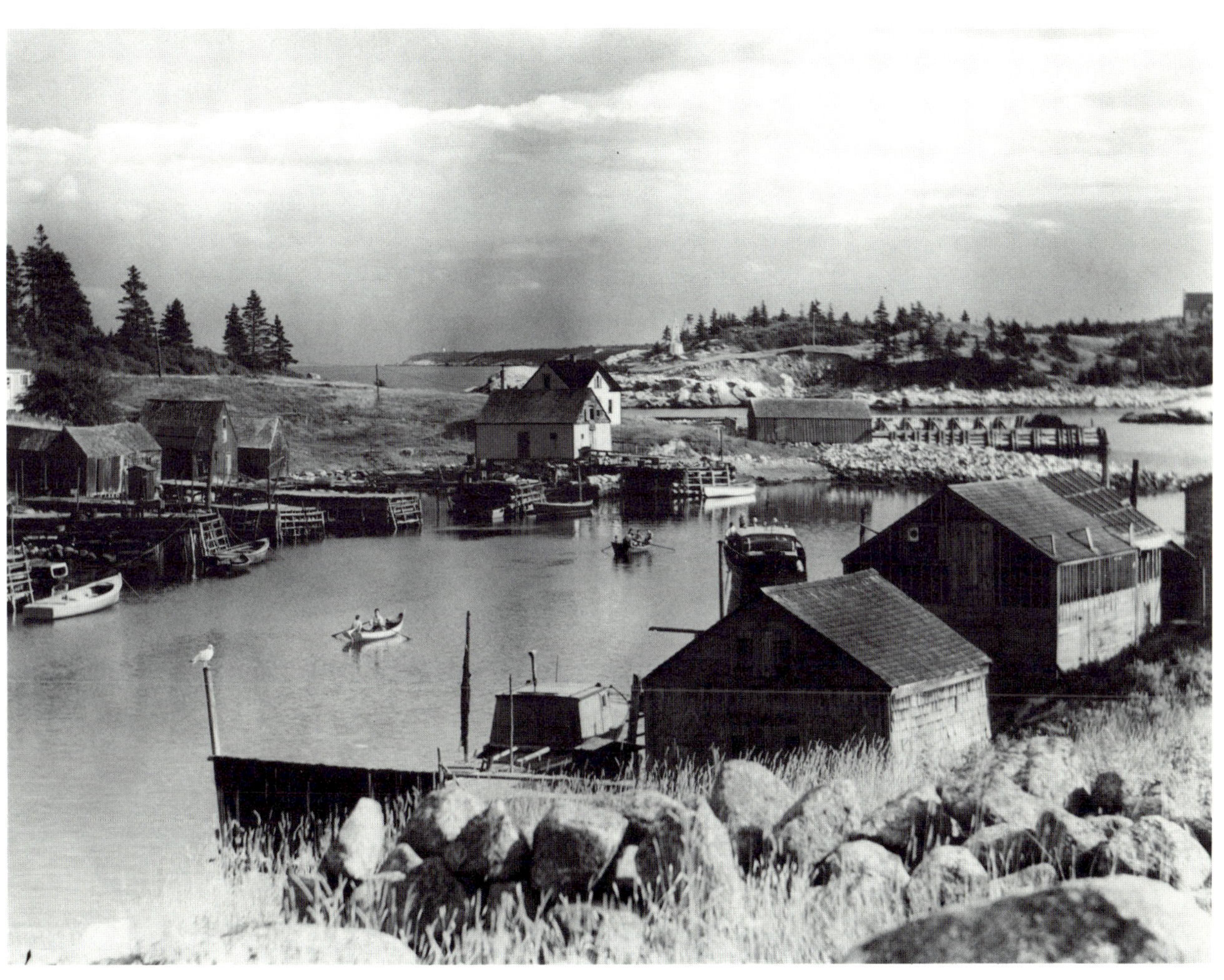

Herring Cove

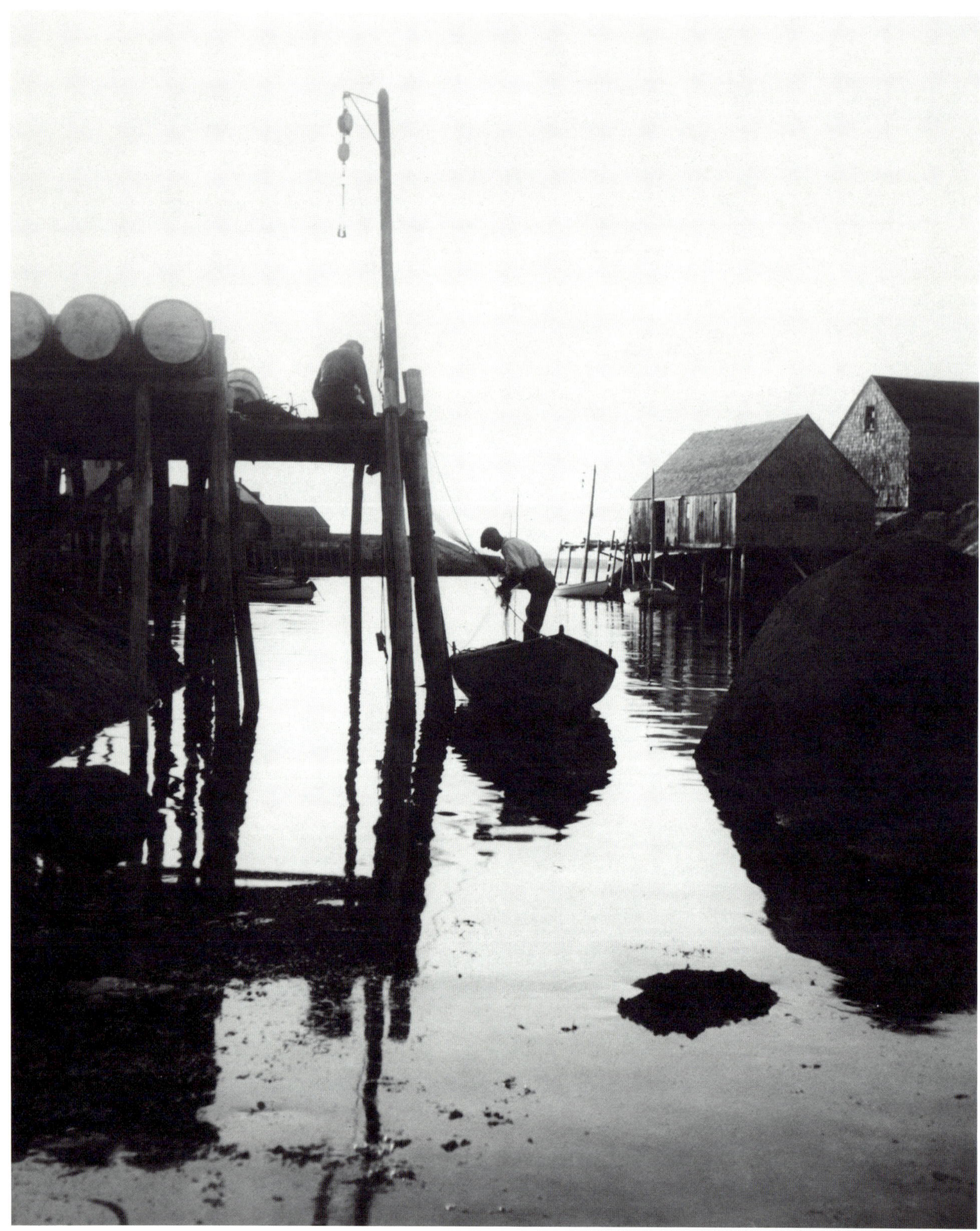

Low tide

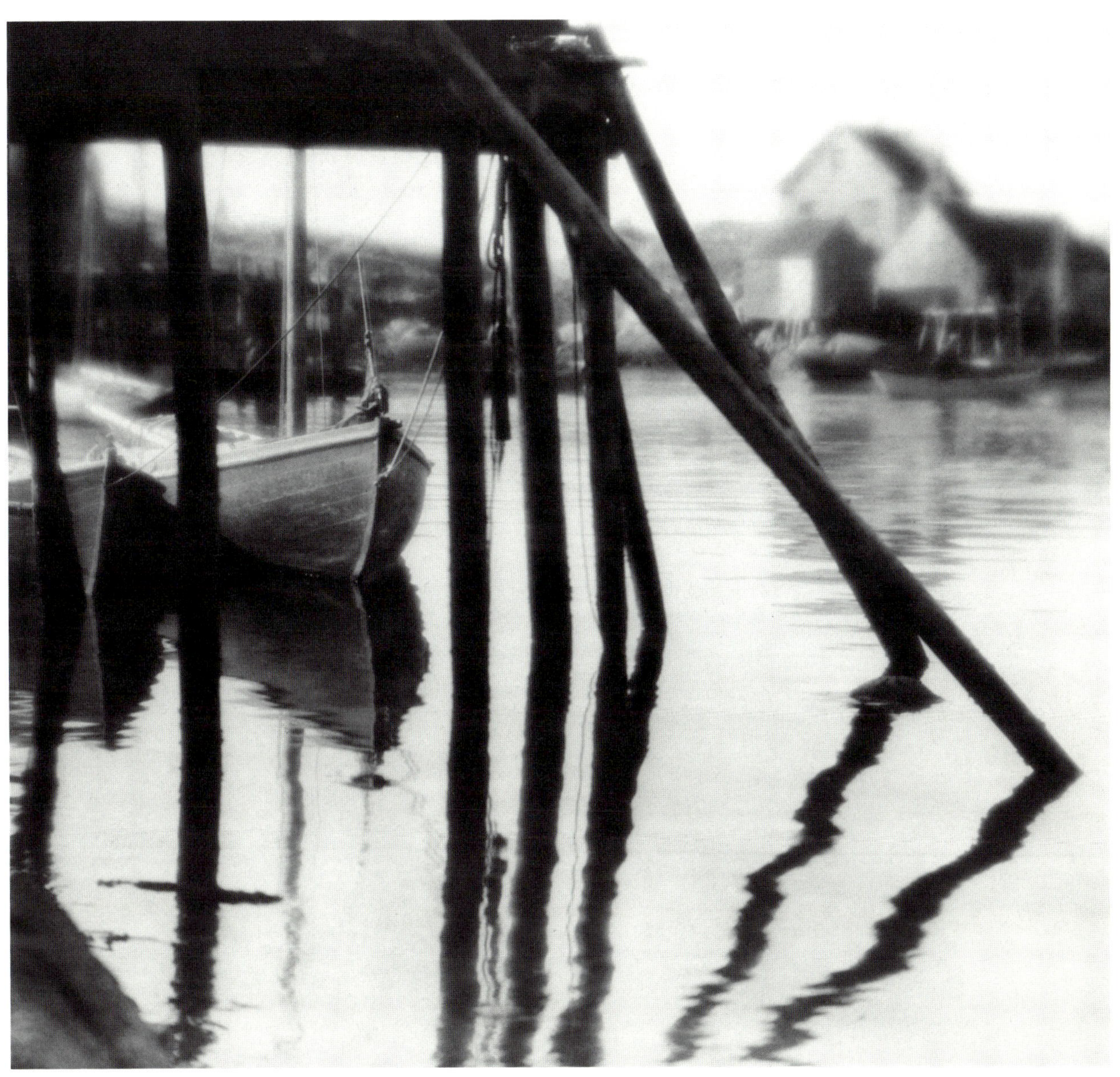

Secure at the wharf

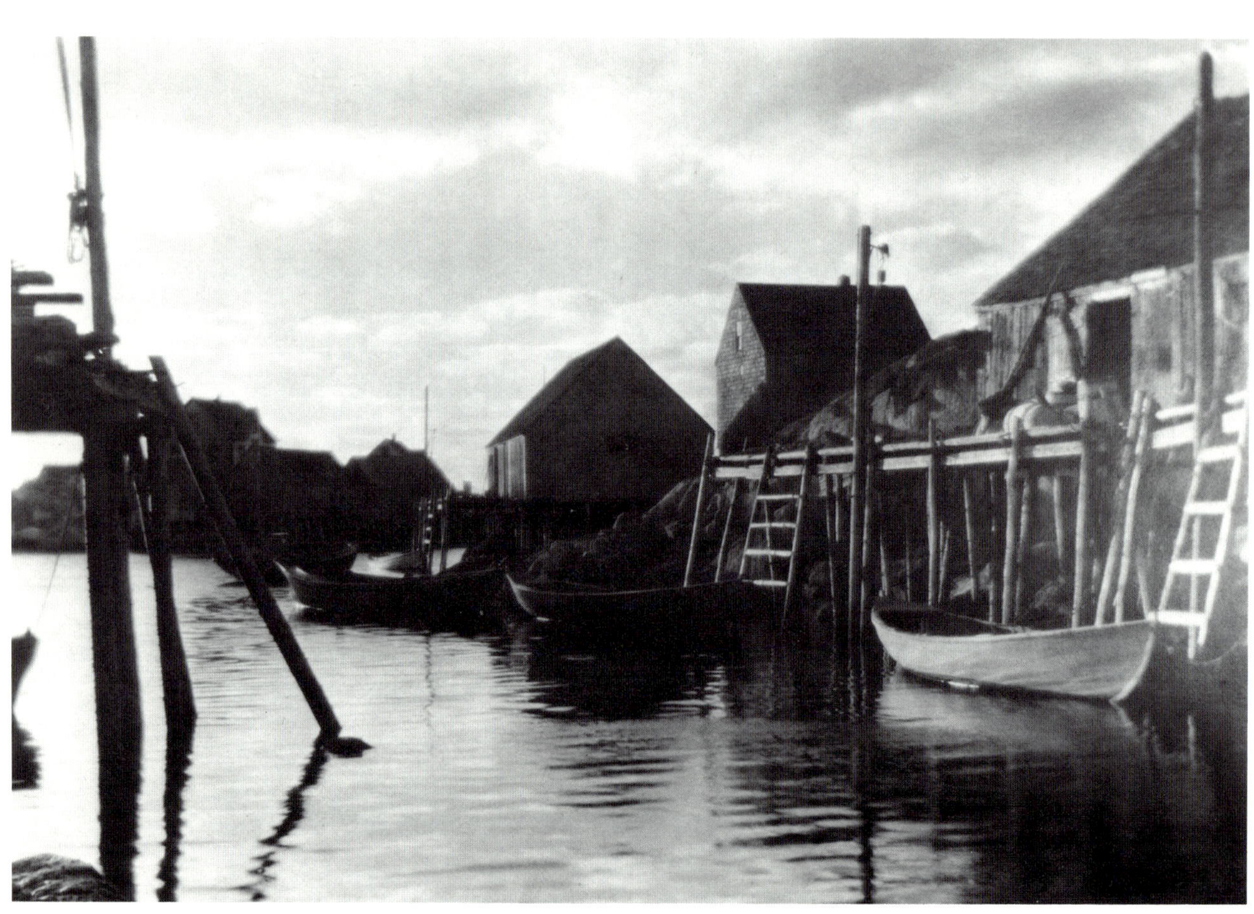

Peggy's Cove

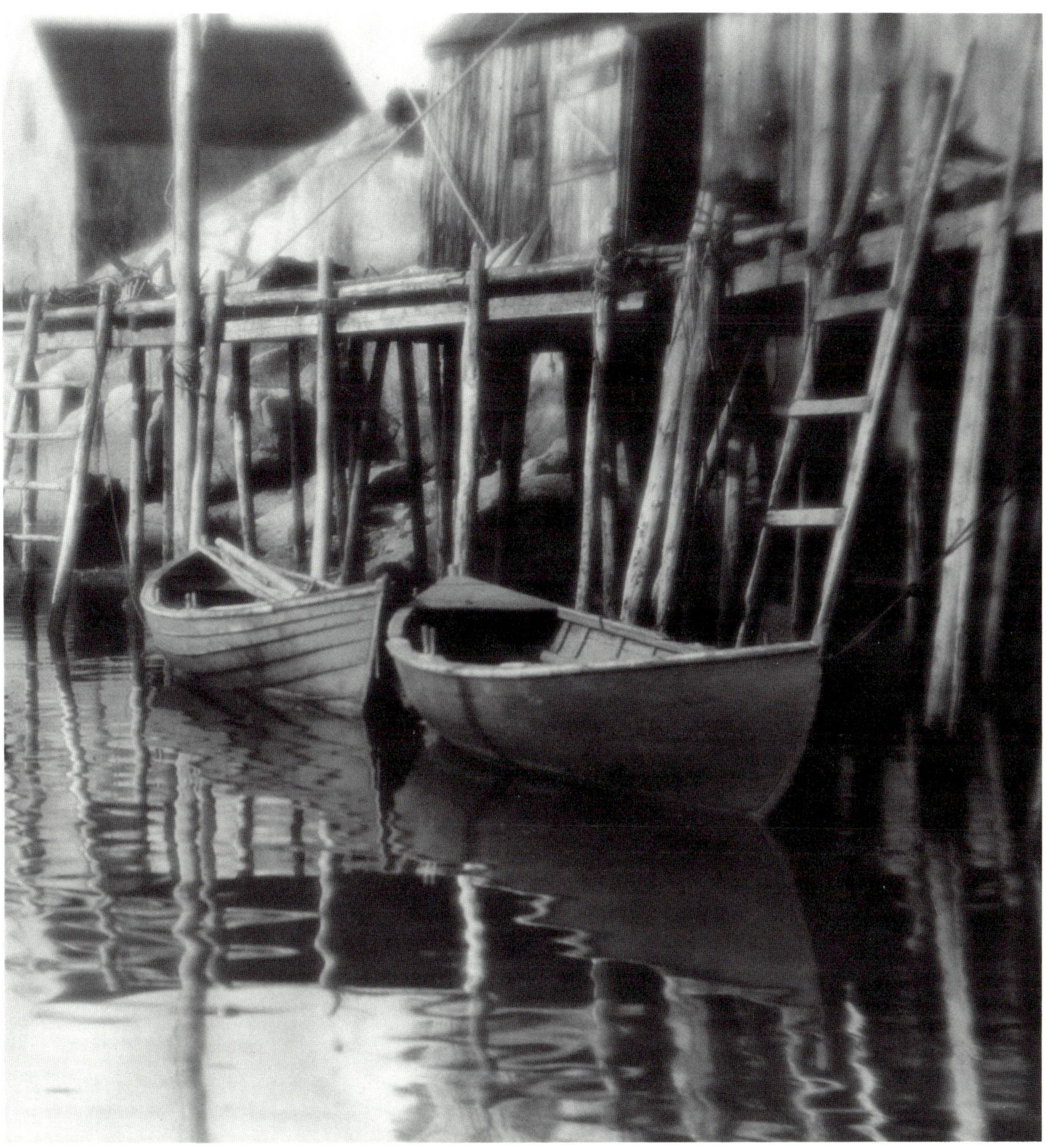

Waiting at the wharf

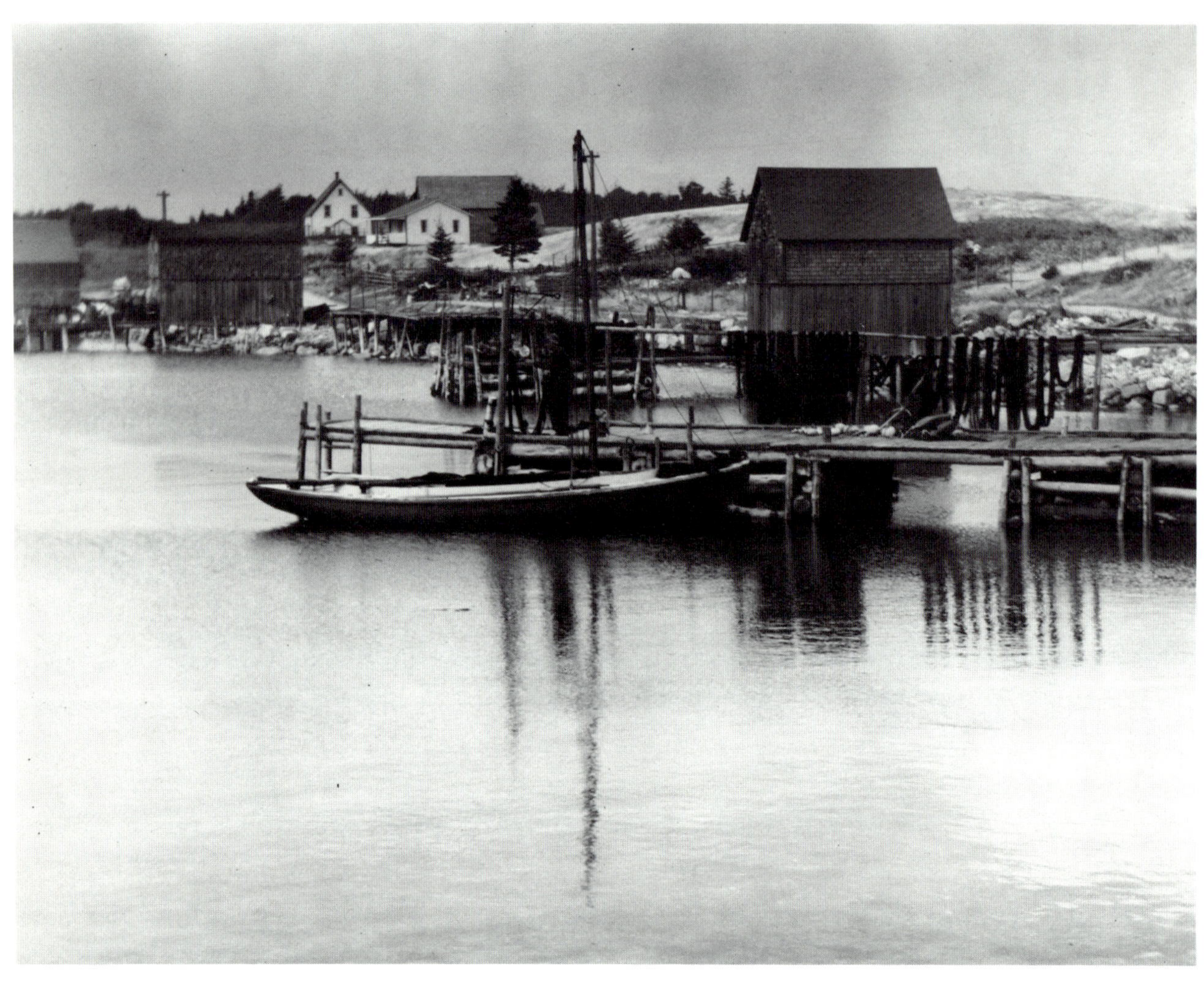

Hanging nets to dry

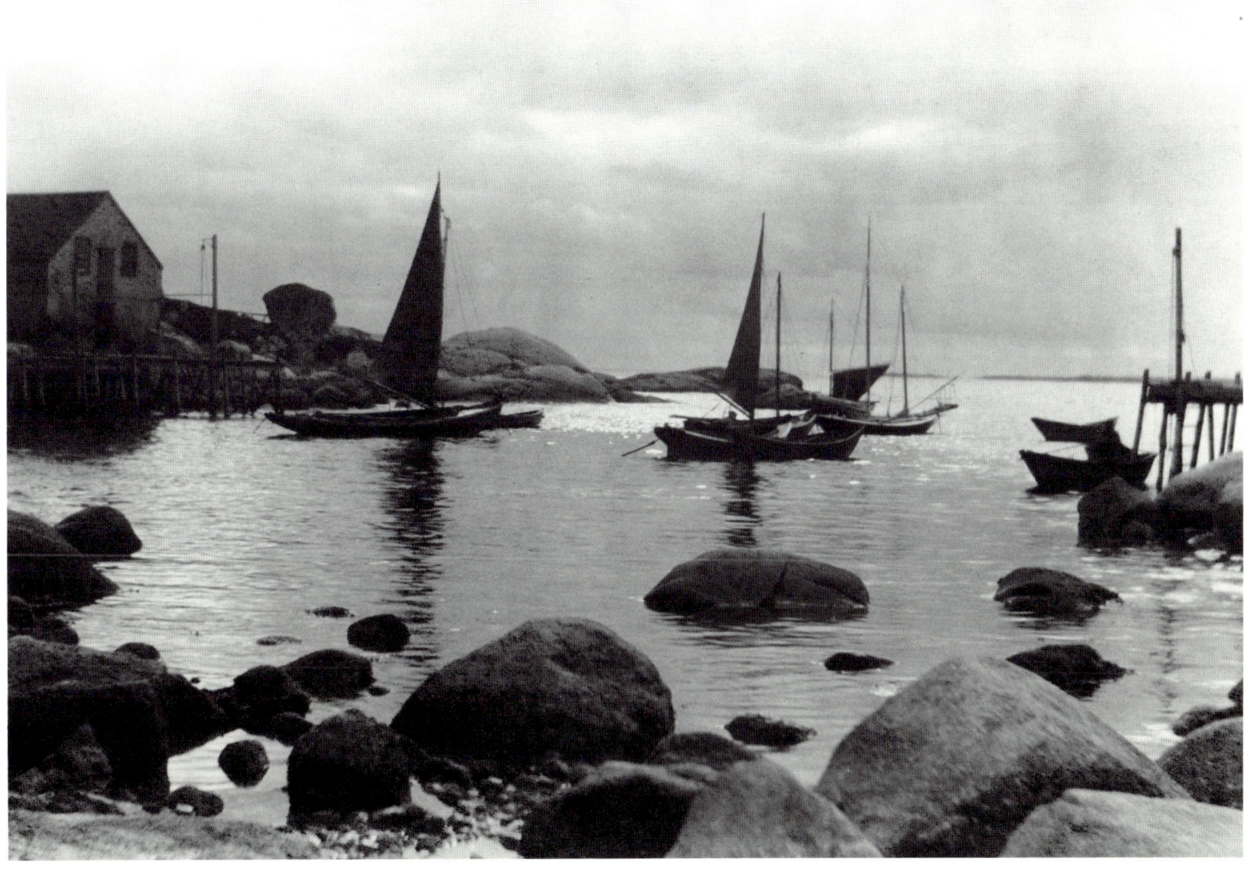

Slipping their moorings

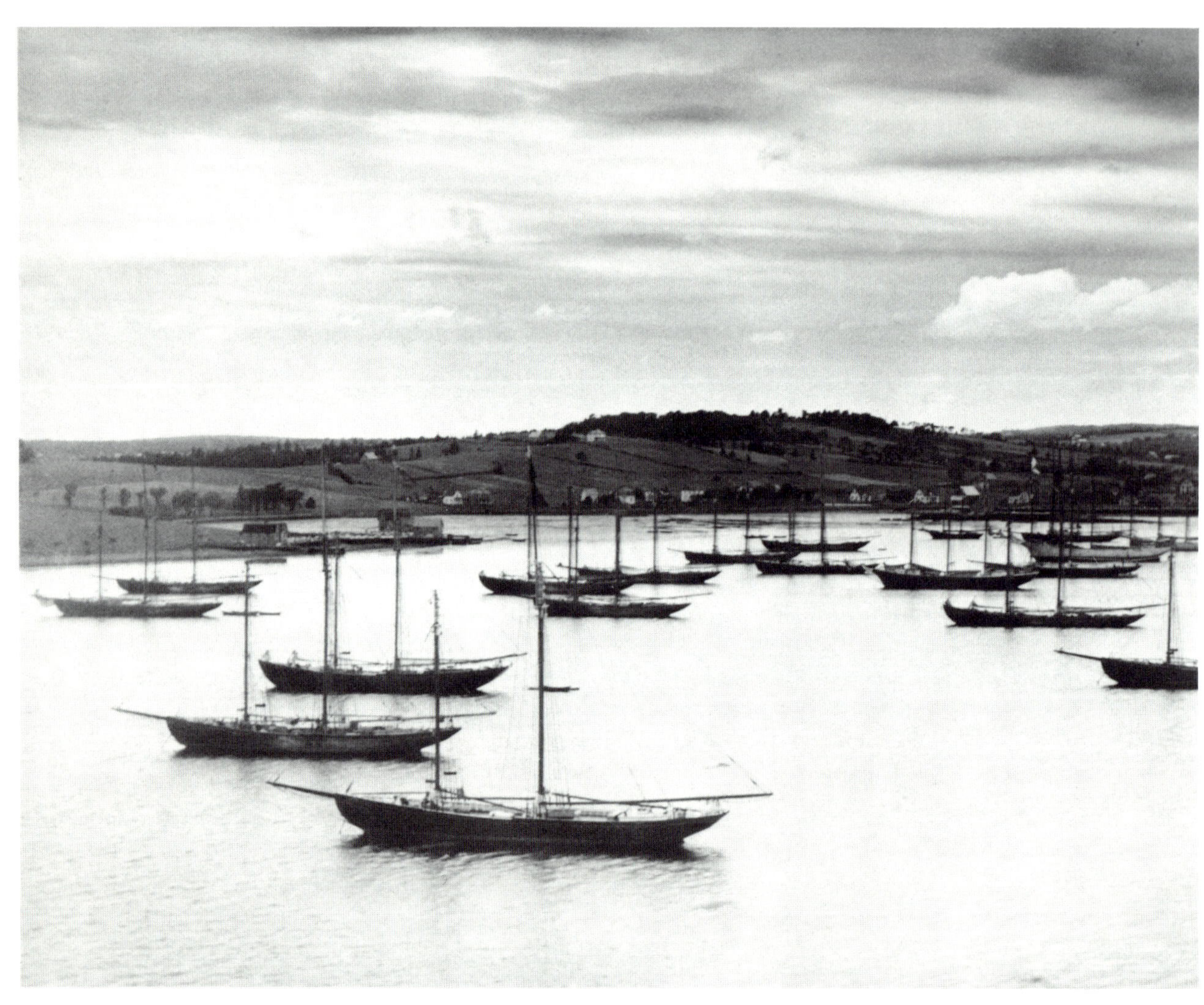

Schooners moored for the winter, Lunenburg

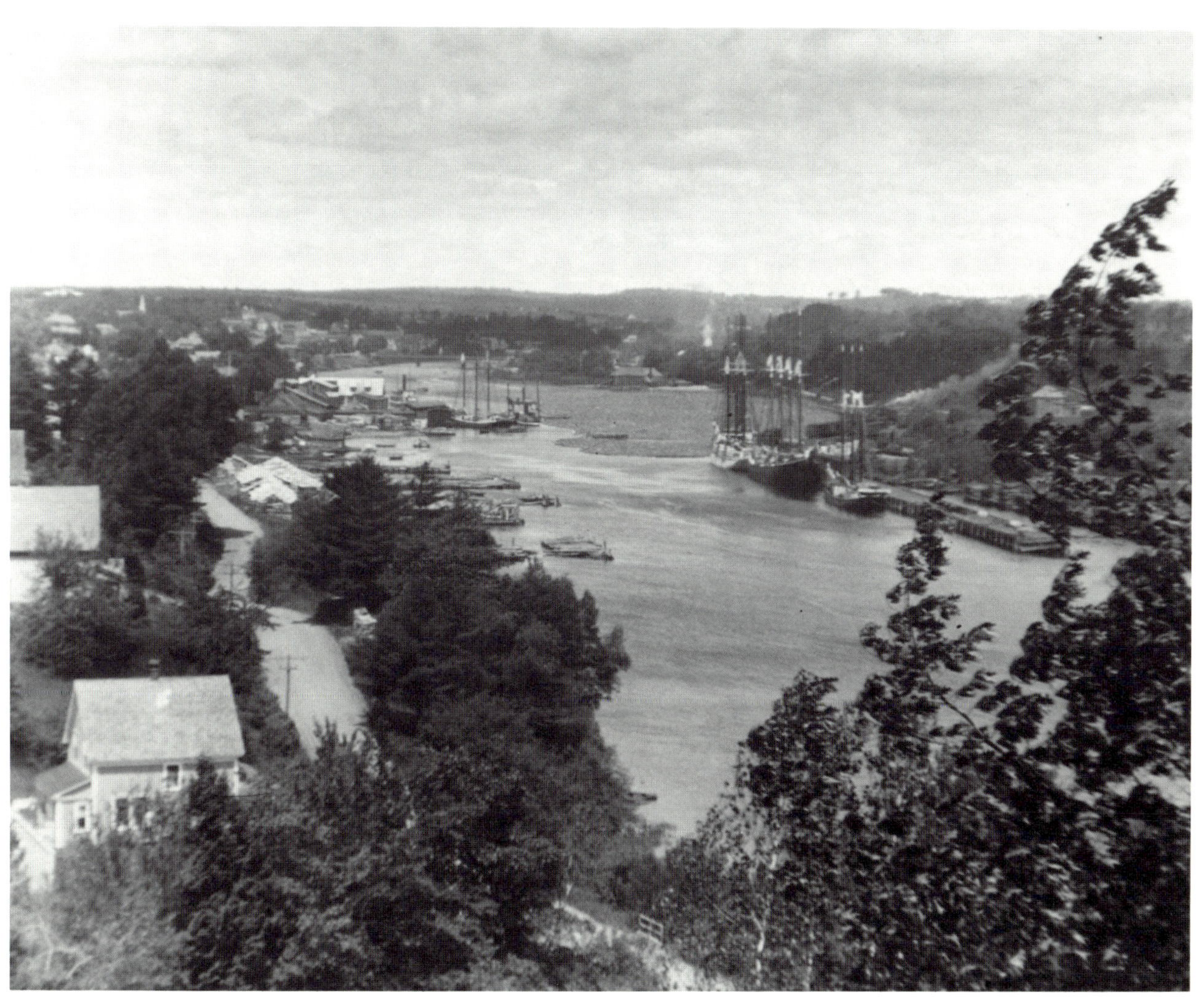

Ships and log boom, Bridgewater

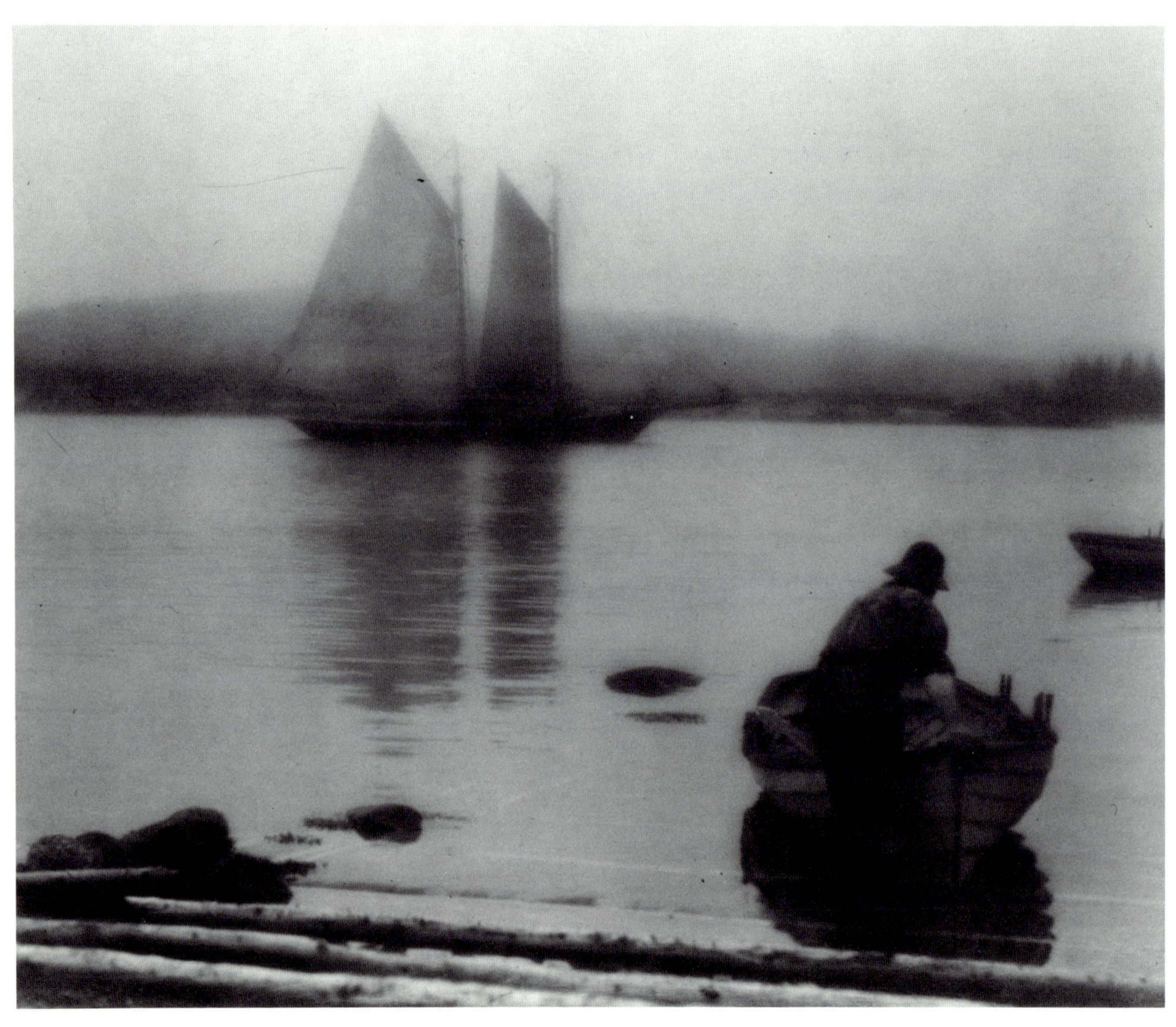

Launching a flat, Newfoundland

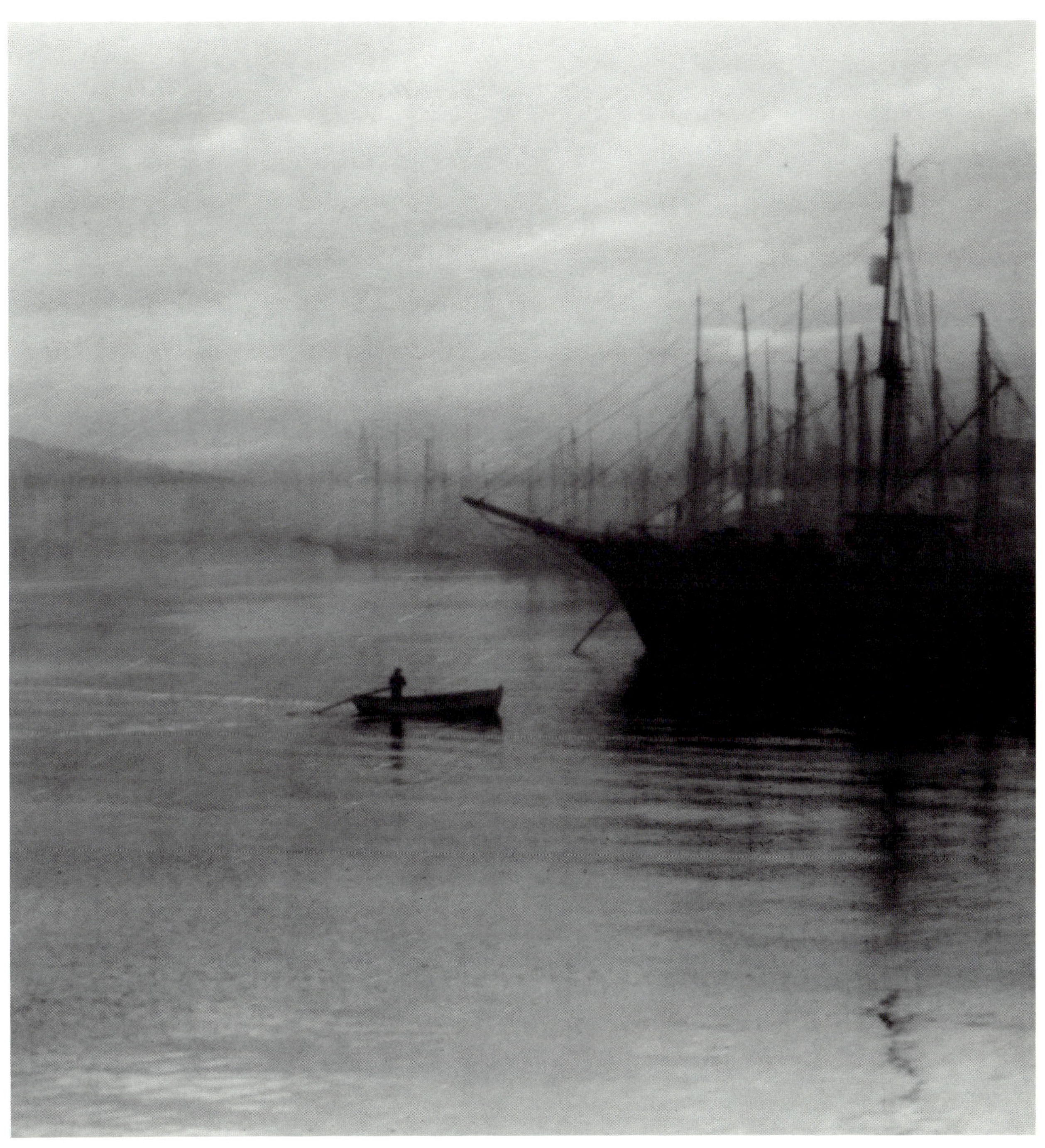

Sealing ships, St. John's, Newfoundland

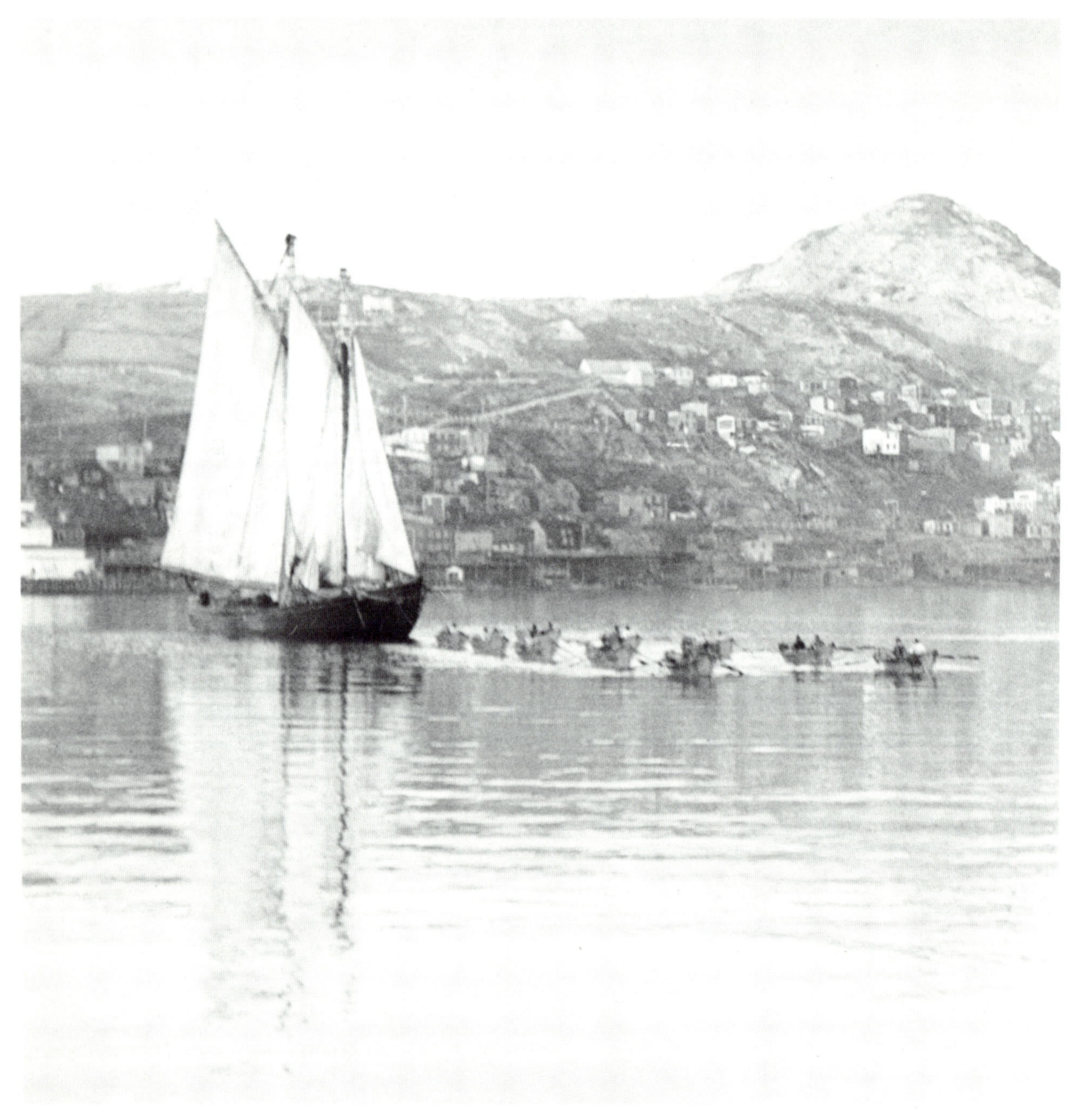

Towing a schooner out of St. John's, Newfoundland

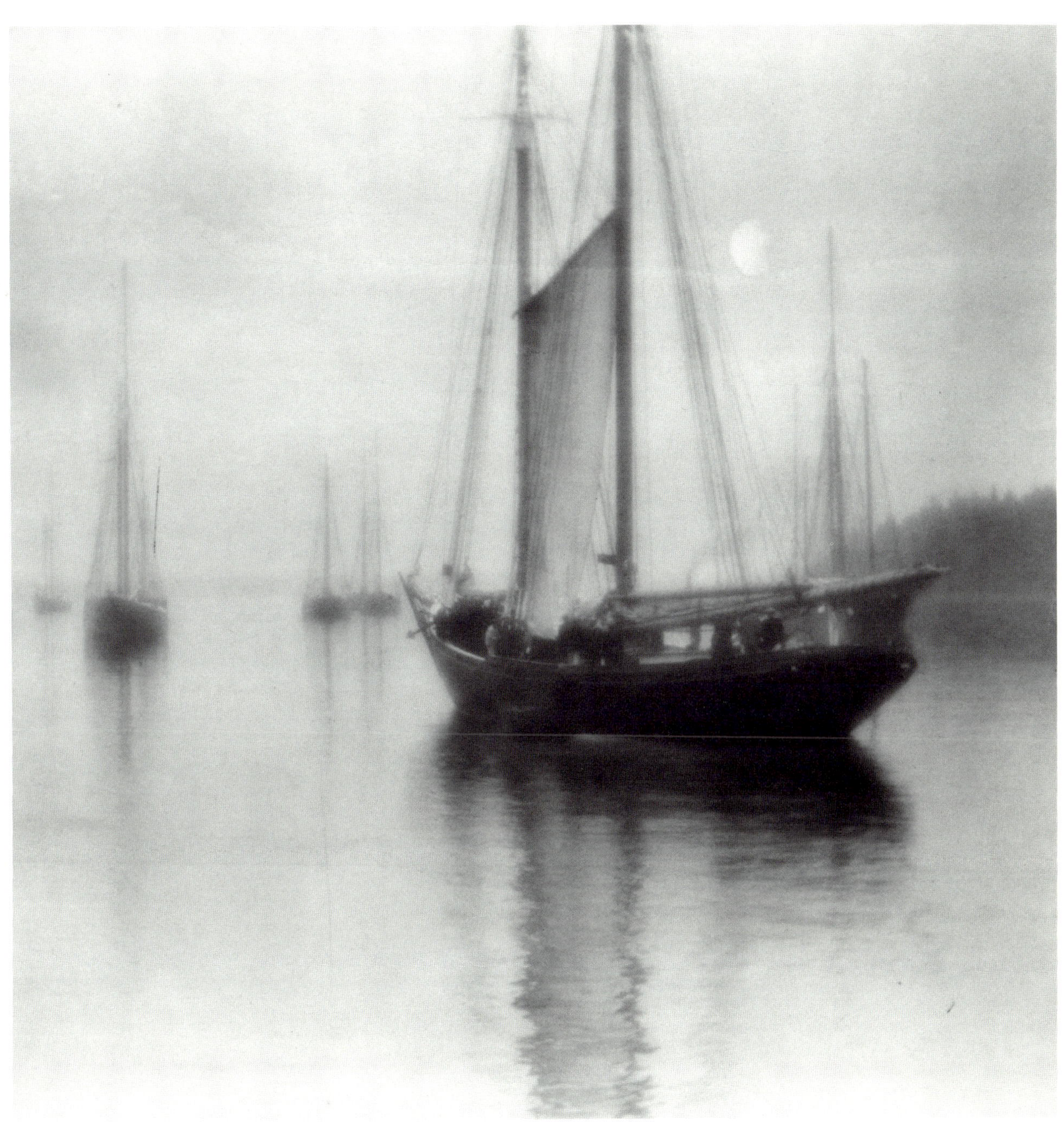

Heading out of Lunenburg for the spring trip

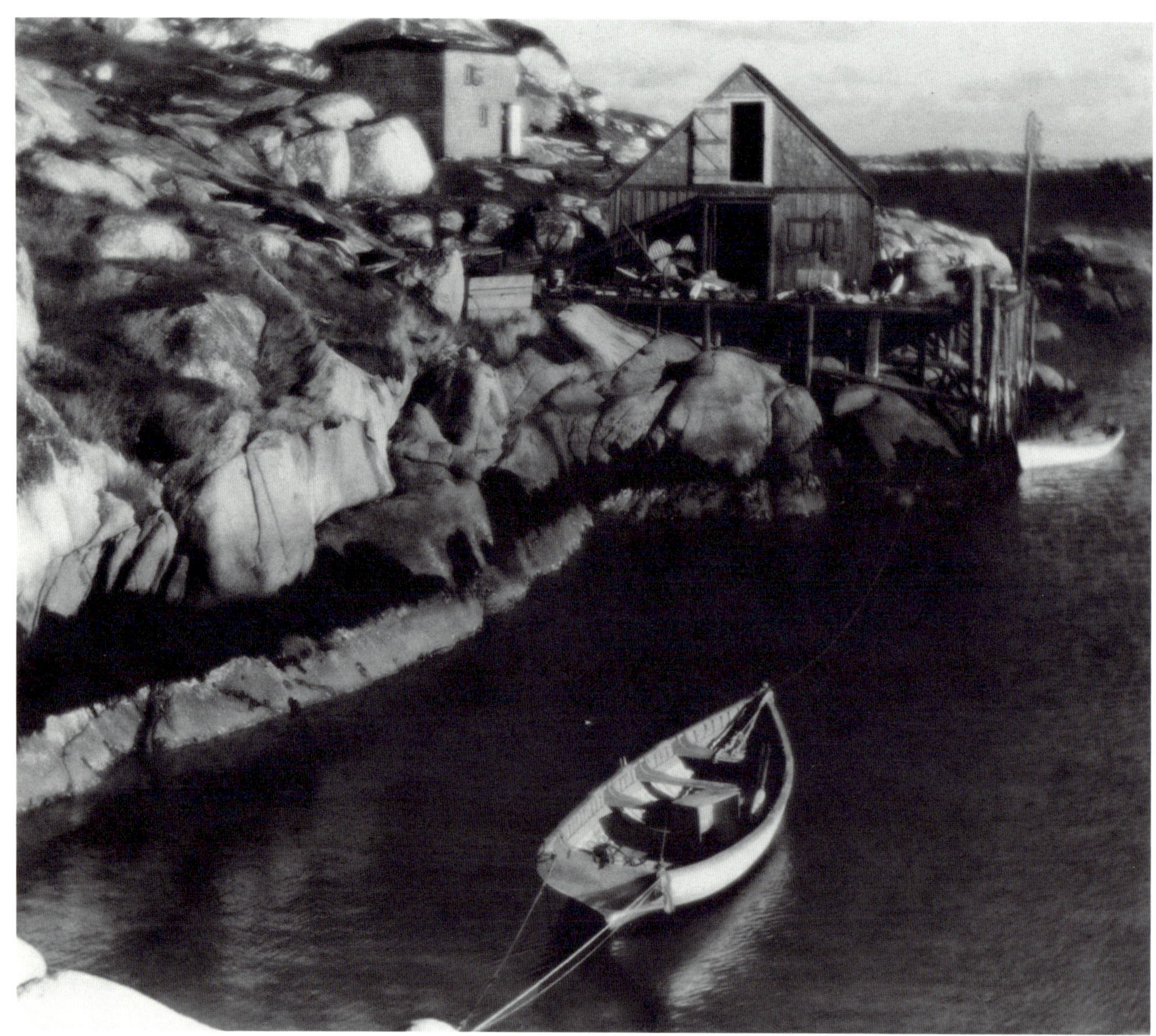

Trap boat moored on a rocky coast

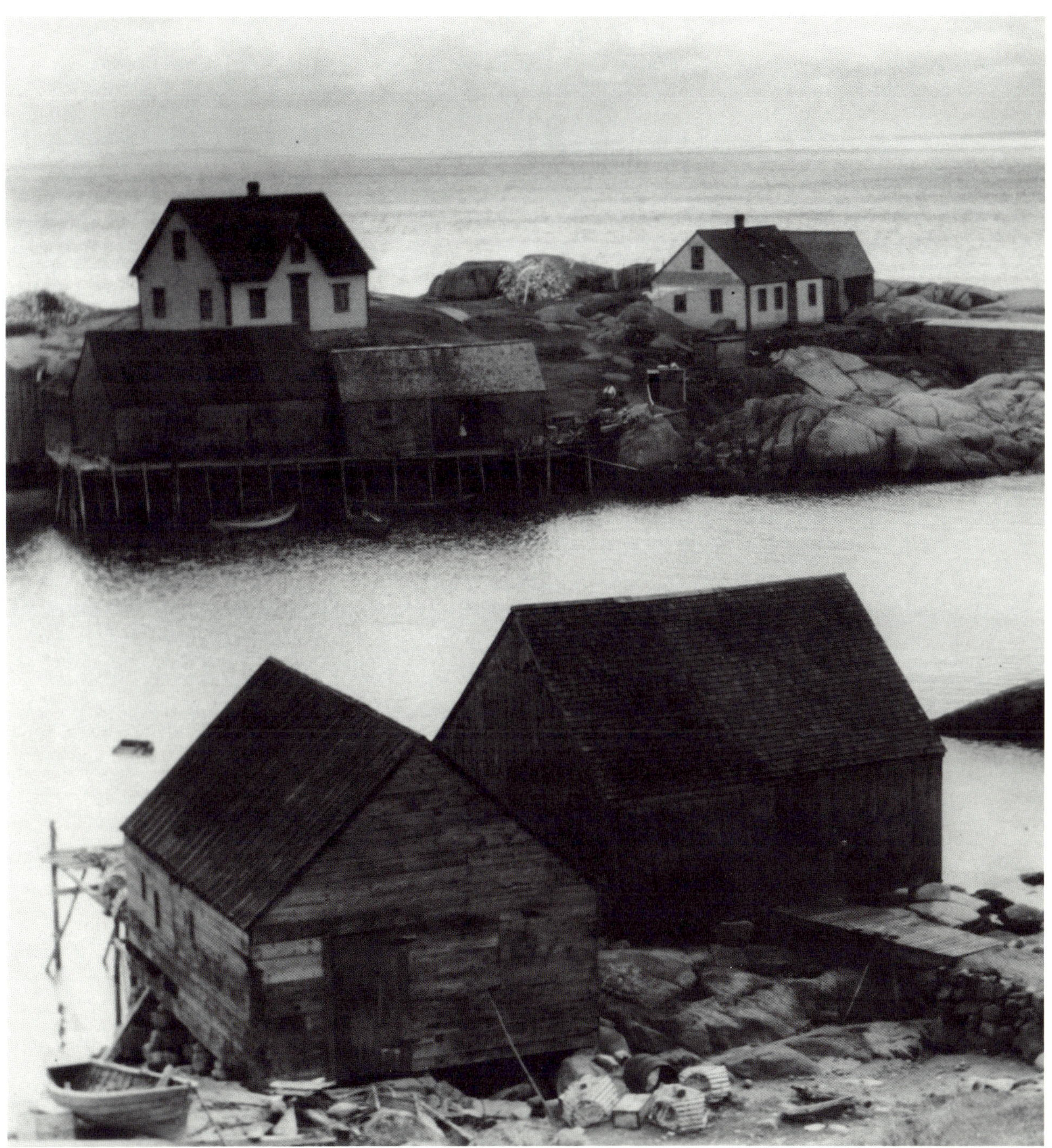

Peggy's Cove

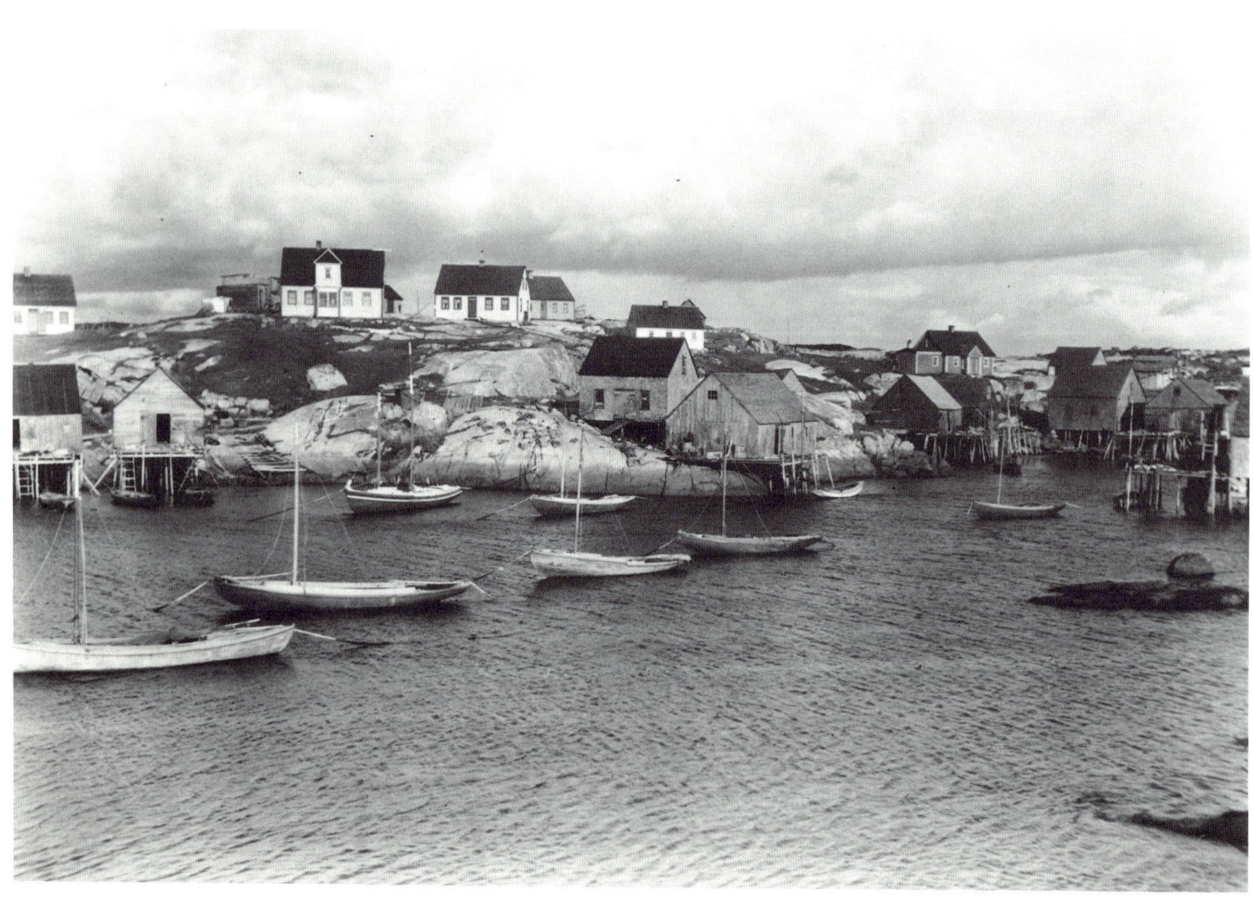

Peggy's Cove

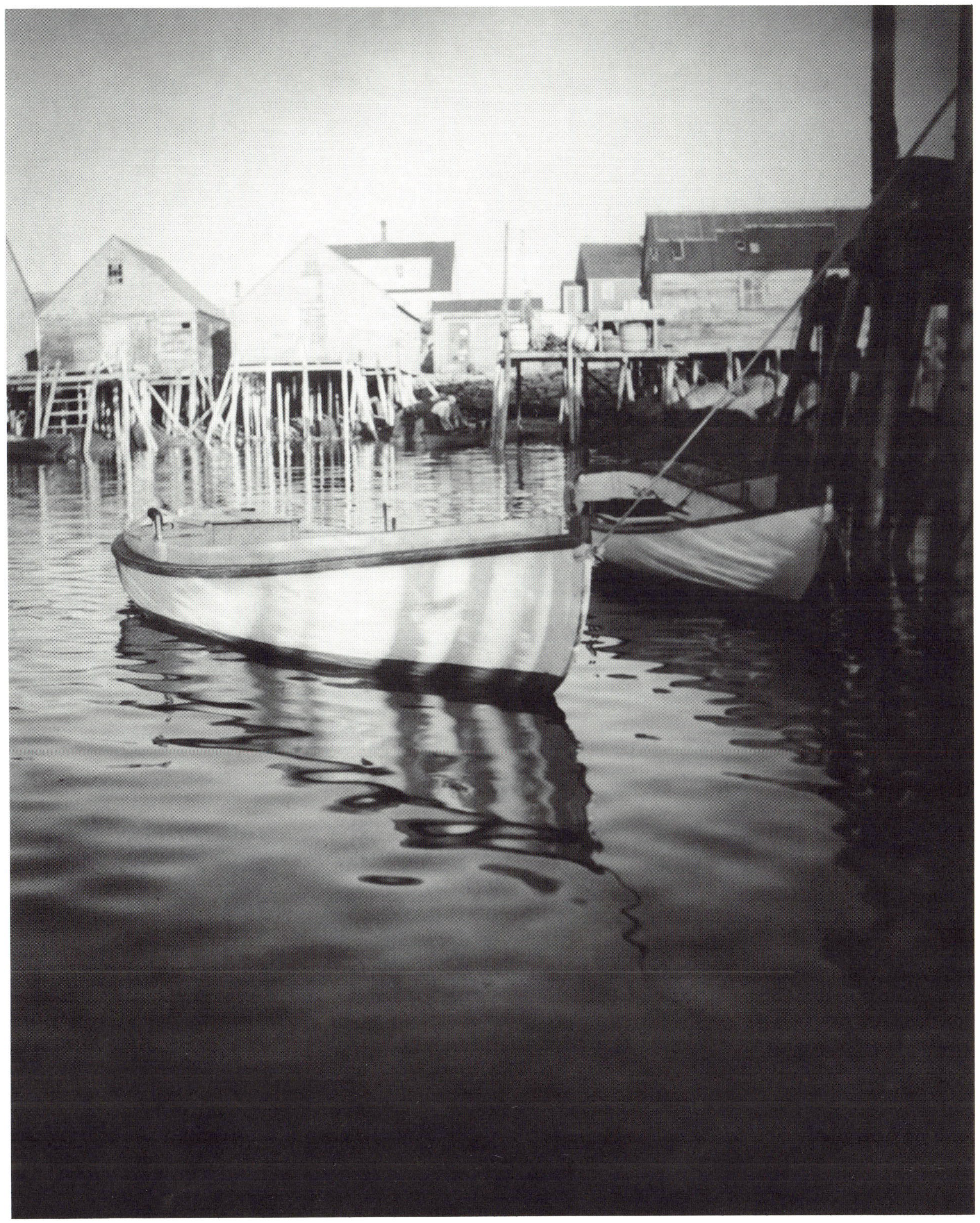

Peggy's Cove

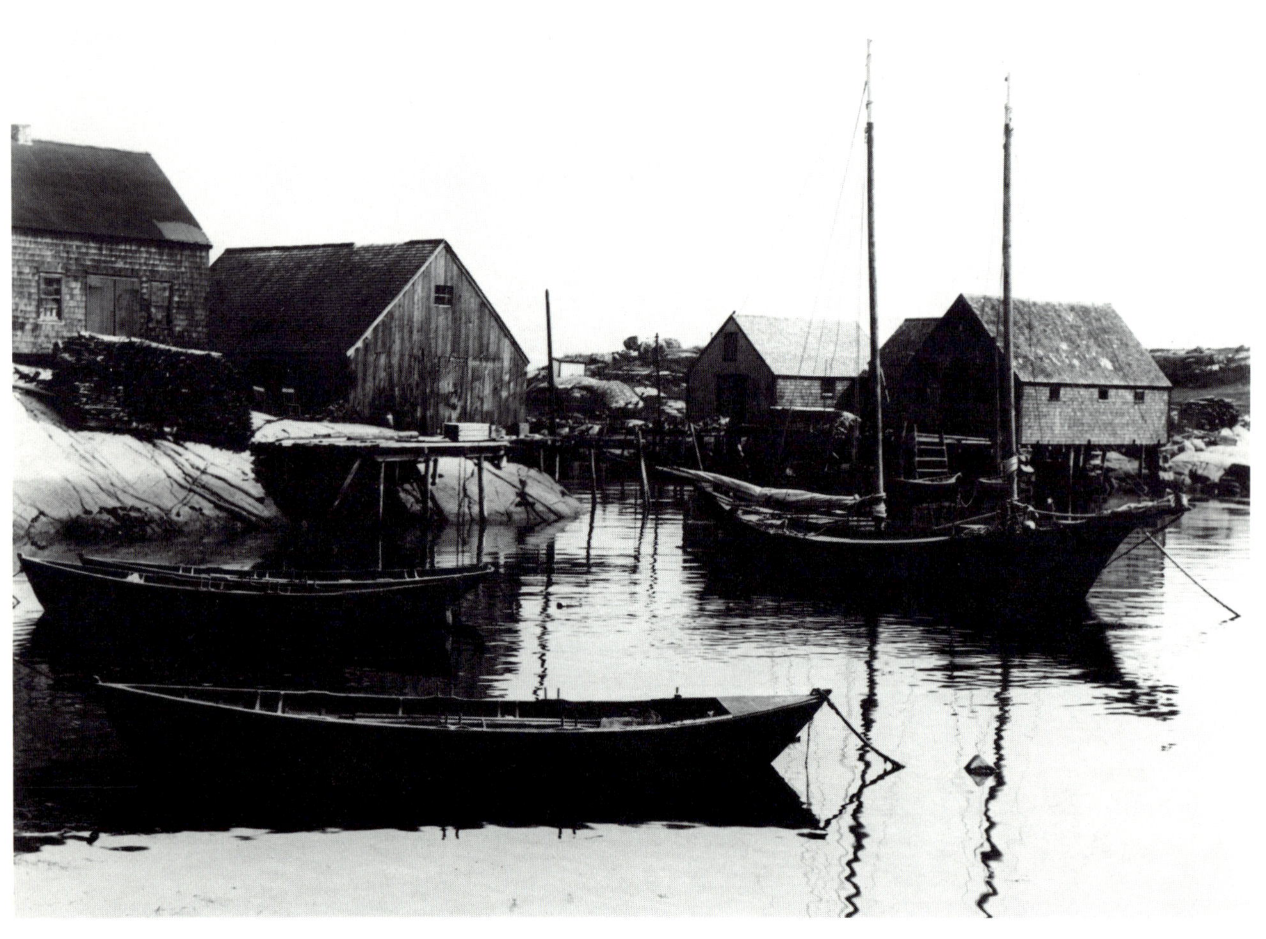

Peggy's Cove

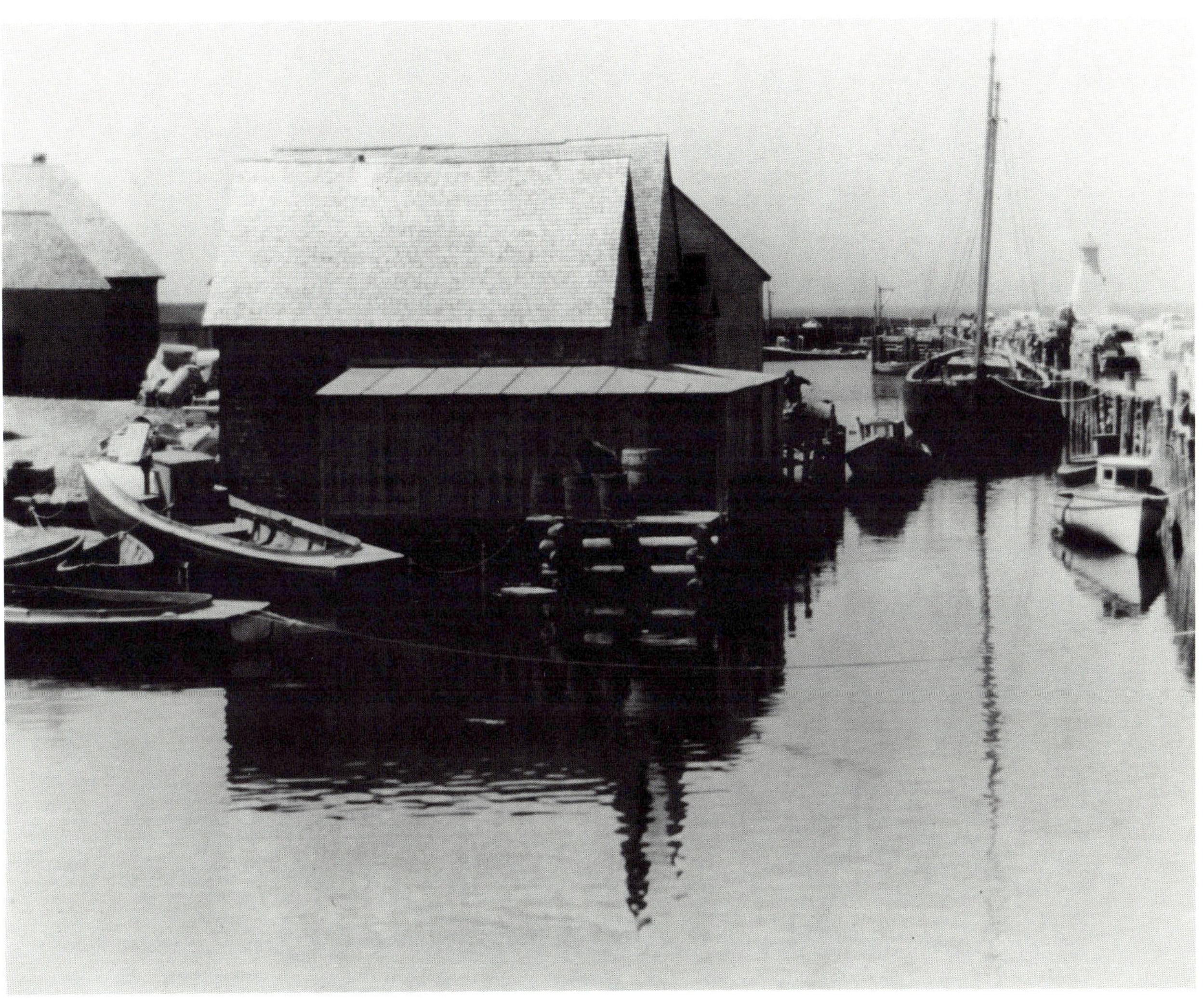

Port Maitland

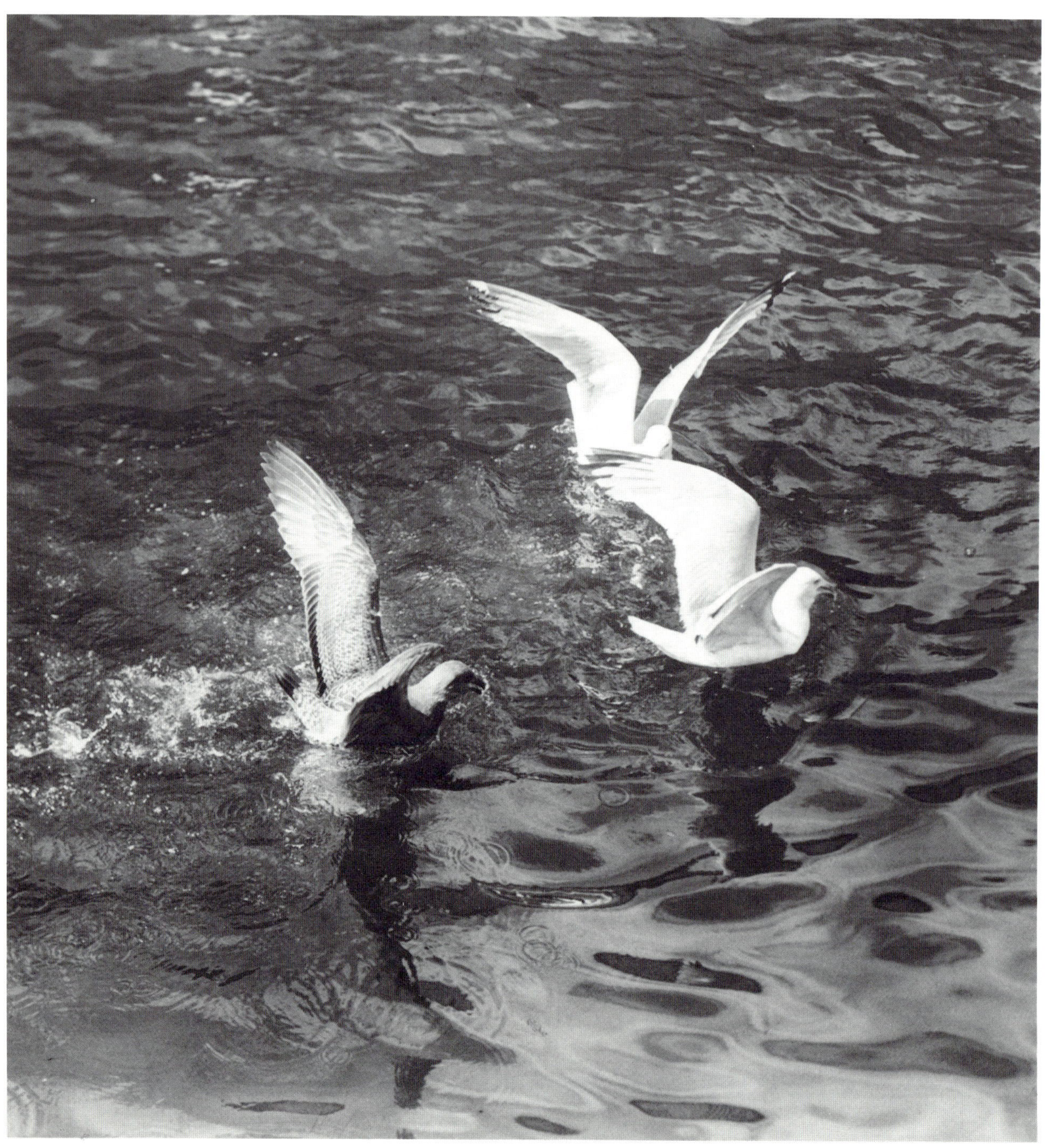

Gulls in the harbour

Fishermen

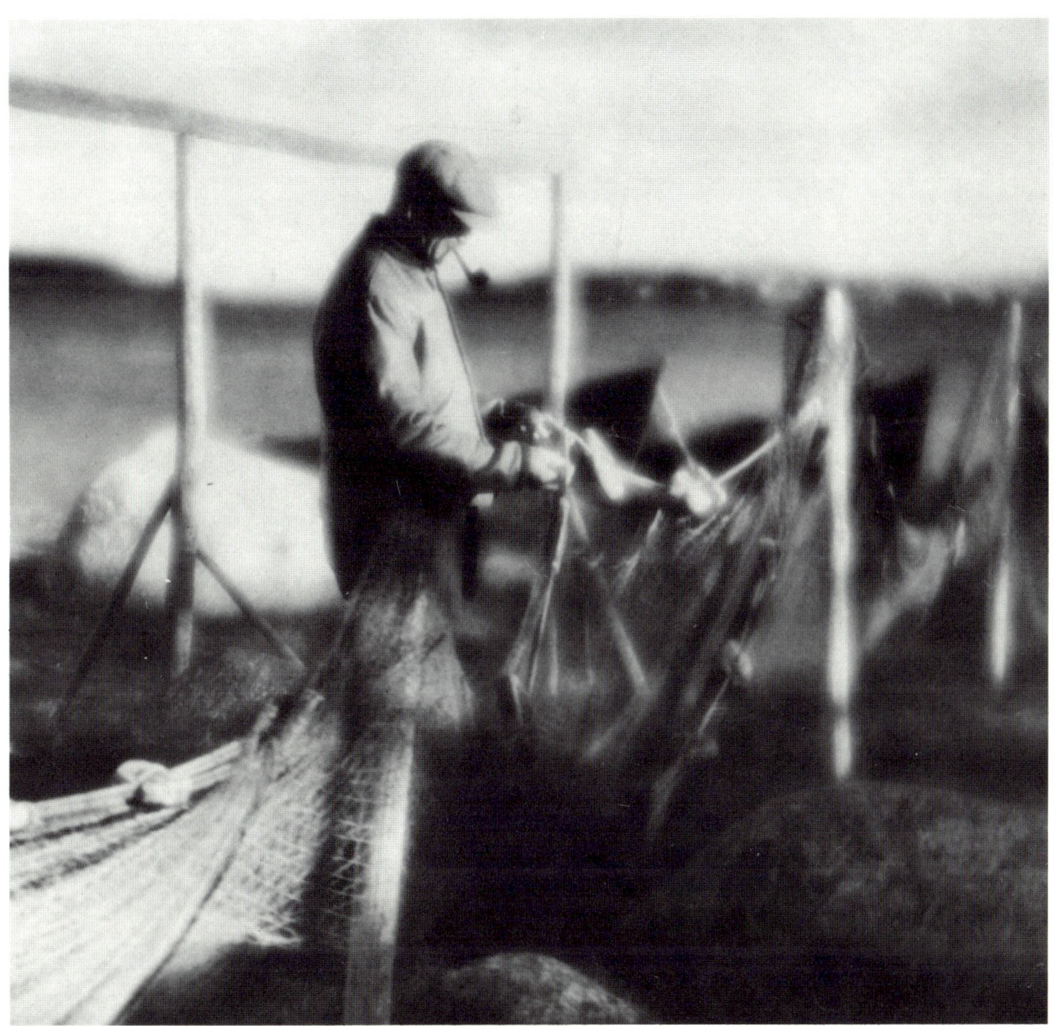

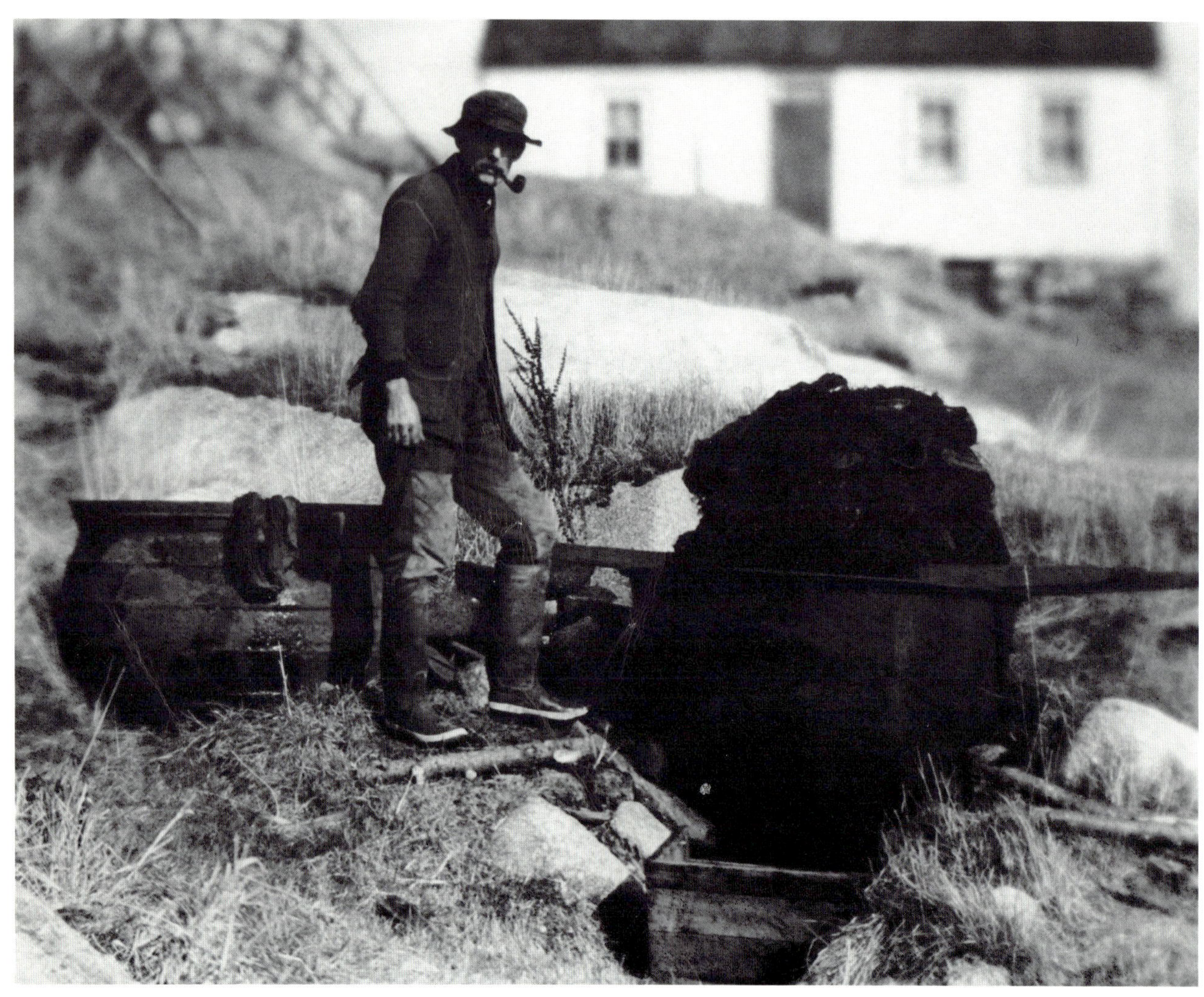

Tanning nets

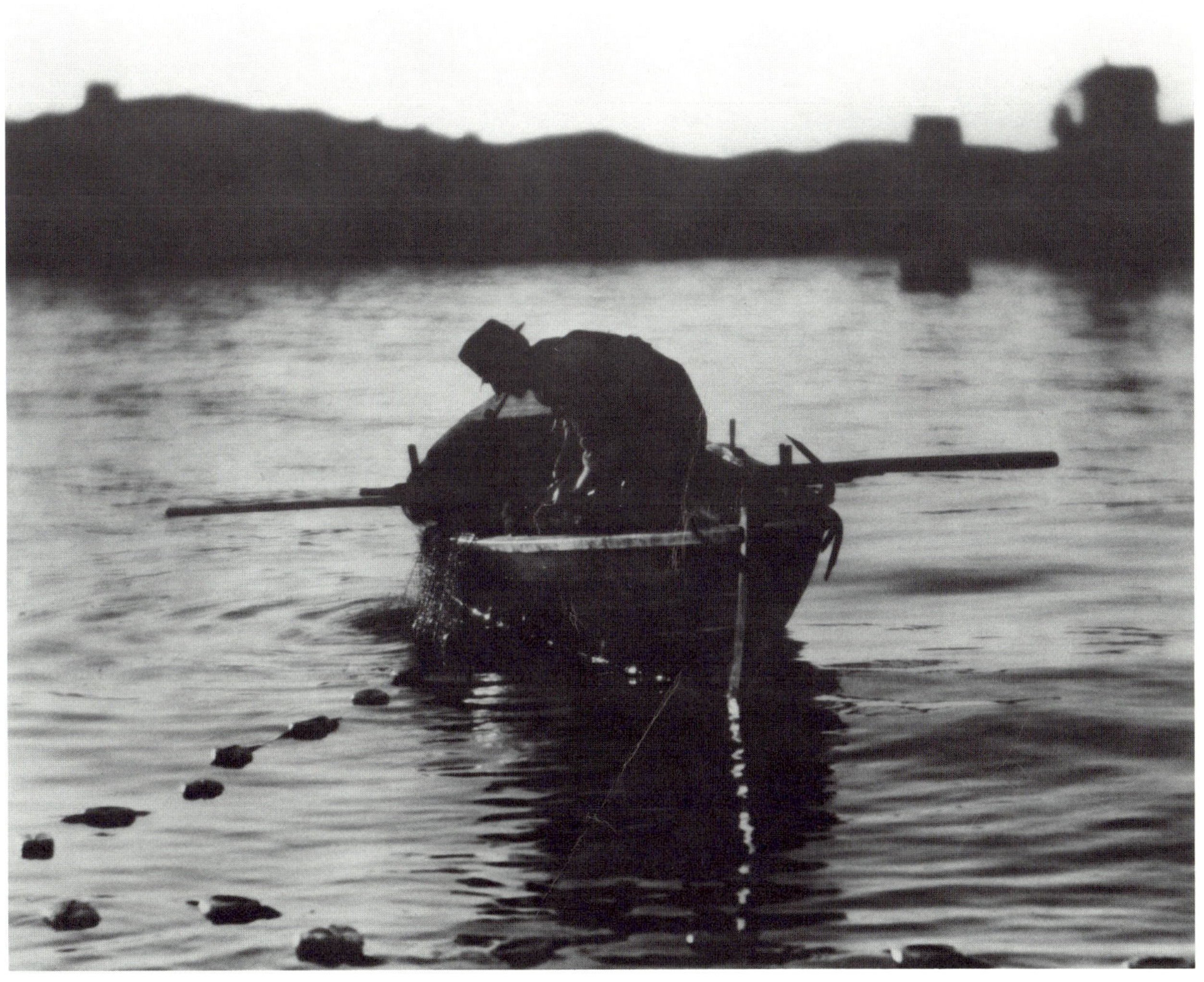

Setting a salmon net

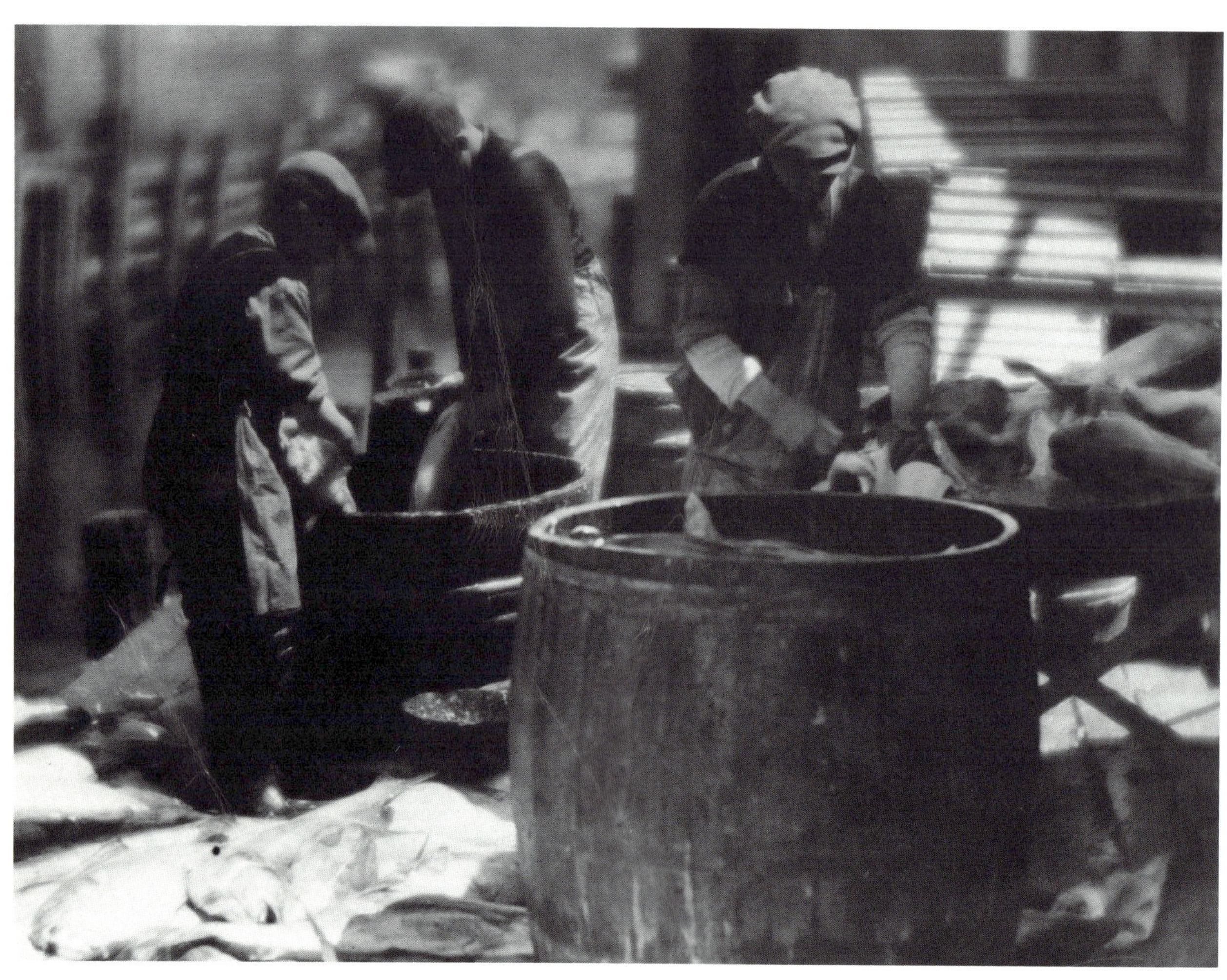

Cleaning and salting fish

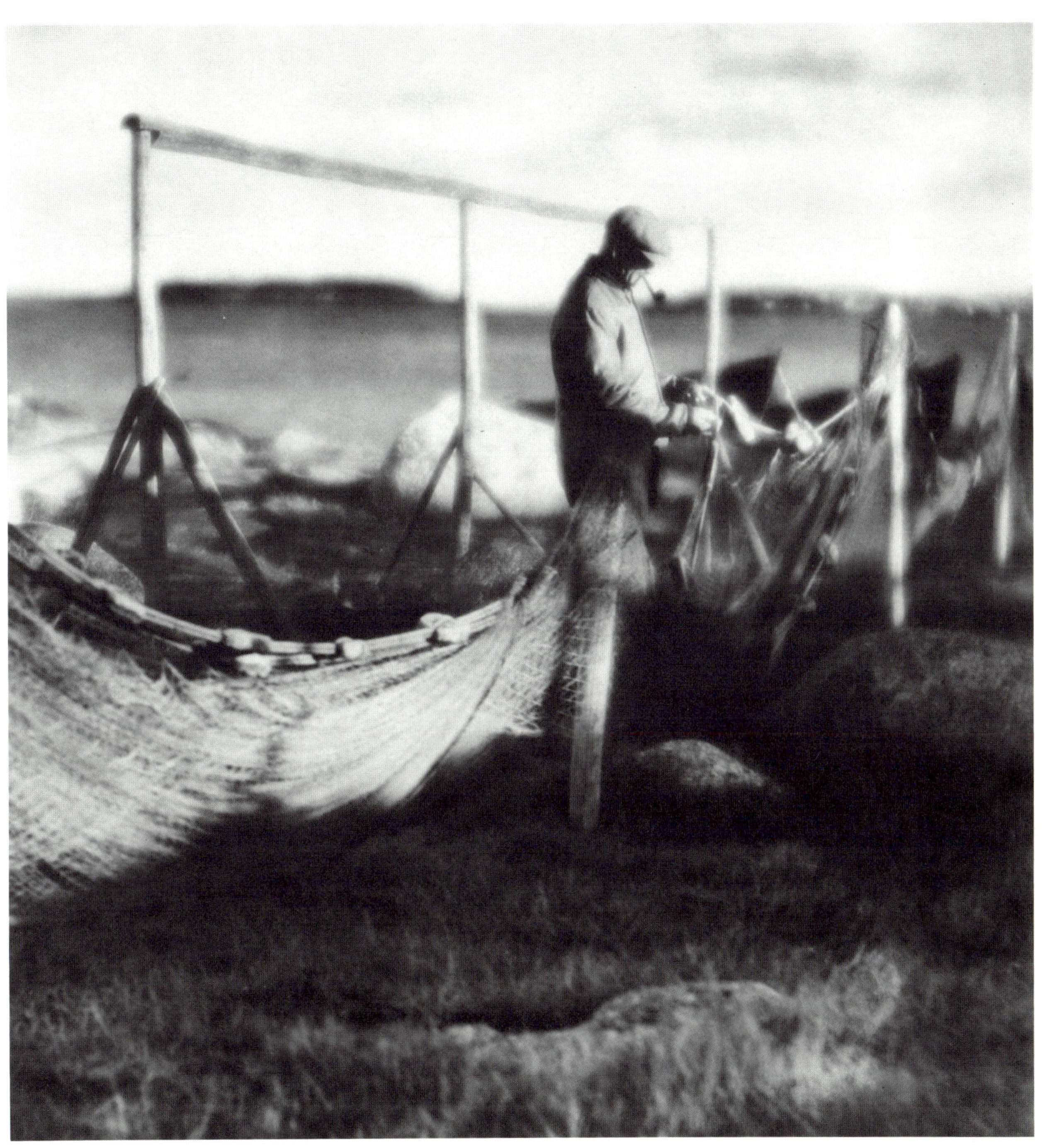

Drying and mending nets

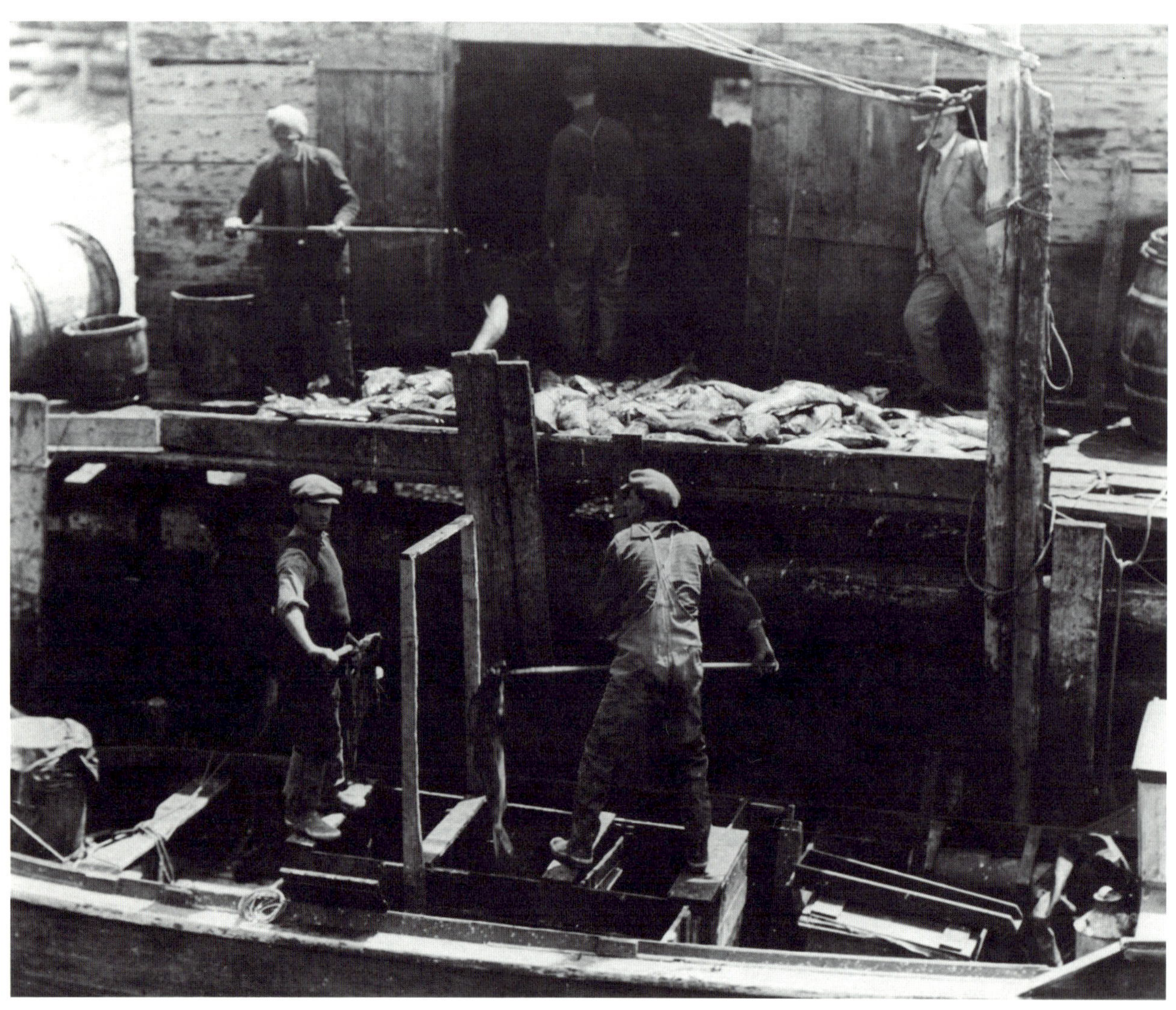

Unloading fish from a "smoke" boat, Yarmouth

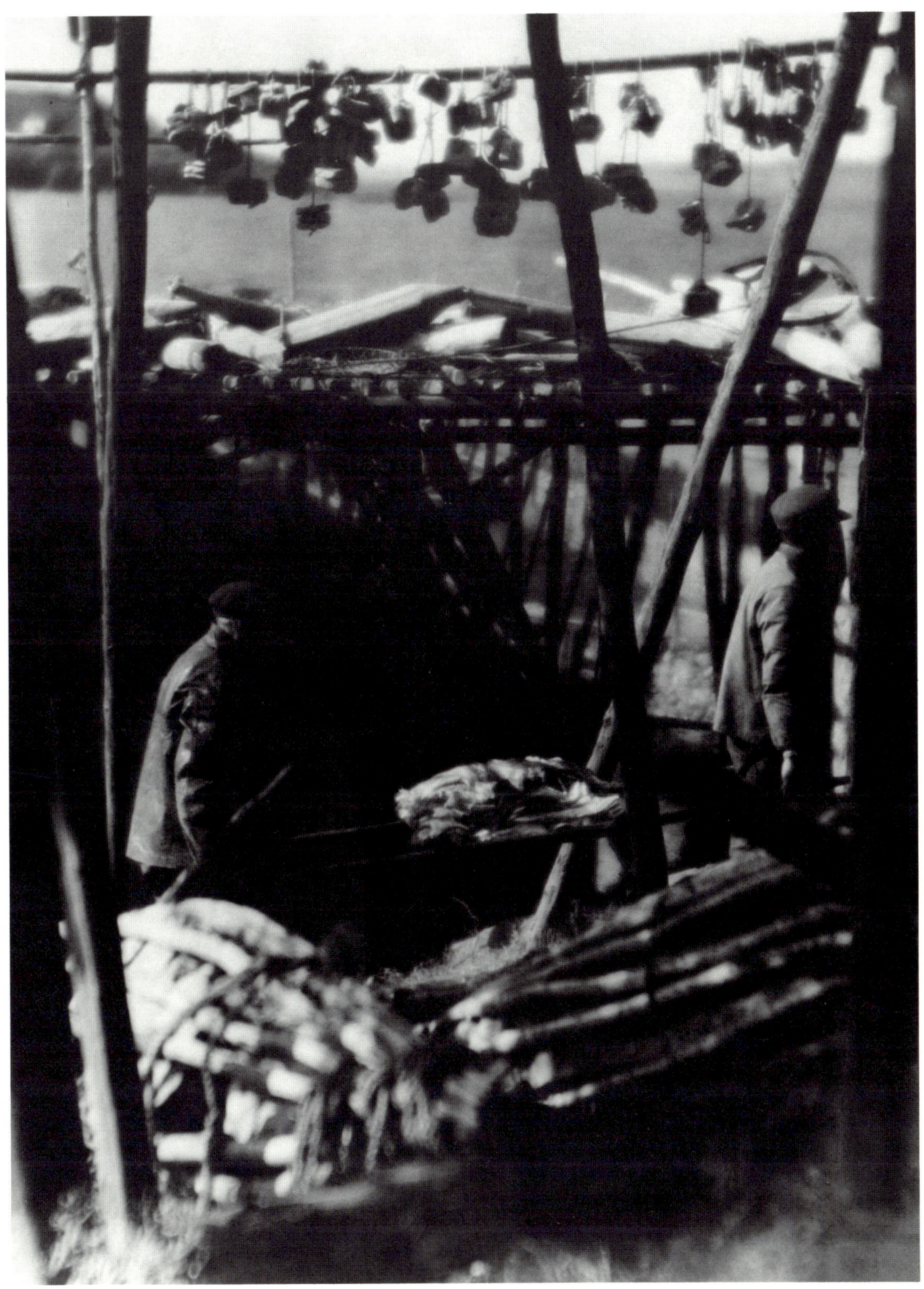

Moving fish with a handbarrow

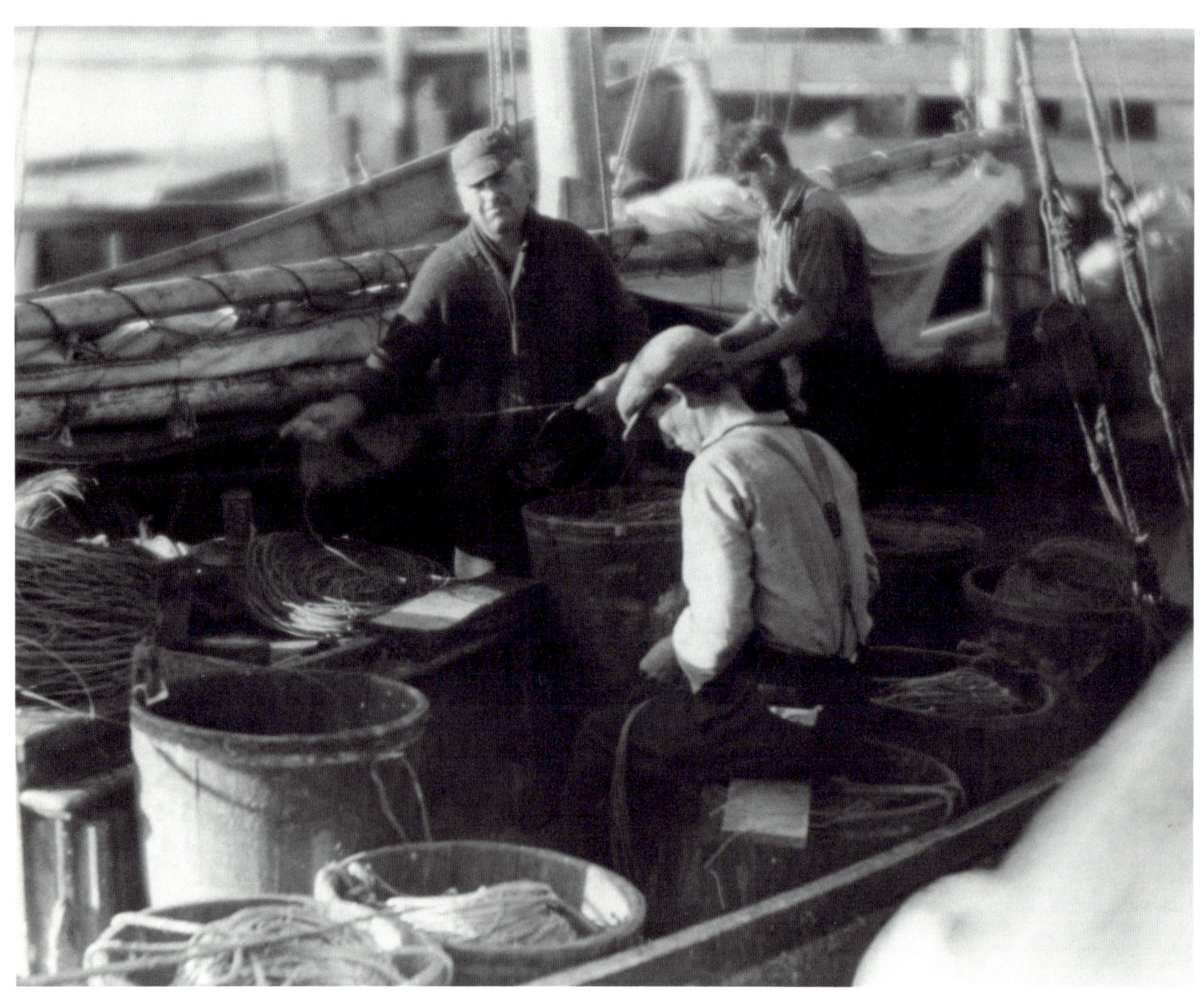

Overhauling trawls on a schooner

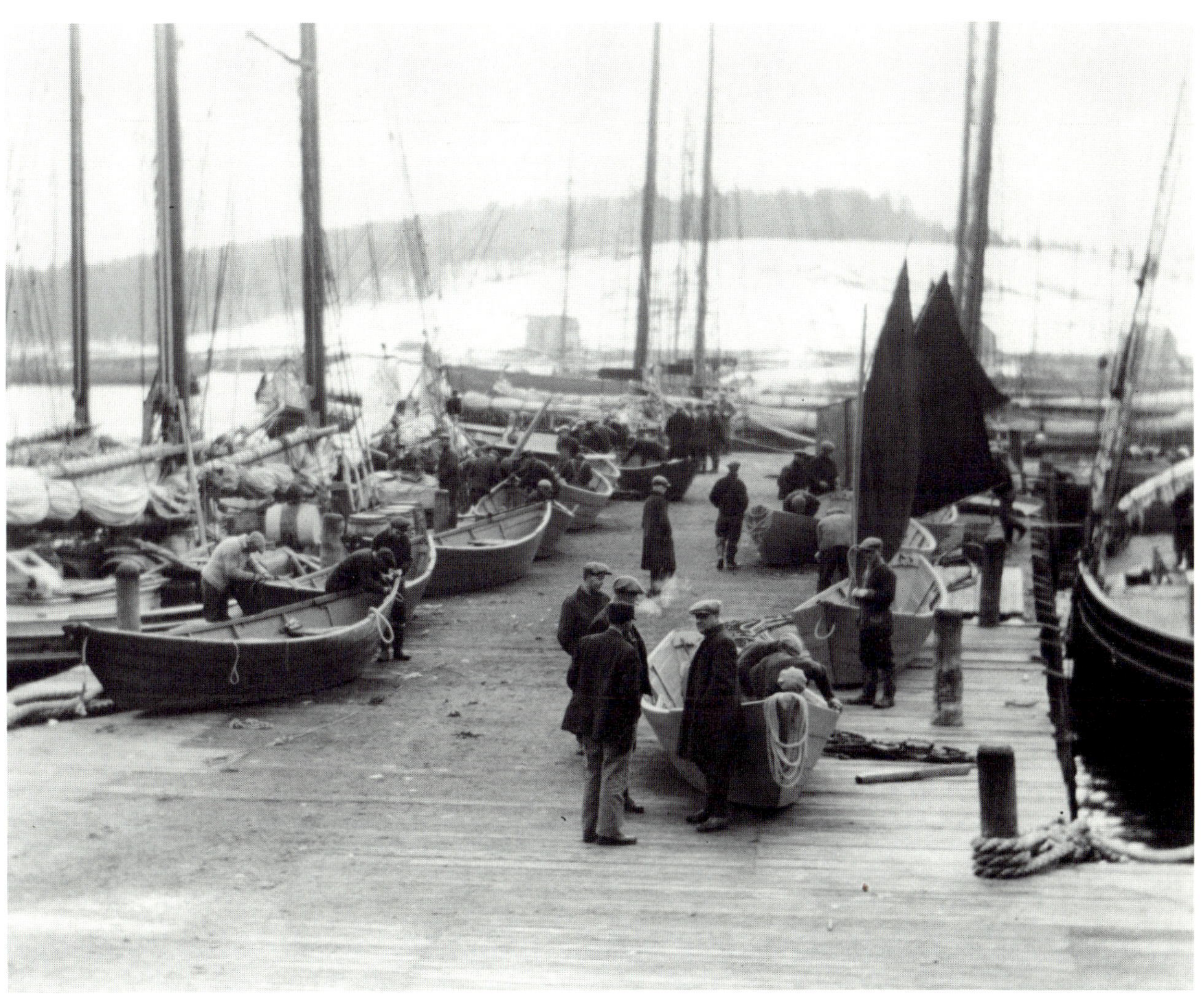

Preparing for the spring trip, Lunenburg

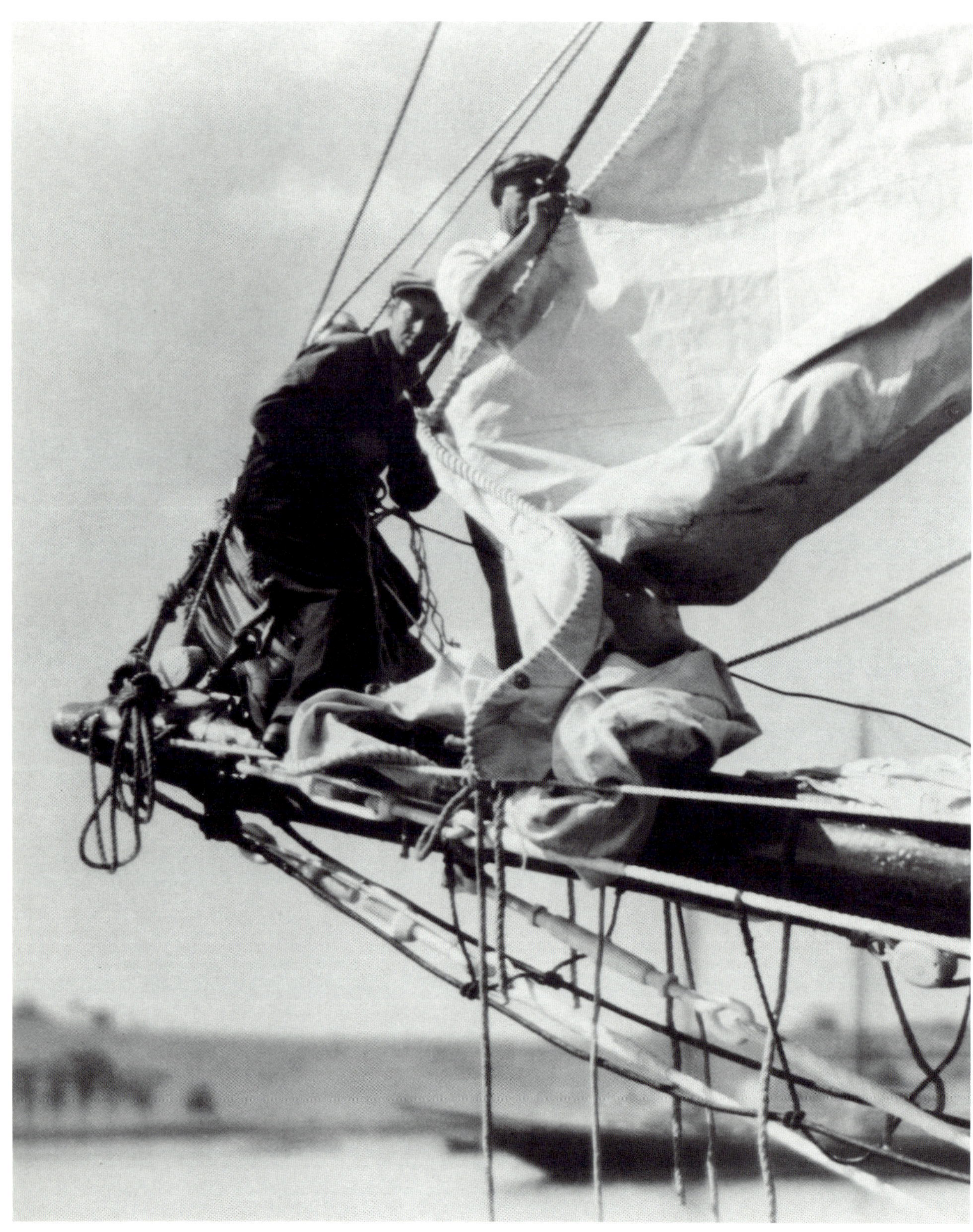

Bending on a jib, Lunenburg

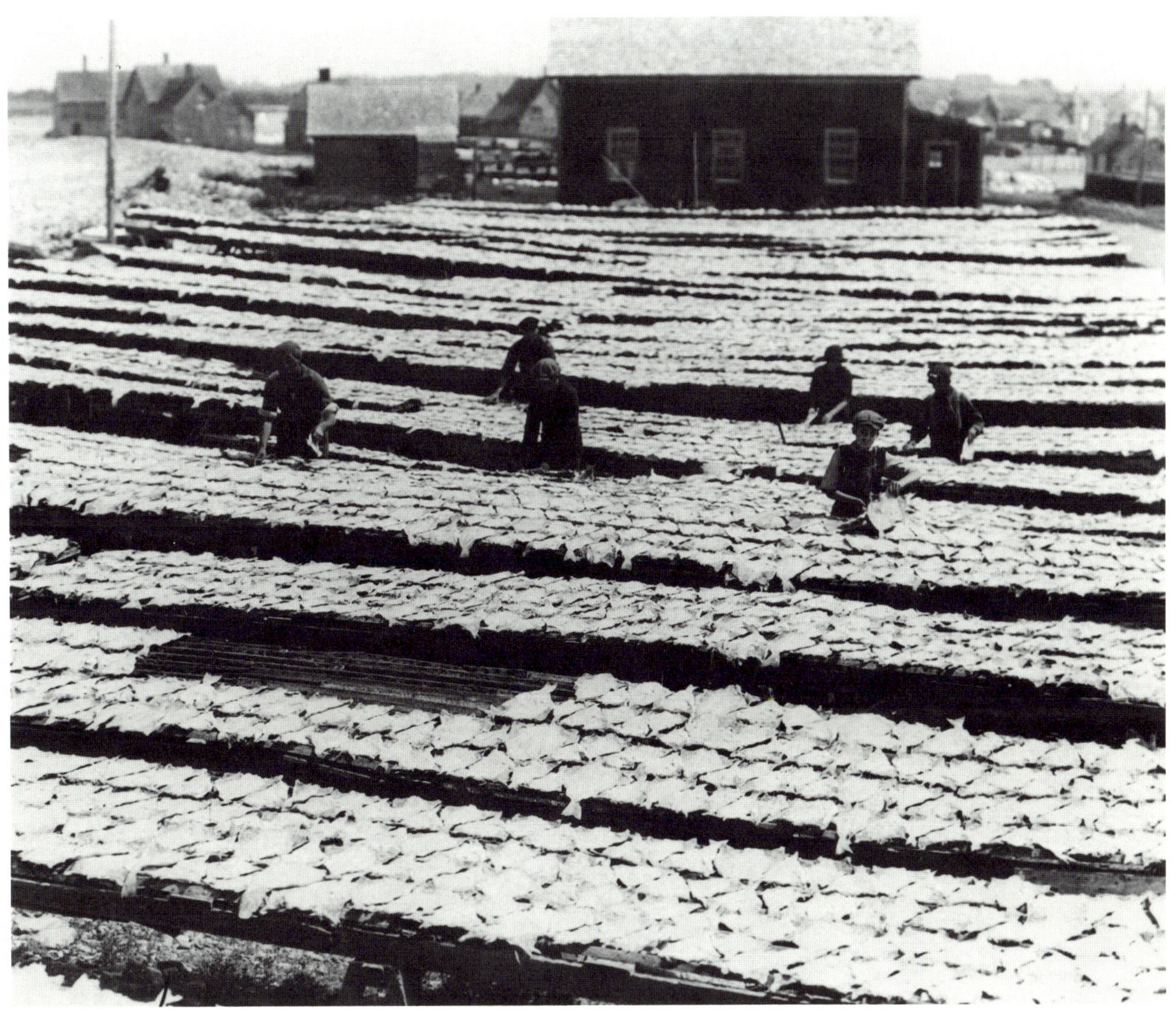

Drying codfish on flakes

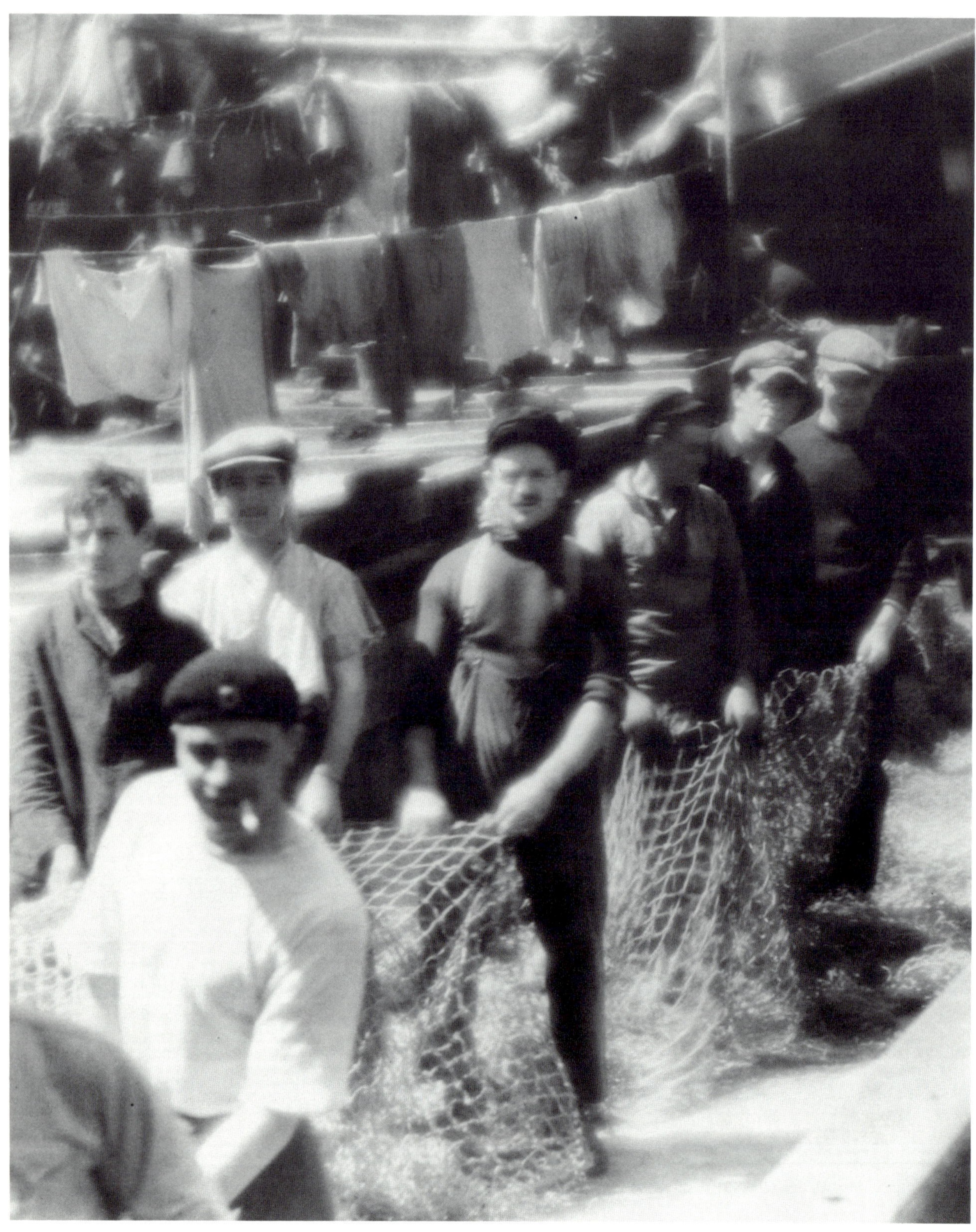

Portugese fishermen, St. John's, Newfoundland

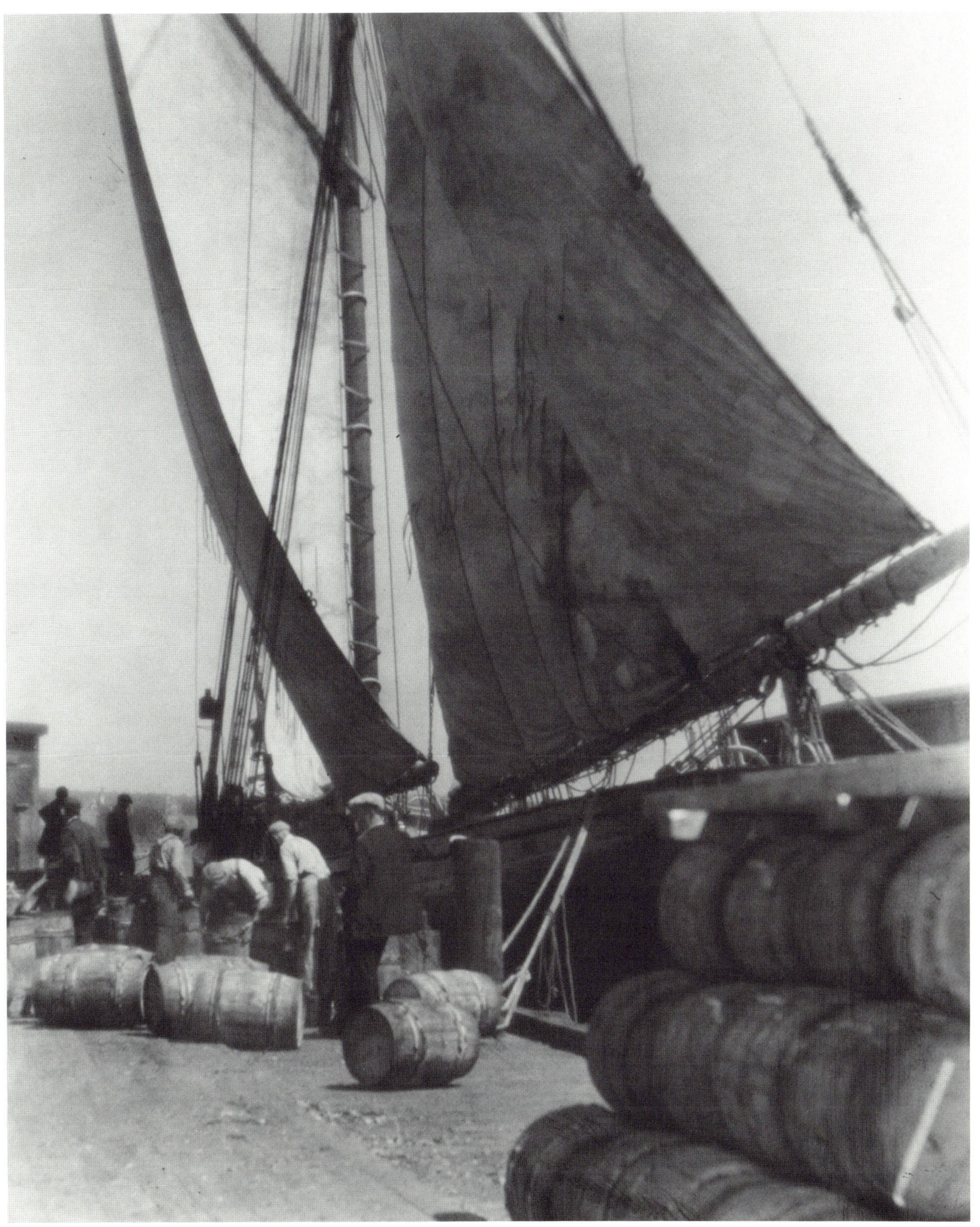

Drying sails

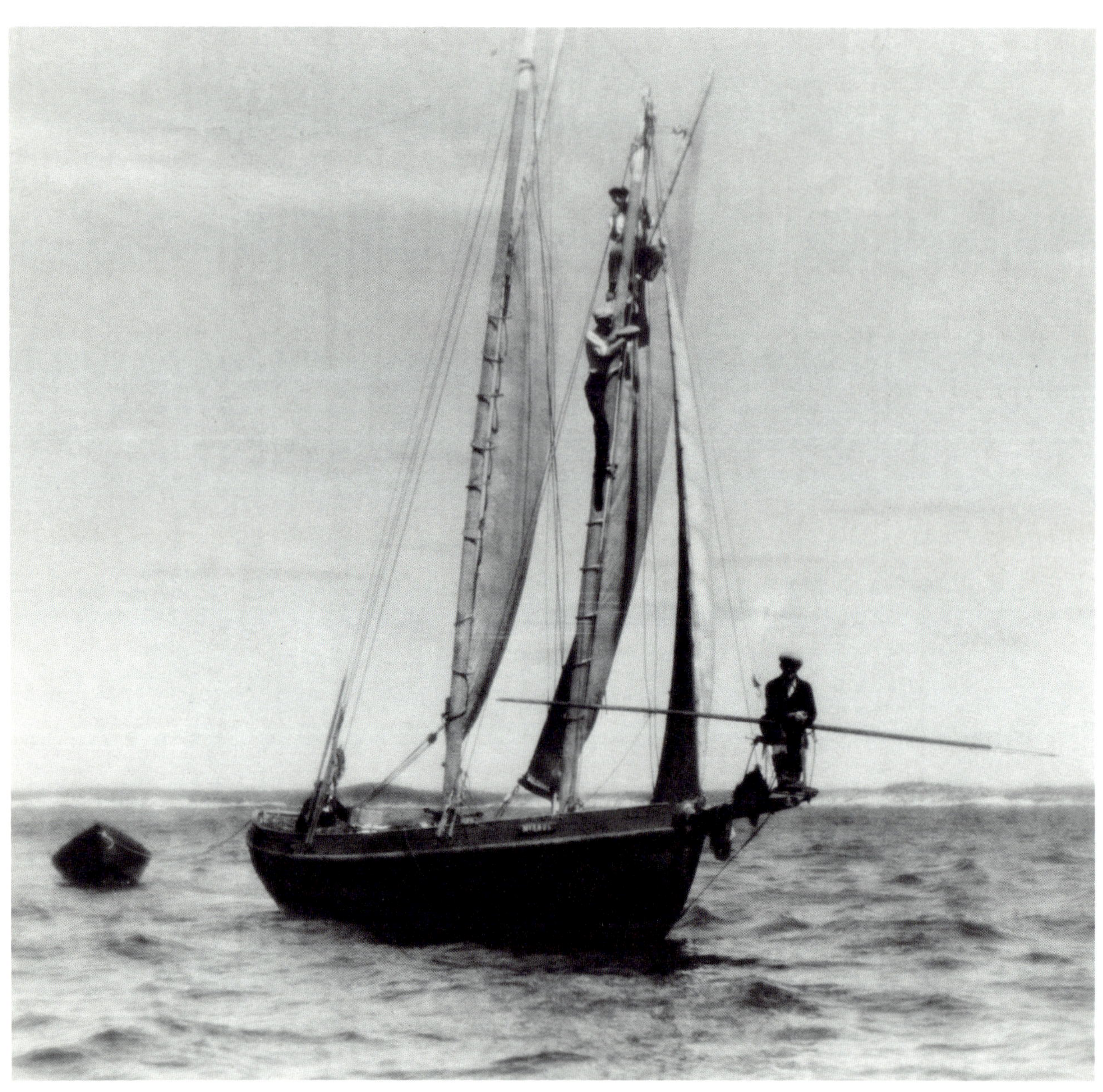

Swordfishing off the South Shore

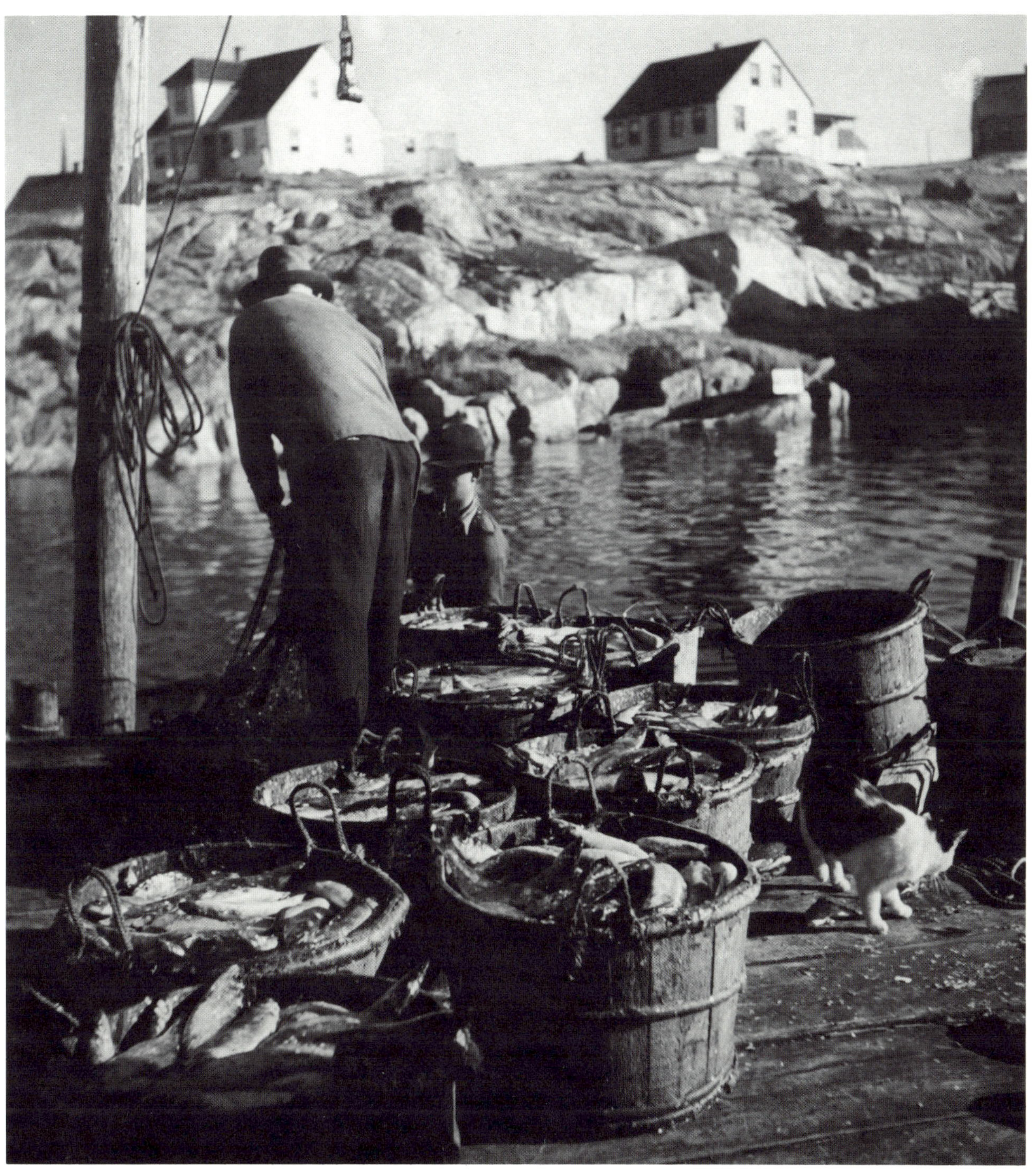

Unloading fish and nets

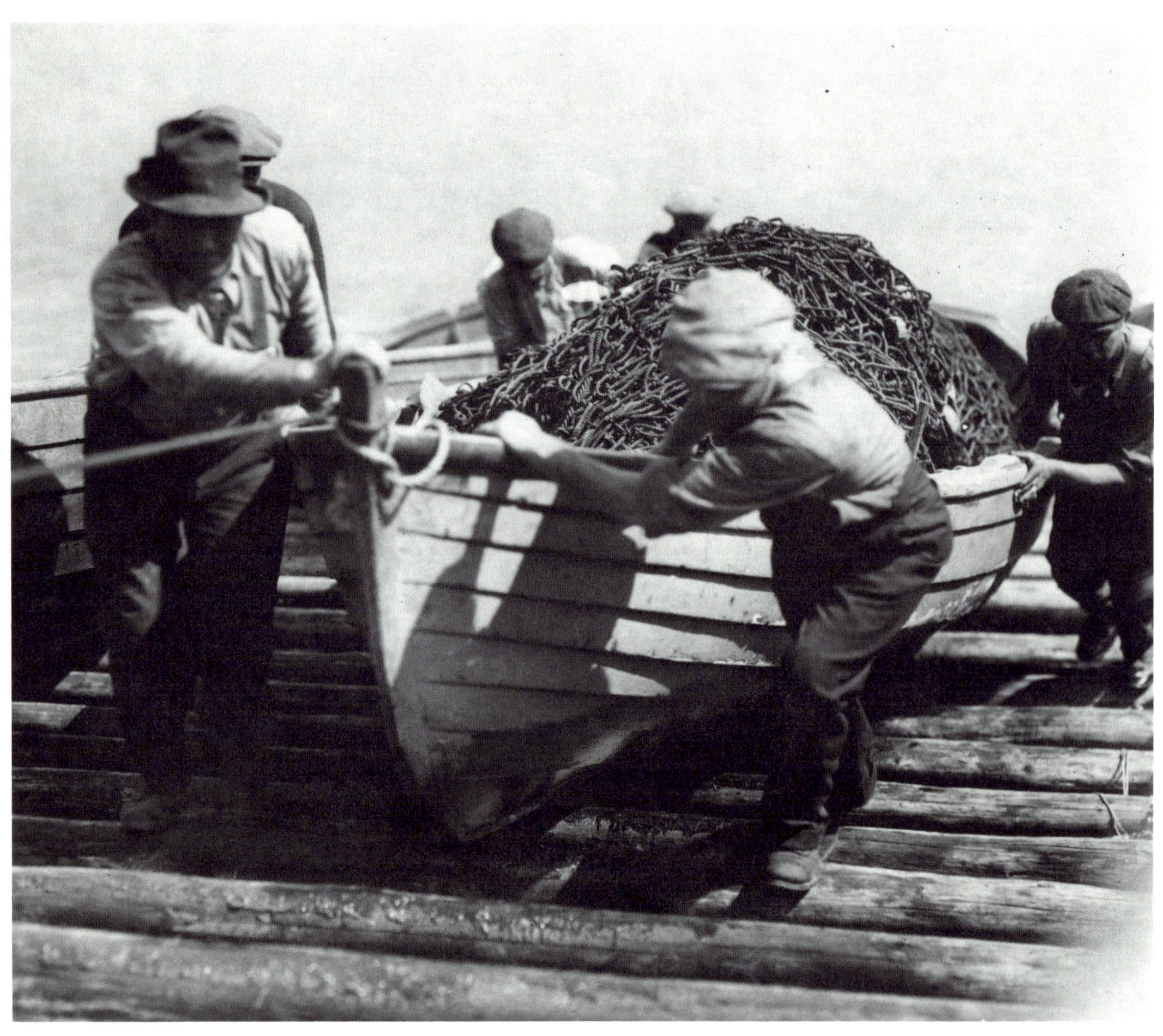

Hauling a tuna trap up the skidway

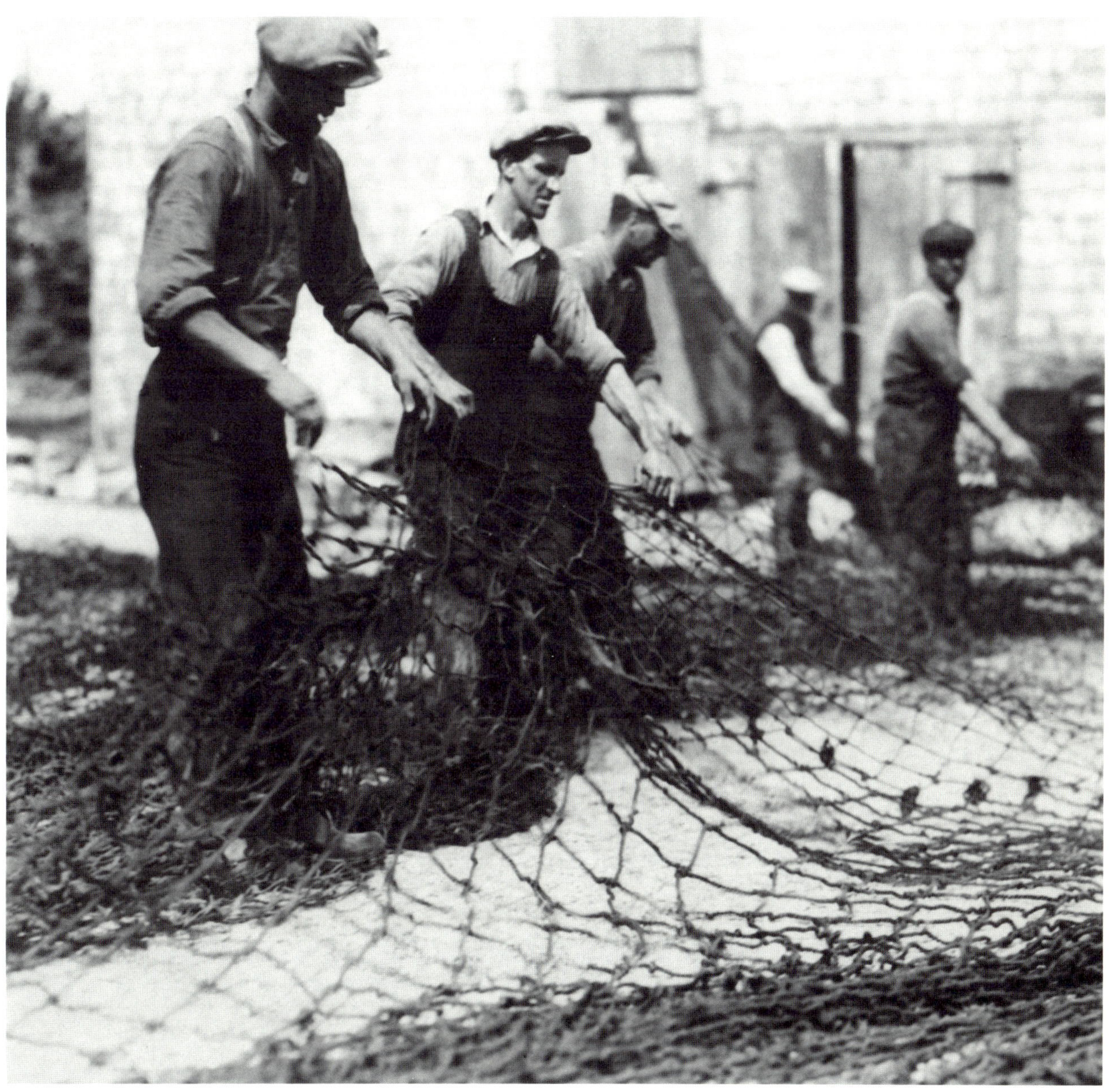

Fishermen overhauling a tuna trap

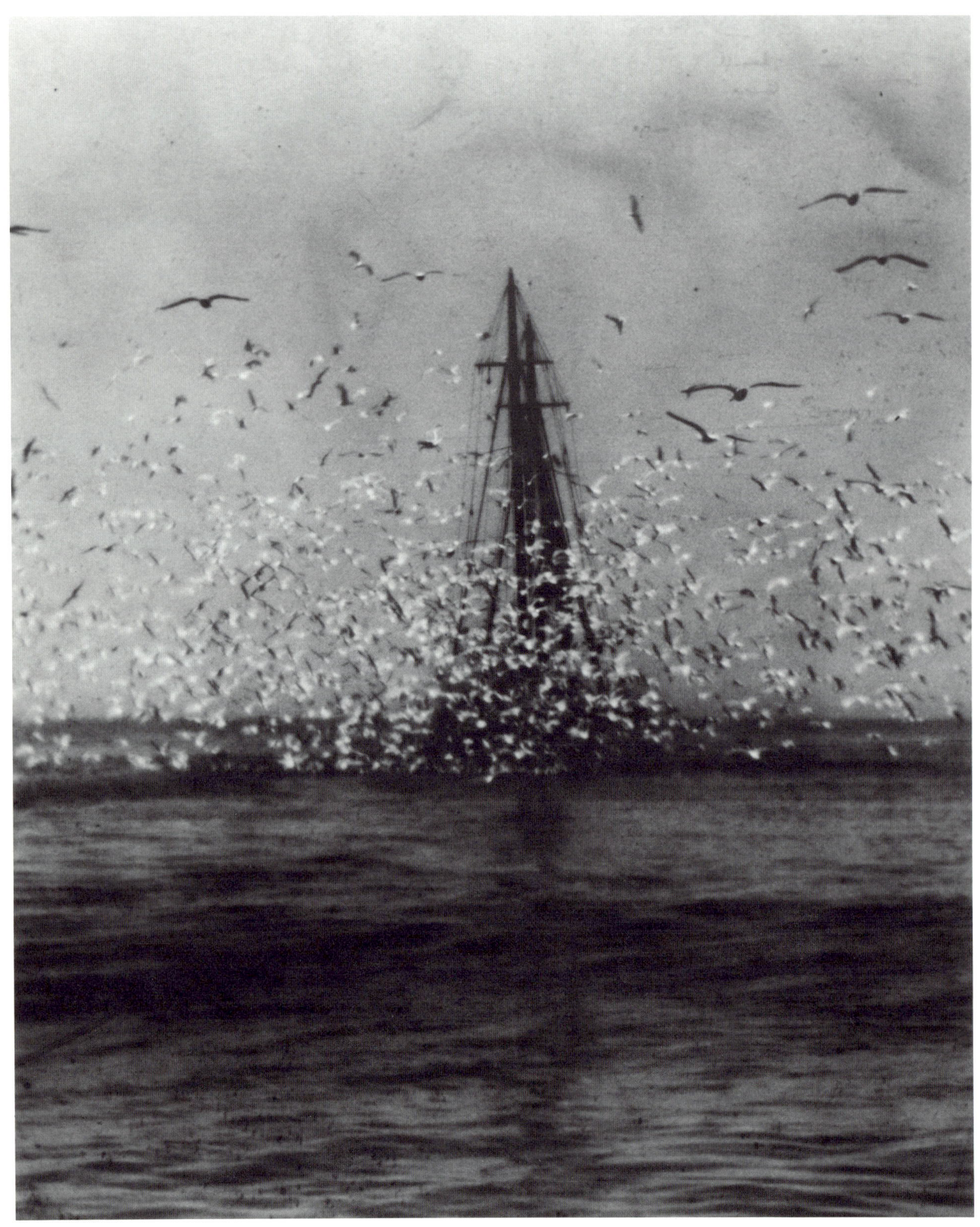

Gulls following a schooner into port

The Schooner Races

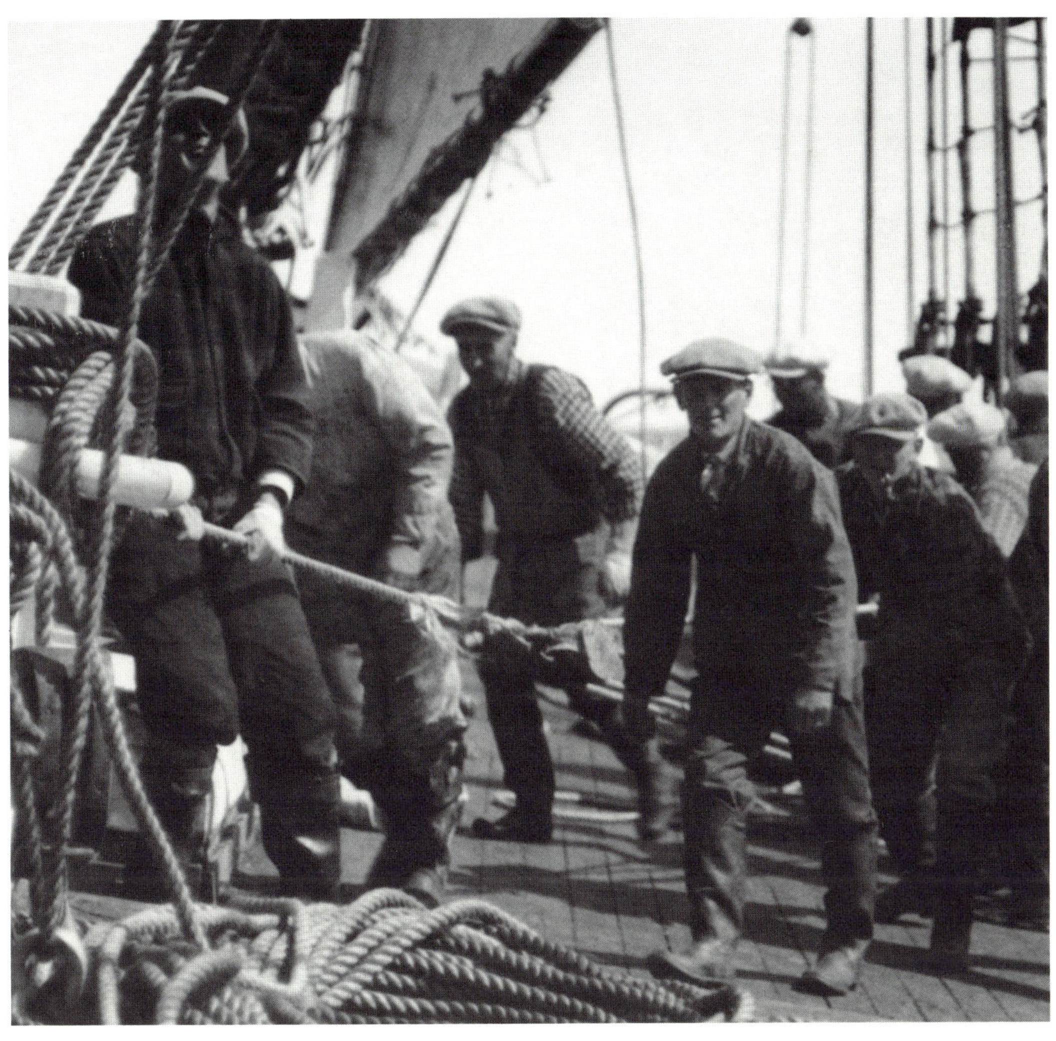

When speaking of the International Fishermen's Schooner Races, 1920-1938, between Atlantic Canadian deep sea fishing schooners and their counterparts from the New England States, we should view the competition as a challenge rather than a professional sporting event, simply because of its origin. It all came about because of a casual but intensifying controversy among Grand Banks dorymen from Massachusetts to Newfoundland over the cancellation of a deciding race for the Americas Cup due to 20 knot winds. The committee's decision to cancel may have been reasonable — but explain that to deep sea schooner fishermen who after years of fishing on the banks considered 20 knots a fresh breeze and sailed dories loaded with codfish back to the schooner laying at anchor under similar conditions.

Mr. William Dennis, proprietor of the *Halifax Herald* which covered the waterfront, was well aware of the controversy. Deciding it was time to turn words into action, he came up with a Cup, a cash prize and a challenge: the fastest schooner from Lunenburg would meet the best from Gloucester and decide a winner — within a time limit over a 45 mile triangle.

The event was unique, and it is safe to say that no other sea-going contest has ever attracted greater interest. Nor has any one sailing vessel achieved greater renown than the Lunenburg, Nova Scotia schooner *Bluenose,* with her famous Captain, Angus Walters. Together they became legendary and to this day continue as such in the archives of Canadian maritime history.

Bluenose, like all ships, was a calculated creation in volume, coefficient, stability and sail plan, and she was perfect in every sequence. For 18 years Captain Angus Walters was in command. Captain Angus and *Bluenose* were never outclassed or beaten. Together they retired as champions.

Bluenose was the 121st schooner to be launched from Smith and Rhuland shipyards of Lunenburg. Her construction, based on skill and experience, was of high standard. Her design was slightly different from the previous conventional schooners. Men who worked on her building were said to have remarked: "She was a fine vessel but different to the others in the fleet."

Some schooners, carrying full sail under strong wind force, will bury and drag water. Too much green water will tumble on deck. The excess weight causes awkward and difficult performance. Other schooners will heel to a degree where the equilibrium is unstable. *Bluenose* tended to heave out, but shipped no water on deck and maintained a stable equilibrium at all times. When she was under full sail and the gusts of wind had a force of 35 knots coming in from forward of the beam, with sheets trimmed she would show a high windward side, while the lee side maintained a stable center of buoyancy, enabling her to cope with and benefit from the wind force. Under these conditions, she would show safe stability and good response to the rudder angle. Very few schooners are capable of that sort of performance. Hove to, under foresail only, in gale force conditions, she would range ahead and maintain a windward position. This explains what the experienced shipwrights were talking about when they referred to her as "different." They recognized something new in the underwater profile.

Operating out on the fishing banks, the crews averaged 20 men (two to a dory, eight dories plus header, throater, cook and captain). When engaged in international race events, the crew averaged 28 to 30 men. Considering the fact that the fishing fleets in the ports of Lunenburg and LaHave had more than 50 schooners, it was not difficult to find enough skilled seamen to make up a race crew. Sometimes captains of other schooners temporarily forsook the dignity of rank for the dramatic thrill of being crew members onboard a racing schooner. It was not unusual that a highline fishing captain be observed wearing a cook's cap and apron and carrying out the forecastle cooking duties for the event. When fully rigged, a schooner has approximately 29 halyards, with sheets and downhauls secured to belaying pins. Each one has its own place and purpose. A crew member must know them by name and also know where to find them. He must also be ready to go aloft when required. These rules were not laid down but were understood as necessary qualifications.

To what extent Captain Angus Walters personally realized the outstanding qualities he possessed in the art of sailing large schooners is unknown. He acted modestly but there was the power of command in his orders and 'suggestions.' His colleagues, the captains and the dorymen, had great respect for his judgement and seamanship. He was never openly critical of the way in which other people operated. Any opinion he had of them was kept to himself.

Nova Scotians built at least six new deep sea fishing schooners with the emphasis on fast sailing qualities: *Bluenose, Haligonian, Canadia, Keno, Mahaska* and *Mayotte.* The first three were rated in that order. *Mahaska* was not up to it. *Keno* and *Mayotte* were short-lived and had little or no opportunity to be tested.

The New England states built seven beautiful schooners, of which *Columbia* and *Mayflower* were, undoubtedly, the fastest. It was fatal to make a mistake or have a 'misfortune' aboard *Bluenose* when competing with *Columbia. Mayflower* was disqualified and never did compete, but she was a good and fast vessel. Regardless, *Bluenose* continued to be the fastest and most able schooner. After 18 years and 12 potential challengers, she remained the champion sailer of the North Atlantic fishing schooners, 1921-1938.

The last series, off Gloucester and Boston, might well be considered a glorious finale to the Grand Bankers from Cape Cod, U.S.A. to Cape Bauld, Newfoundland. *Bluenose* beat *Gertrude L. Thebaud* to win that series on October 26, 1938, off Cape Ann, by two minutes and fifty seconds.

Gertrude L. Thebaud returned to her berth in Gloucester. *Bluenose* returned to Lunenburg. Both schooners were stripped of topmasts and mainbooms. Sail was reduced to 'jumbo,' 'foresail' and 'stormsail,' and diesel engines were installed. There were no others of the conventional sailing fleets to be found. It was the end of an era. The 'topsail schooners of the Grand Banks fleets' had disappeared.

Claude Darrach

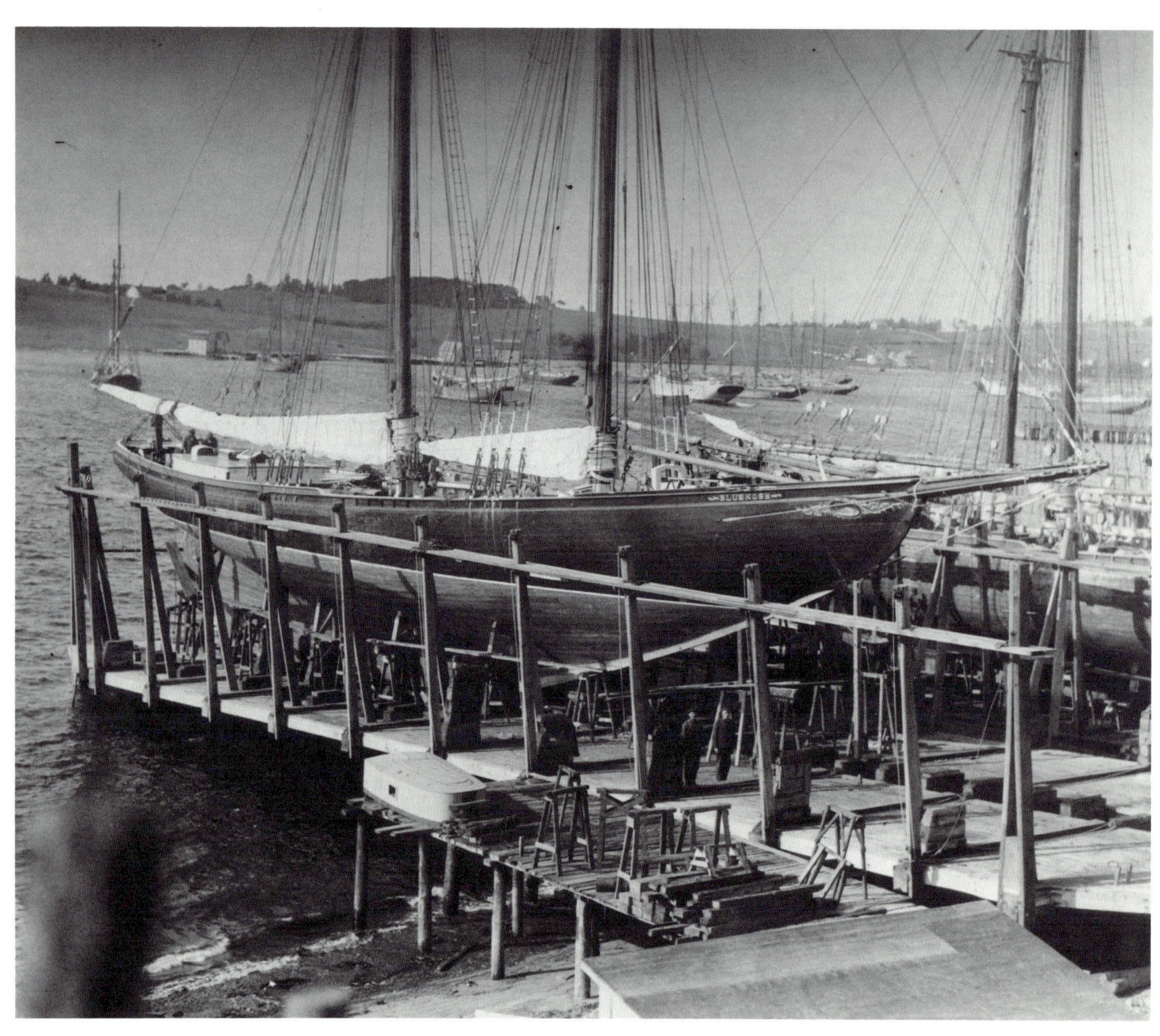

Bluenose on the slip in Lunenburg

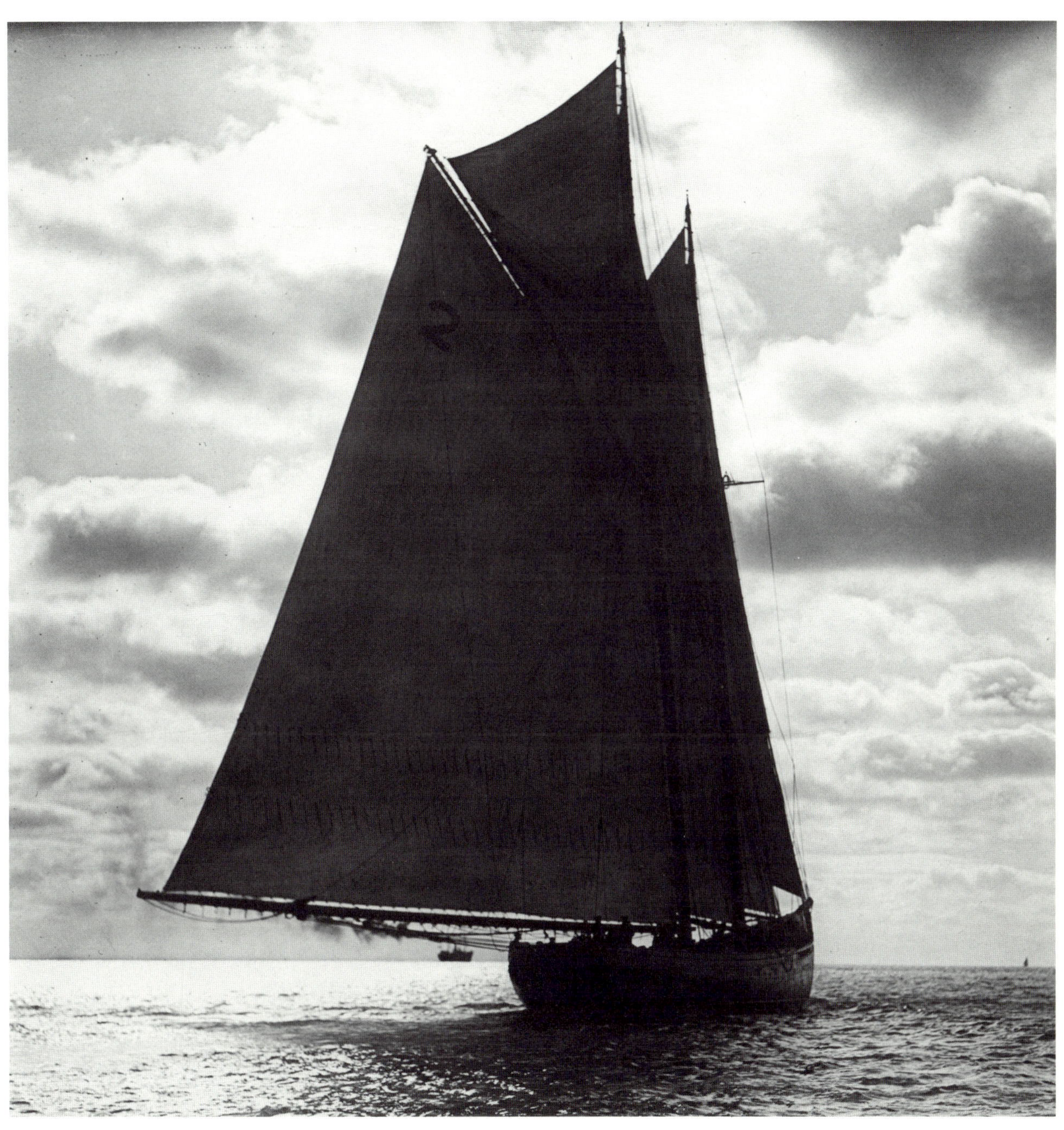

Bluenose running with the wind, 1921

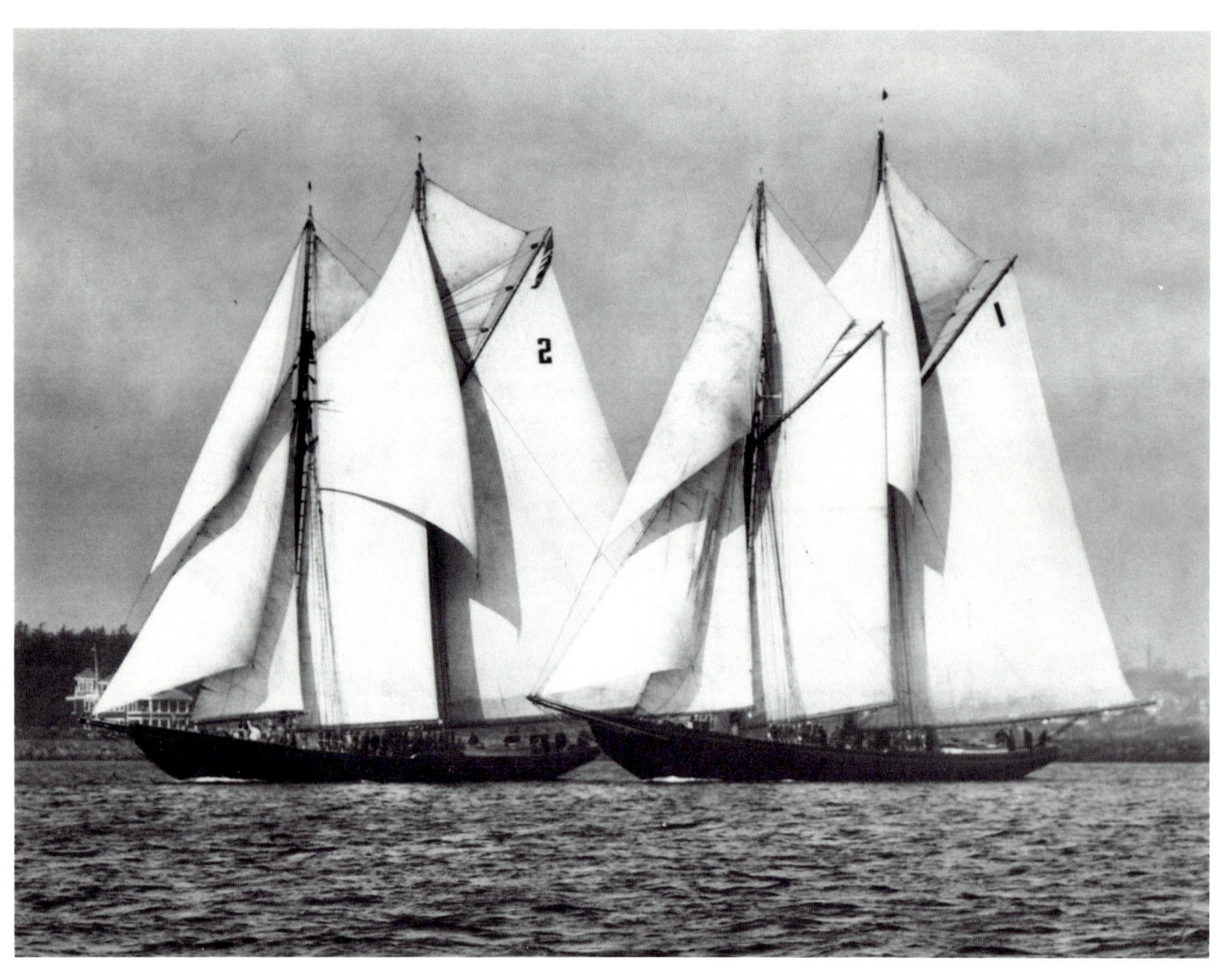

Gertrude L. Thebaud and *Bluenose,* 1931

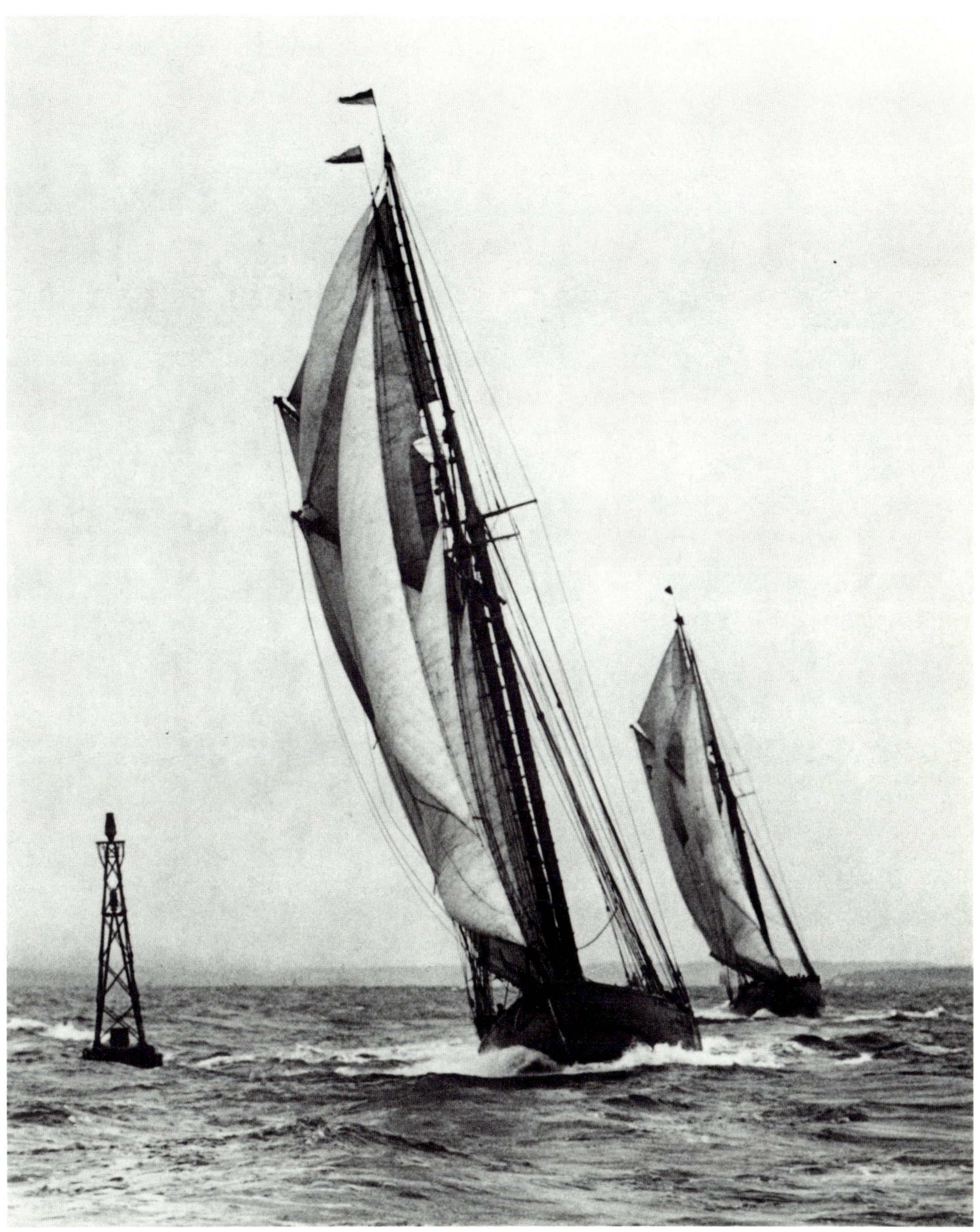

Bluenose racing for the buoy, 1922

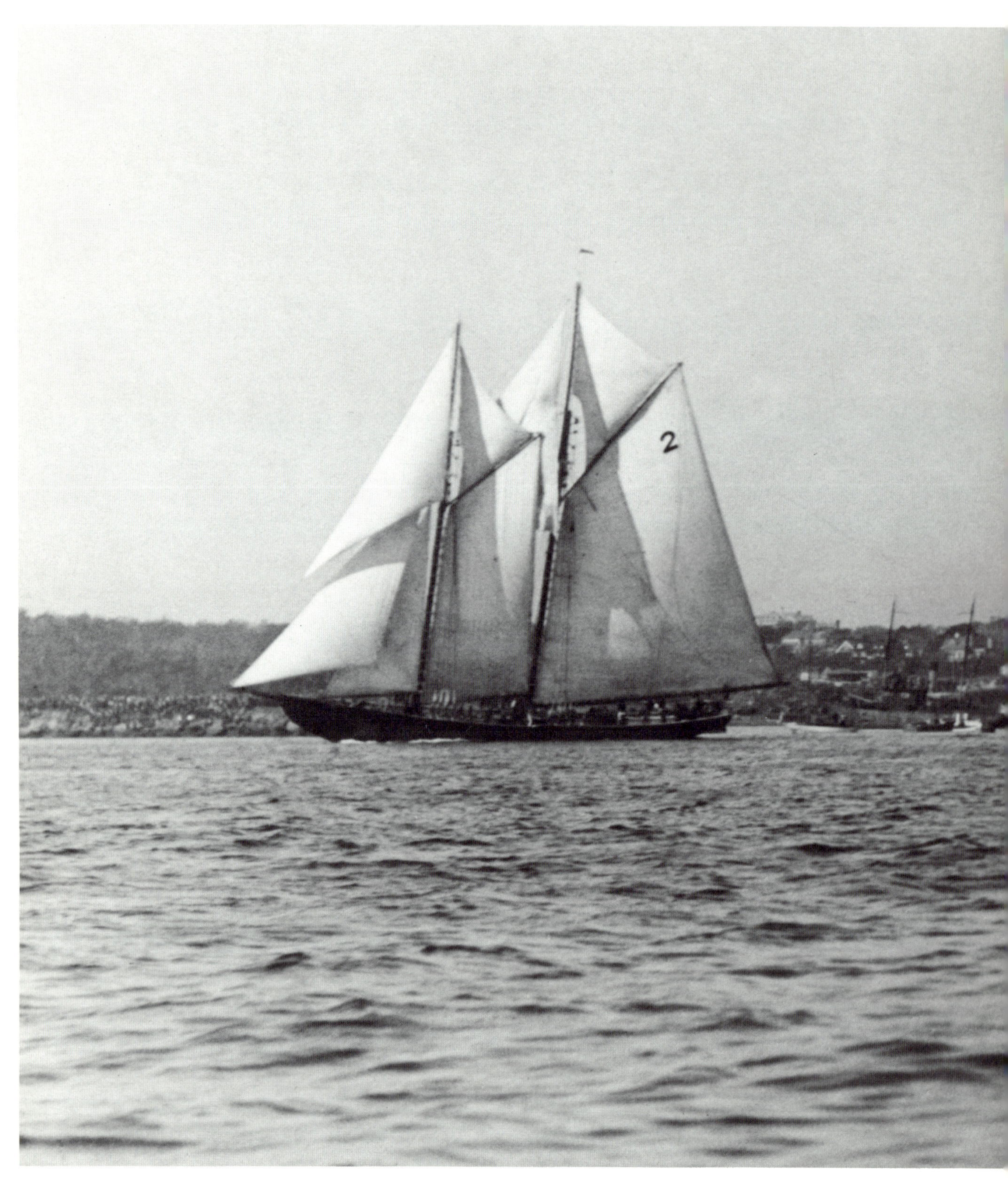

Bluenose, Canadia and *Alcala,* 1921

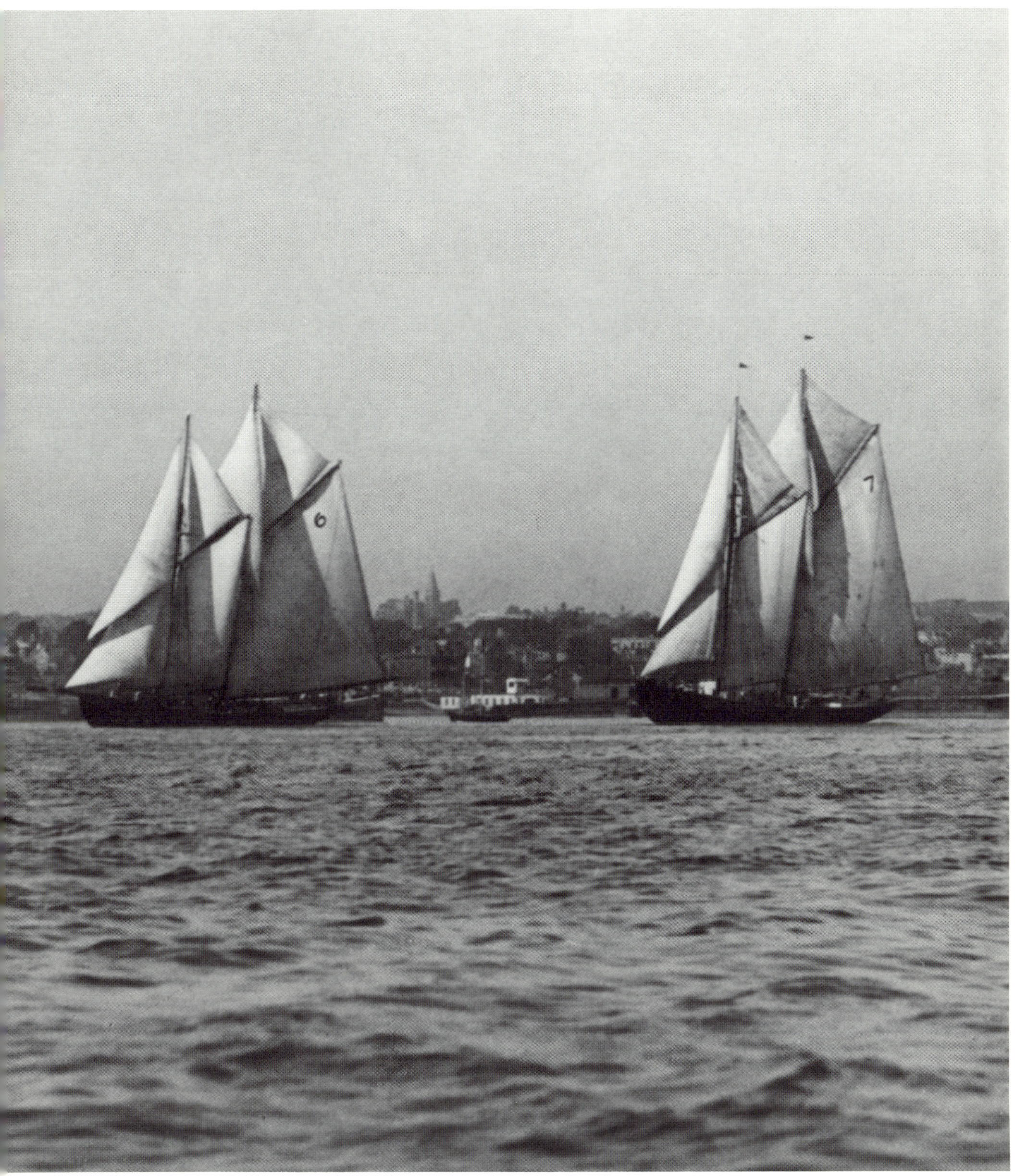
6
7

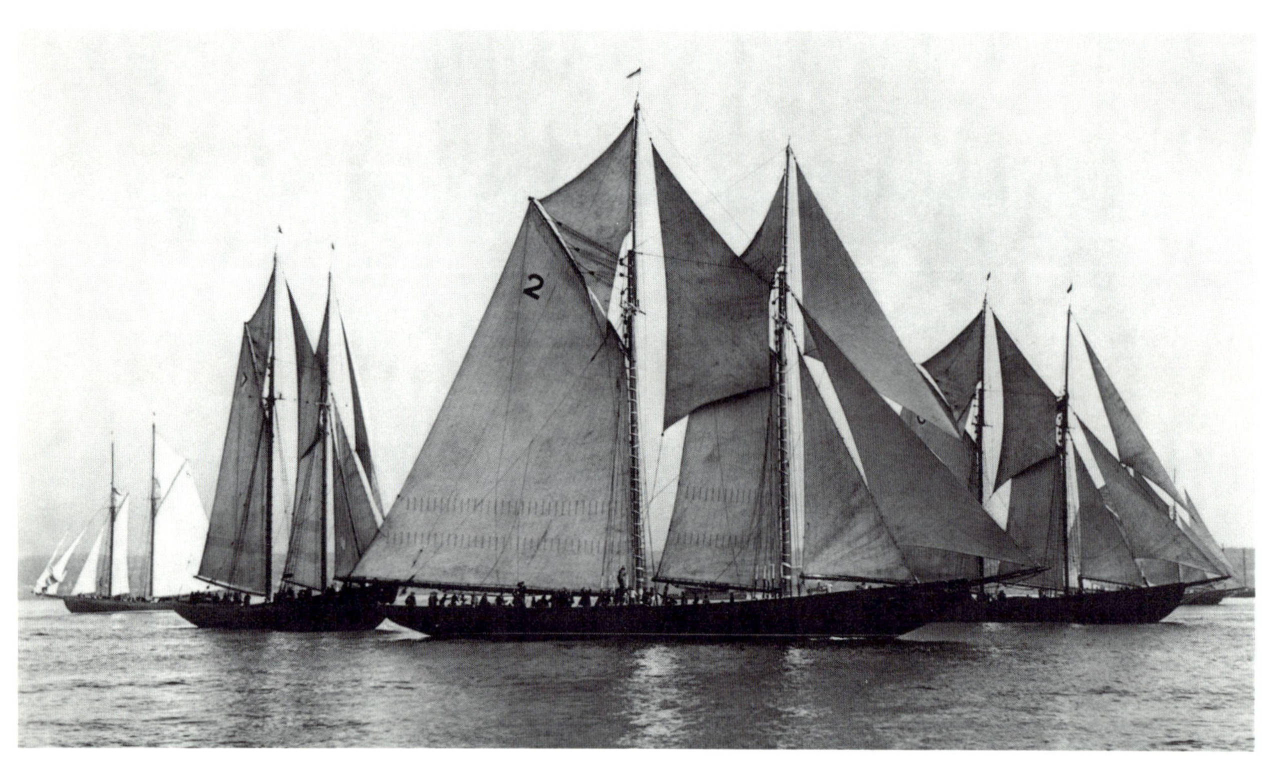

Independence, Alcala, Bluenose and *Canadia,* 1921

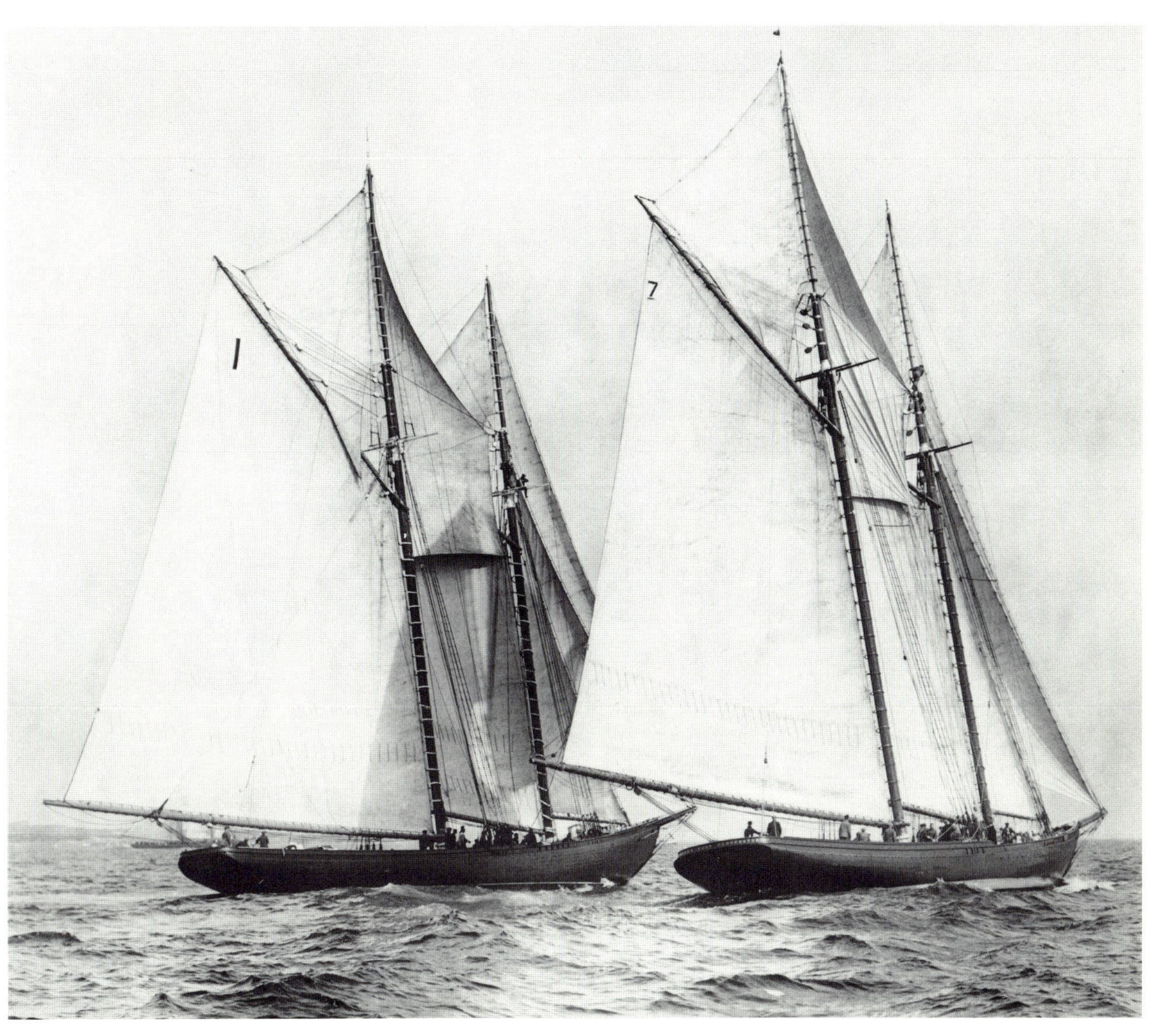

Bluenose and *Henry Ford,* 1922

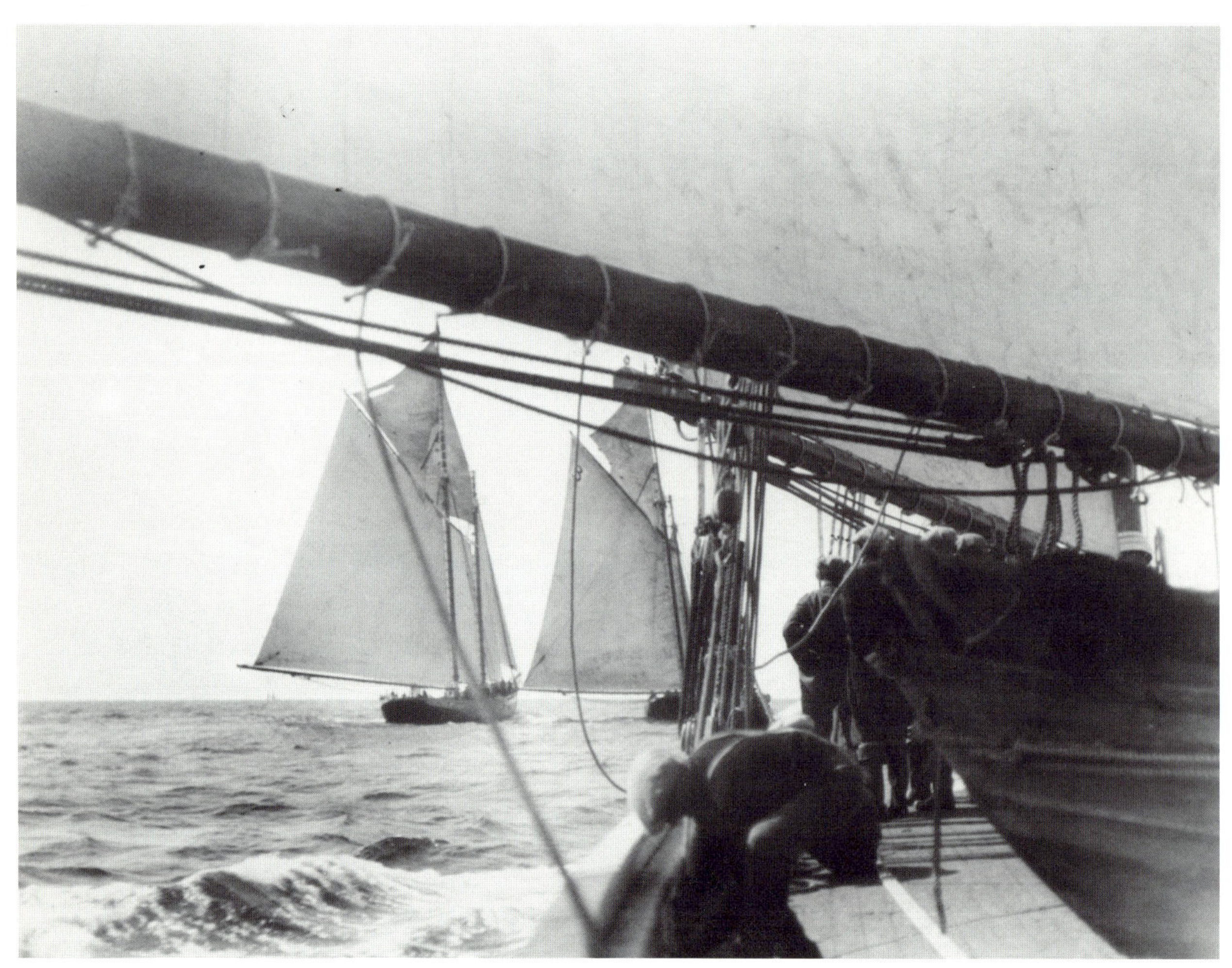

Under the main boom

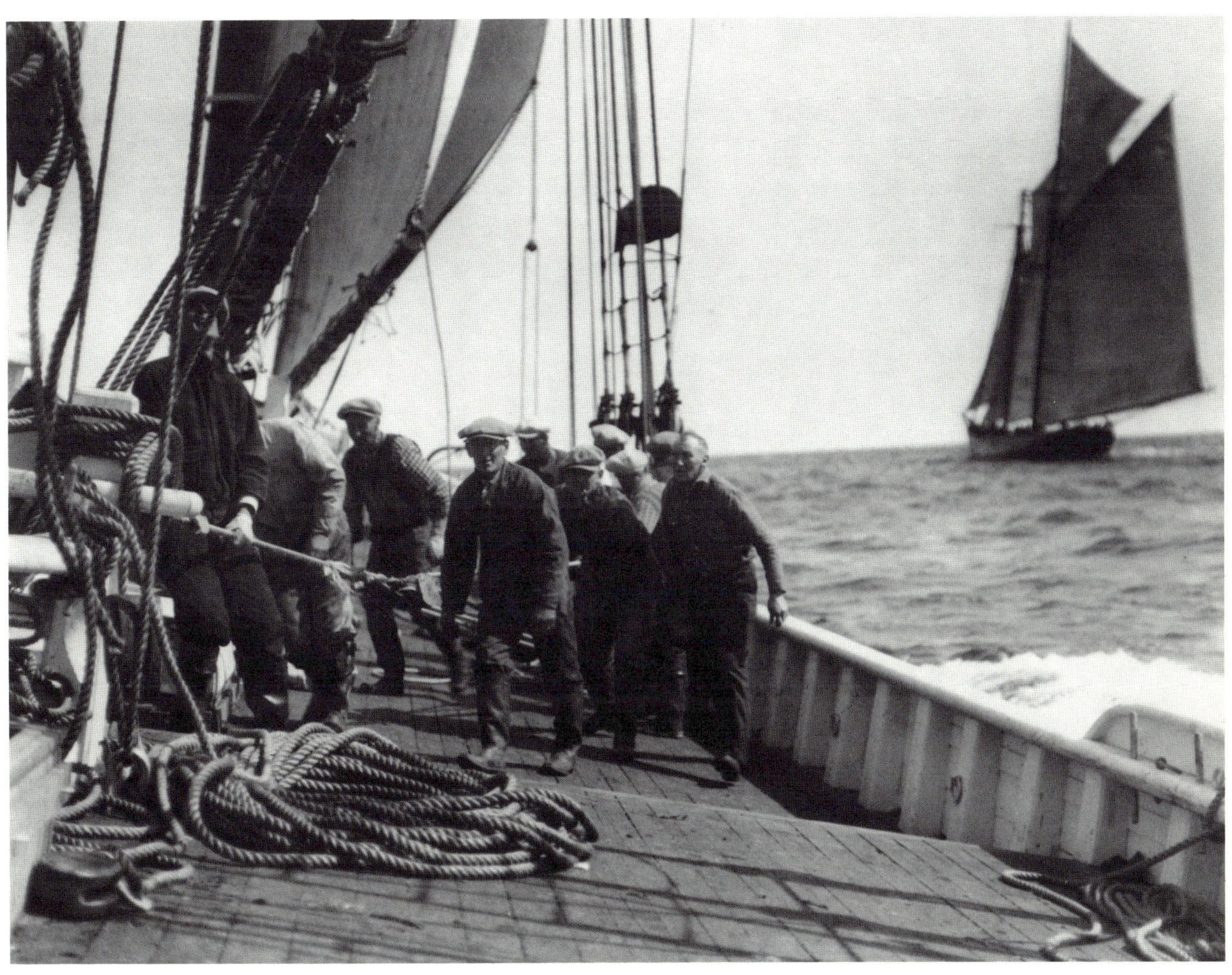

Setting the fore topsail

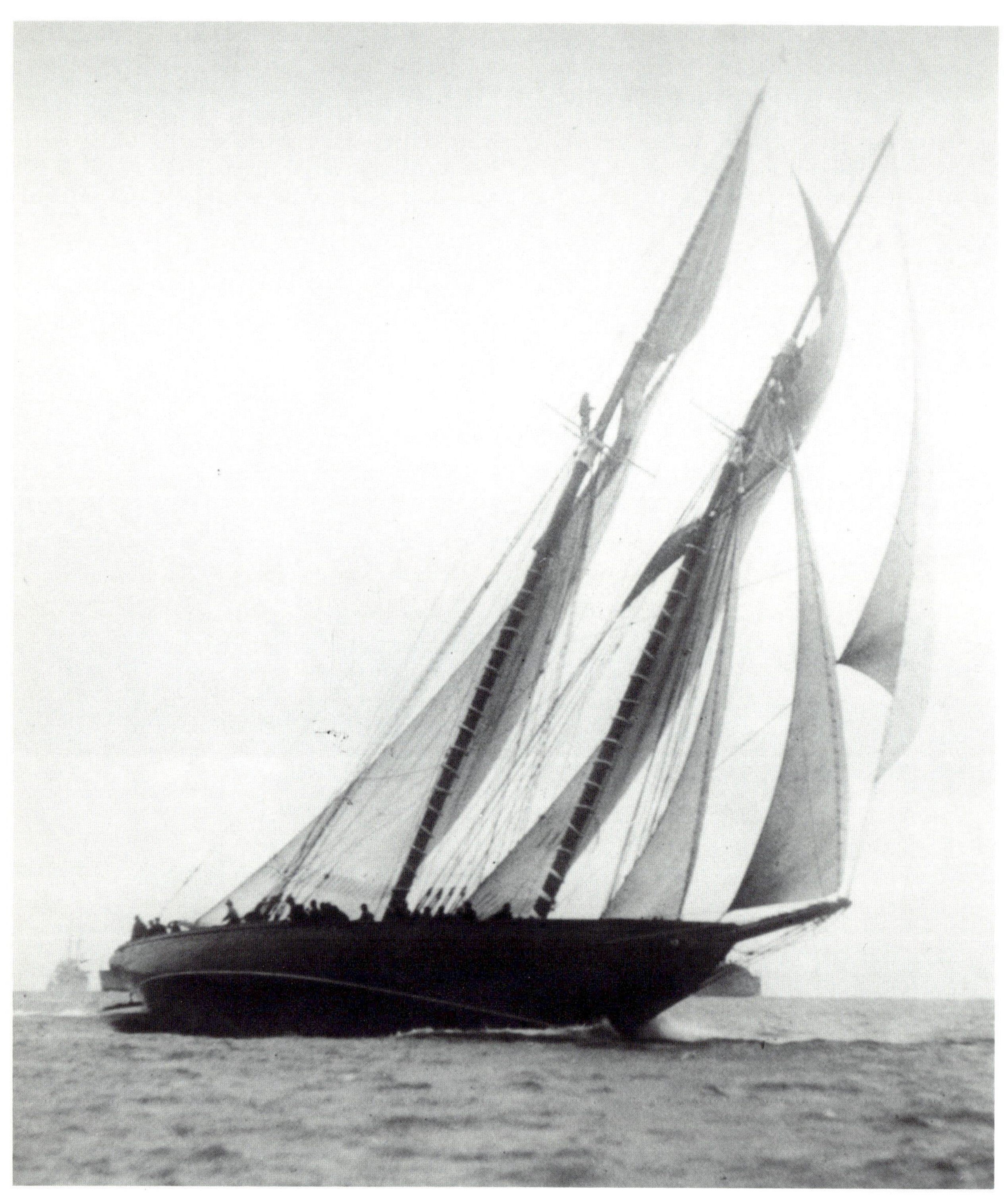

Bluenose races for the finish line, 1931

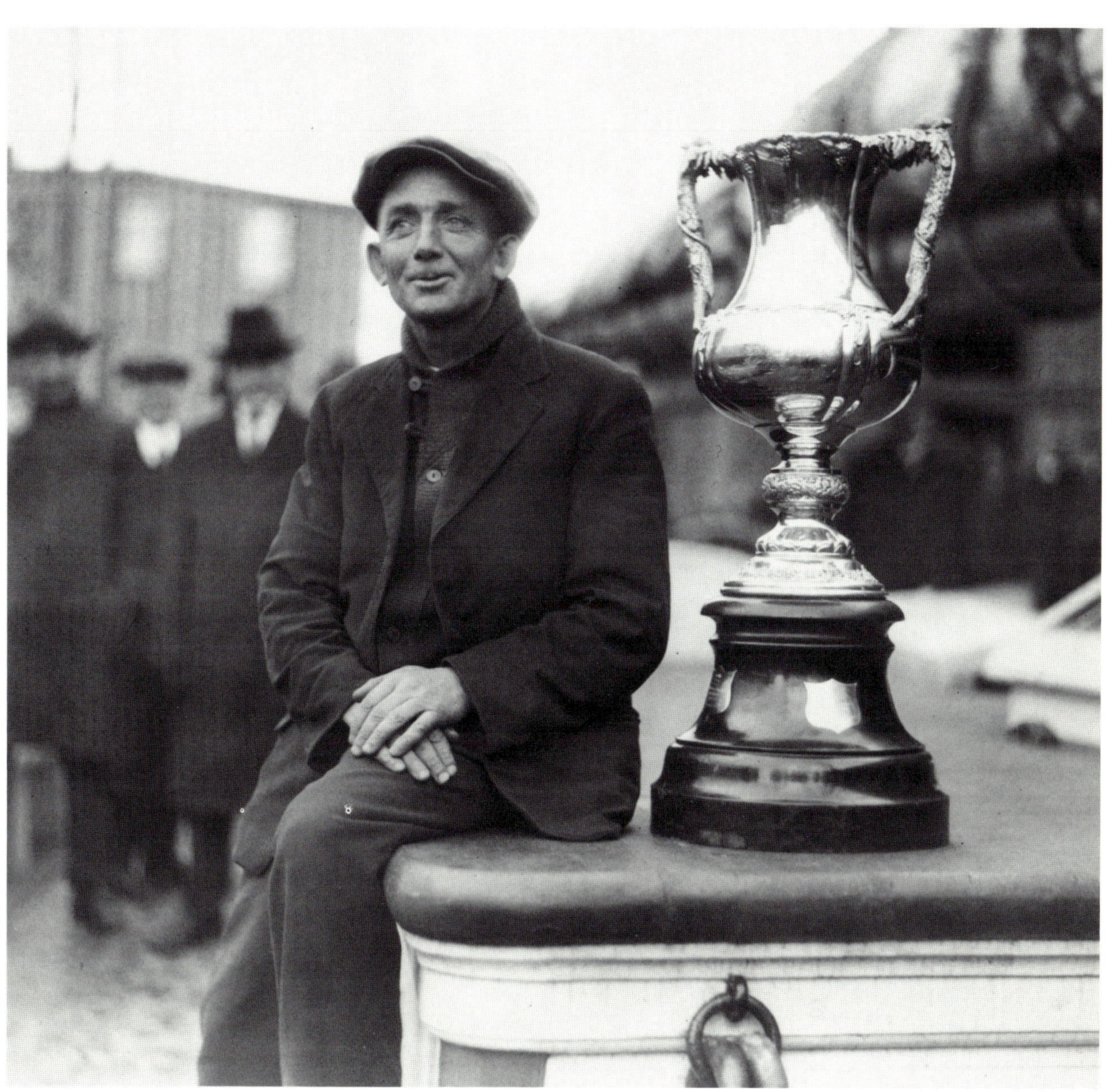

Captain Angus Walters and the *Halifax Herald* trophy

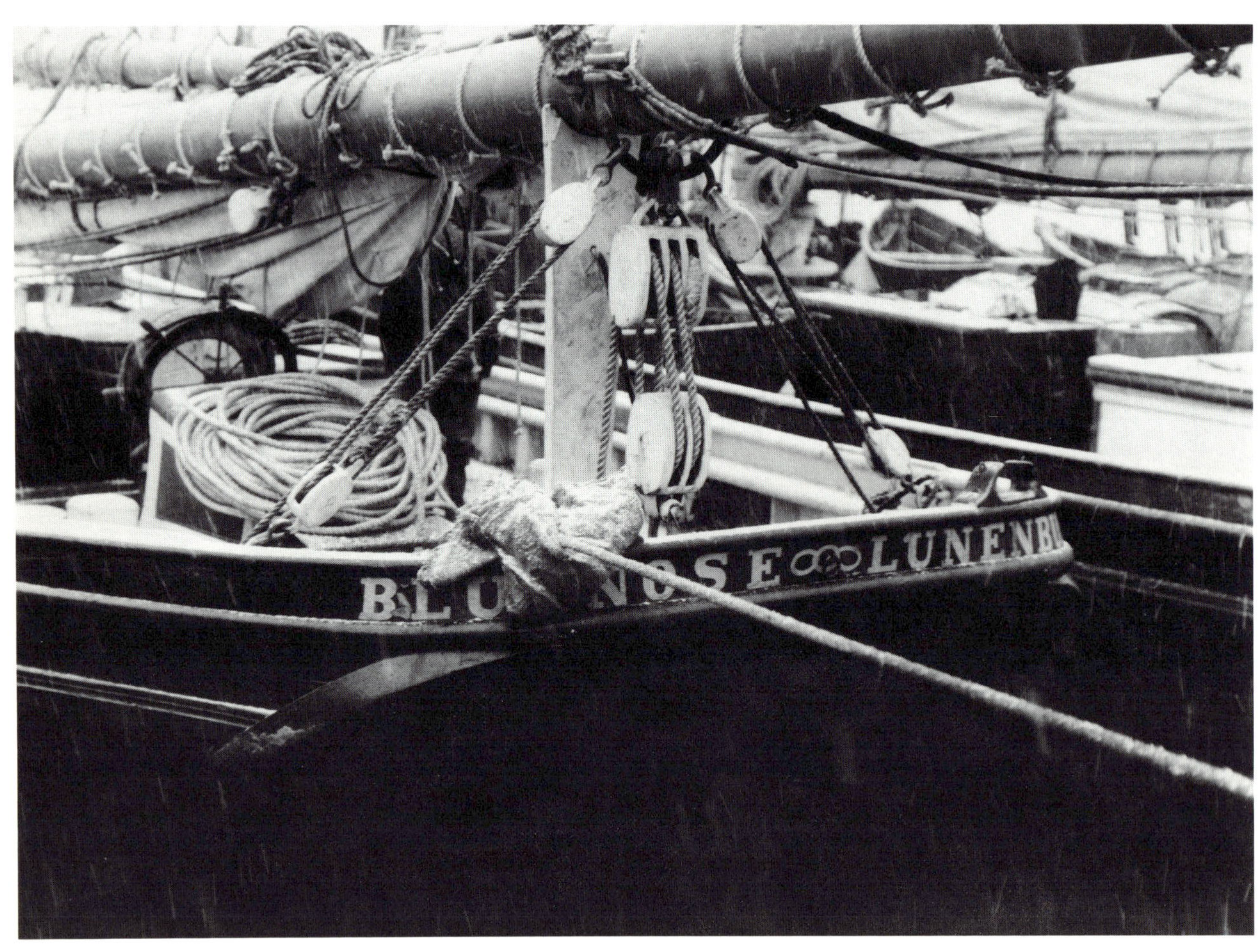

A name made famous